Between Known Men
and Visible Saints

Between Known Men and Visible Saints

A Study in Sixteenth-Century English Dissent

M. T. Pearse

Madison ● Teaneck
Fairleigh Dickinson University Press
London and Toronto: Associated University Presses

Associated University Presses
440 Forsgate Drive
Cranbury, NJ 08512

Associated University Presses
25 Sicilian Avenue
London WC1A 2QH, England

Associated University Presses
P.O. Box 338, Port Credit
Mississauga, Ontario
Canada L5G 4L8

The paper used in this publication meets the requirements
of the American National Standard for Permanence of Paper
for Printed Library Materials Z39.48-1984.

Library of Congress Cataloging-in-Publication Data

Pearse, M. T. (Michael T.), 1955–
    Between known men and visible saints : a study in sixteenth-century English dissent / M.T. Pearse
        p.   cm.
    Originally presented as the author's thesis (doctoral)—University of Oxford, 1991.
    Includes bibliographical references and index.
    ISBN 0-8386-3563-6 (alk. paper)
    1. Dissenters, Religious—England—History—16th century.
2. Separatists—England—History—16th century. 3. Radicals—England—History—16th century. 4. England—Church history—16th century. I. Title.
BR377.P43 1994
280'.4'094209031—dc20
                                                                94-16045
                                                                CIP

FTW
AGR 4850

PRINTED IN THE UNITED STATES OF AMERICA

For Annie (Proverbs 18.22)

Contents

Abbreviations

APC	*Acts of the Privy Council* (46 vols. London, 1890–1964).
Bradford	*The Writings of John Bradford,* ed. A. Townsend (2 vols., Cambridge: Parker Society, 1848 and 1853).
EED	C. Burrage, *The Early English Dissenters in the Light of Recent Research* (2 vols., Cambridge, 1912).
Foxe	J. Foxe, *The Acts and Monuments of the English Martyrs,* ed. J. Pratt (London, 1563, 1576, 1870).
LPFD	*Letters and Papers, Foreign and Domestic, of the Reign of Henry VIII,* eds. J. S. Brewer, J. Gairdner, and R. H. Brodie (21 vols. in 36, Vaduz, 1965).
PRO	Public Record Office, PCC-F.8 Tashe.
TBHS	*Transactions of the Baptist Historical Society.*

Map Showing Areas of Free-Willer Activity

Preface

THIS book is the fruit of my doctoral research, and was submitted to the Theology Faculty Board of the University of Oxford in 1991. The original intention, begun with the naïvete of many new research students, was to paint something on a far broader canvas. I wanted to look at the relationship between the ecclesiologies of English radicals and their acceptance or rejection of Reformed theology in the period from Mary's reign to the English Civil War. My tutor humoured me in my high designs, and allowed me to discover for myself that such a wide-ranging task as I envisaged would demand a superficiality that comports ill with the first requirement of the doctoral student: original research. In any case, Henry Hart and his free-will men soon absorbed me so much that they could not possibly be dismissed in the three or four pages that would have been their allotted space had I seriously tried to follow my original plan. Perhaps I will manage it some day. In the meantime, the much more modest task actually completed, and presented on these pages, has been a satisfying—and hopefully significant—one.

Most prefaces such as these wax eloquent about the merits of research supervisors. Perhaps some of this eloquence is mere humbug, but having been through that particular mill myself I am well aware that most of it cannot be. If I never succeed in becoming the courteous and witty model of a Christian scholar, at least Dr. Barrie White, at that time Principal of Regent's Park College, Oxford, will have shown me the ideal to aim at. Frequently when dealing with my own students, and even when writing, I pull myself up short and realize that I am playing at being Barrie!

Unintentional mimicry may be the most embarrassing form of appreciation, but it is also the most sincere. It should be added, and not just as an afterthought, that Dr. Alister McGrath of Wycliffe Hall, Oxford, kindly eased me through the final stages of the work, and calmed my frayed nerves through some anxious moments. Preferring to live riskily, I have not always taken their advice, and any errors that remain in this book are, alas, a testament to human incorrigibility.

I am very grateful to a number of institutions and libraries who have permitted me, not only to use their excellent facilities, but to cite their original documents in this work. The Public Record Office, the Manuscripts Department of the British Library, Lambeth Palace Library and Dr. Williams's Library (all in London) as well as the Centre for Kentish Studies, Maidstone, have been helpful in this respect. Mrs. Alison Sproston of Gonville and Caius College, and Dr. Frank Stubbings and his staff at Emmanuel College, as well as the staff of Cambridge University Library, were all particularly kind, and helped to make research trips to Cambridge an enjoyable experience. The staff of the Bodleian Library, Oxford (particularly those in Duke Humfrey) provided invaluable assistance, and sometimes a guiding hand through the intricacies of the index.

Dr. Andrew Turner was very kind in allowing me to use a room in his house as a base for research operations, and in which to write many, perhaps most, of the following pages. The staff of Associated University Presses have been both helpful and patient in turning the thesis into a book.

Probably most of our family's longtime friends are the people of Linden Christian Fellowship in Swansea, among whom I learned, not only what it meant to be a Christian, but also, by talking, praying, working—and arguing—together over years, how to think theologically, and how to relate theological ideas to their real-life meanings as lived out in the context of Christian communities. The 'Linden experience' has been formative in my own thinking. How can I ever repay them?

The biggest debts must be mentioned last. If a copy of this book survives the centuries and is auctioned off as a rare relic of the 1990s, the purchaser will still not have to pay as much for it as my family has. My parents, Don and Joan Pearse, paid with three years of worry, and with crucial moral and financial support, without which we could not have managed. My wife Ann, and children Ieuan, Bethan and Rhian, paid with three years of relative poverty in a one-bedroom flat, and an all-too-often absent or preoccupied husband and father. What can I say but "Thank you, and I promise never to do it again"?

Introduction

BOTH Lollardy and English separatism have been subjected to increasing scrutiny over the past three or four decades; interest in the latter doubtless owes something to the increased understanding of Elizabethan and later Puritanism that has resulted from the intensive research and burgeoning literature on that subject. The former remains a perennial object of fascination, both as a forerunner of, and an advance fifth column for, the Reformation in England.

In this last respect, in recent years several writers have focused their attention on the "known men" of late Lollardy; J. A. F. Thomson has given his book the title of *The Later Lollards 1414–1520,* while Anne Hudson, in her *Lollards and Their Books,* discusses the tendency of early English Protestants to demonstrate the antiquity of their doctrine by printing medieval texts. Margaret Aston, in her *Lollards and Reformers,* discusses how far the English Reformation itself might be said to be a revival of Lollardy, and how far the latter simply survived into the age of Protestantism.[1] J. F. Davis's study, *Heresy and Reformation in the South-East of England 1520–1559,* is also concerned, to no small degree, with those whose unorthodoxy had an indigenous flavor. He concludes that Lollardy provided at least some of "the seeds of all the future growths" within the Church of England, and "proved a reservoir that flowed into many channels."[2]

The Lollard idea of "known men" is connected, not only with the Lollards' need for secrecy to avoid their persecutors, but also with the need to preserve the purity of their clandestine fellowship. Reginald Pecock, bishop of Chichester, writing in the fifteenth century, had noted the dual use of the concept; if a Lollard was assured that a new acquaintance was a "known man," "al is saaf, perel is not forto dele with him," but also "if eny man knowith not . . . the writing of the Bible, as it lijth in text, namelich the writing of the New Testament, he schal be vnknowen of God forto be eny of hise."[3] Lollardy sought to distinguish between the truly godly and the rest, and thus to provide a means of elite fellowship for those "known" to God and to one another.

15

The history of early English separatism had been authoritatively traced by B. R. White in 1971, but it was only more recently, in 1988, that Stephen Brachlow provided a thorough exposition of its distinctive theological and ecclesiological traits in his book, *The Communion of Saints: Radical Puritan and Separatist Ecclesiology 1570–1625*. Brachlow discusses at length the relationship between church membership and saving faith, emphasizing that, for most separatists and radical Puritans alike, the church was to be composed of "visible saints," discernible on the basis of their confession of faith and outward manner of life.[4] E. S. Morgan, in his 1963 book *Visible Saints: The History of a Puritan Idea,* had covered the subject of "visible sainthood" before Brachlow, though the two do not agree on all points. The essentials, however, seem clear enough: all of these later, Puritan and separatist, radicals were agreed that no certainty could be attached to human judgments in respect to who should, or should not, be admitted to church membership, and Augustine's distinction between the visible church of the professing and the invisible church of the eternally forechosen was upheld. The visible church, as Morgan puts it, "should have in appearance the same purity that the invisible church had in reality: it should admit to membership only those who appeared to be saved, only those who could demonstrate by their lives, their beliefs, and their religious experiences, that they apparently (to a charitable judgment) had received saving faith."[5] The nearness or otherwise of the approximation made by the visible church to the invisible, depended on the ecclesiological strictness of the particular separatist whose views are being examined; this could vary from a simple demand that members should be able to give some account of the Christian verities, accompanied by good behavior, to an insistence that the would-be member should give an account of his own experience of saving faith. John Robinson, the early seventeenth-century separatist leader, argued that only those could be members who were "visibly, and so far as men in charity could judge, justified, sanctified, and entitled to the promises of salvation, and life eternal."[6] Even so, he intended the judgment of charity to be extended reasonably liberally.

Both Lollardy and separatism, then, were concerned to one degree or another with purity of fellowship and with discerning the godly from the godless. Lollardy, of course, entailed doctrinal dissent from the pre-Reformation Catholic church in England. The separatists, on the other hand, found themselves in rather less conflict with the credal formularies of the established Protestant church than with the church structure itself. Both movements have had their historians and theological analysts. The subject matter of the present work, however, is those mid-Tudor radical activists and writers who, like the Lollards, had doctrinal concerns of their own, but who were also generally committed to gathering the worthy out from the unworthy, and who operated in England after Lollardy had begun to lose itself in the wider English Reformation, and before the emergence of separatism as it broke away from the left wing of English Puritanism.

To be sure, there is a fair degree of overlap in respect to chronology. The origins of separatism, for example, can be traced to the Marian exiles, or at least to the Plumbers' Hall congregation or Richard Fitz's church in London in the late 1560s, while the consideration of the Family of Love in this book entails discussion of a period rather further into Elizabeth's reign than that. There again, Joan Bocher, whose life and opinions are considered here, is generally counted as a late Lollard. What qualifies her for inclusion in this work is her refusal to be subsumed by the official Protestantism of the established church. The present work seeks to encompass the whole of the radical challenge to the emergent "official" Protestantism of the period.

It is not as if this has never been researched before, of course. J. W. Martin, an American scholar, has published a number of articles on those radicals who remained consciously separate from, or antagonistic toward, the emerging state Protestantism of the 1540s–1570s, and these articles have recently been reprinted in one volume, under the title, *Religious Radicals in Tudor England*. Martin's friend and mentor, A. G. Dickens, has also acknowledged the growing importance of these radicals by considering them in some depth in the recent second edition of his masterpiece, *The English Reformation*.[7] Even in respect to Henry Hart and his circle, concerning whom Martin and others have written extensively, a fair amount of important fresh biographical evidence, is considered in the present work. As will be seen, some of that fresh material is of the greatest import in assessing the significance of Henry Hart's circle.

The main purpose of this study, however, has not been attempted before: to analyze the actual religious ideas of the radicals themselves, and to compare these with the positions adopted by the magisterial Protestants whom they attempted to refute. The theological and ecclesiological import of the views pronounced by Henry Hart, John Trew, and their fellows, is weighed against those of John Bradford; Robert Cooche is compared with William

Turner; a nameless Anabaptist (possibly also Cooche) with John Knox, and so on. The writing of John Champneys is not so much contrasted with some particular antagonist, as simply analyzed for theological content, in which it abounds, rather than for biographical detail concerning Champneys, in which it does not. In several cases—and Champneys is one of the best examples—a veritable gold mine of information concerning the inner world of mid-Tudor radicalism can be gleaned from this approach. So much—arguably too much—of previous writings concerning these dissenters, has contented itself solely with extracting narrative material from the sources. J. W. Martin tends to use this data to make sociological points concerning the phenomenon of the religious conventicle, the encouragement given to it by the growth of printing, and so forth. There is nothing wrong with this approach, of course; indeed, it is extremely helpful as far as it goes. But the central concerns for which the radicals themselves stood, and often suffered, have been comparatively neglected in the process. This study is more concerned with asking exactly what the dissenters believed, and why. Other important questions relate to the coherence, or otherwise, of those beliefs, their ecclesiological implications, and what elements of their ideas the radicals held in common.

The writings of Robert Cooche, and of his critics, yield at least some biographical information as well as a coherent, developing, and closely integrated theology and ecclesiology. More than any other English writer of this period, he appears to have been influenced directly by, and in favor of, Continental Anabaptism.

John Champneys hasn't been given much concentrated attention in his own right by historians. His work, *The Harvest is at Hand VVherin the Tares shall be Bovnd, and cast into the fyre and brent,* is remarkable for the ideas which it expresses, and is here subjected to a theological analysis. Champneys's later career, early in Elizabeth's reign, is discussed, as is the assumption by some historians that he is the author of *The Copie of an answere.* That work is also discussed here, since its antipredestinarianism appears to have been of a religiously radical, rather than a conservative, kind, its later republication as propaganda for seventeenth-century Laudianism notwithstanding.

English Arianism and other types of ultraradicalism in the Edwardian and Marian periods are considered, for it was these groups which formed the seedbed for the growth of Hendrik Niclaes's Family of Love in England. The Familists have already been covered by excellent recent histories[8] and so in discussing the Family of Love here, the accent is placed very firmly upon theological analysis, and attempts to trace the interplay of ideas and the terms of the debate between the Familists and their state-church antagonists. The Familists are a very different group from most of the others examined in these pages, since their ideas are a blend of spiritualism and rationalism, rather than containing the strong biblicist element general among the radicals. Even so, there are definite connections, both personal and theological, with the mid-century radicalism considered earlier in this work. The origins of English Familism, its view of religious authority, and its main religious concerns, are all discussed.

What M. R. Watts calls "the Calvinist origins of dissent," as distinct from "the earlier, radical stream," have been deliberately excluded from this study.[9] The story of the "Edwardian" underground congregations in Mary's reign, and of the privy church of Richard Fitz or of the Plumbers' Hall congregation in the 1560s, has been told elsewhere,[10] and this is not a history of proto-separatism, nor of the frustrated English admirers of Calvin, Zwingli, and Bullinger, but rather of the non-Reformed "radical stream."

The subject of predestination recurs frequently in this work, as it is a common subject of debate between radicals and magisterial Protestants, and appears to have had implications for the ecclesiology of both. A chapter is accorded, therefore, to reviewing the opinions of the English reformers on this subject, especially as it connects with their concept of the "invisible church," and thus with their ecclesiology. For the reformers in general, predestination and its associated doctrines appear to have been the inner citadel of their theology, from which they sallied forth to do battle with the pestiferous sectaries who are the principal subjects of our story. As will become apparent, their view of what constituted a sound basis for the church depended upon this theology. The tendency of radicals to reject predestination, for the same reason, is also noticeable though, as will be seen, not quite unanimous.

It should be borne in mind that a number of theological terms applied here, whether to the dissenters or to their opponents— *supralapsarian, sublapsarain, amillennial,* and so forth—are more recent in usage (i. e., from the post-Dortian era) than the people and events under discussion. The terms are not employed under any illusion that the individuals to whose ideas they are applied would readily have adopted them. Rather, they appear to be the most precise analytical tools for understanding those ideas, and sometimes the least cumbersome way of referring to them.

The views of the English radicals who preceded, and ran in a different tradition from, the separatists of the Elizabethan era were vilified by their state-church opponents. If that is understandable, it is unfortunate that those views should meet the scarcely happier fate of being overlooked by posterity. This book is an attempt to help fill that void and thus to contribute to the exploration of the world of sixteenth-century religious radicalism in England.

Between Known Men
and Visible Saints

1

The Free-Will Men

In 1561 Jean Veron, a French reformer who had been invited to England in the reign of Edward VI, and who had returned again at Elizabeth's accession after the Protestant exile under Mary, published *A frutefull treatise of predestination*. It was written, he claimed, "that I might enarm and fence the true churche of God againste the pestiferous sect of the fre wil men of oure time".[1] He explained in *Against the fre wil men,* published at the same time as *A fruteful treatise,* that these enemies of "the free mercy and grace of God . . . ye shall not onely fynde . . . among the papystes, but also amonge them, that wyll be coumpted most perfect christians, & most earnest fauourers of the gospel." A marginal note explained that he meant "the Anabaptistes and free wil men."[2] In other words, the espousers of the doctrine of human free will whom Veron made his target were, to borrow the modern political metaphor, to the left of the official Protestantism in whose service he himself was employing his pen. The right wing—Roman Catholicism—also held to free will; the denial of free will, and a belief in predestination, Veron saw as being a distinguishing feature of the middle ground, the position of state-church Protestants like himself. As will be seen, he was not alone in this perception.

Nicholas Lesse, writing in 1550 in the preface to his translation of some passages of Saint Augustine concerning predestination, also denounced the "corrupt sort of heretiques" who reject the doctrine.[3] Just to make it clear whom he had in mind, he added, "I do mean the anabaptysts and frewyl masters."[4] Anabaptism and a belief in free will tended to be equated with one another. Some of the earliest English dissenters to have been consistently antipredestinarian would have been those who had come under Anabaptist influence. John Bale took it as axiomatic that Anabaptists had "in a maner the same opinion of fre wil | & of justification by workes" that Catholics did.[5] But however impeccable, even archetypal, the Anabaptists' separatist credentials might be, and however emphatic their opposition to the doctrine of predestination,[6] Anabaptism as a source of influence upon the English radicals of the sixteenth century, as in the seventeenth, is not easy to prove. Most of those who fell into the hands of the authorities for Anabaptism were foreigners, often Dutch, and most of the few native-born Englishmen who were consciously committed Anabaptists pass as shadows across the historian's field of vision.

This difficulty has not prevented many historians, from J. M. Cramp[7] in the last century, to E. C. Pike[8] at the beginning of this, to W. R. Estep and I. B. Horst[9] in more recent years, from claiming to discern precise features from these shadows, and definite conclusions of an Anabaptist presence in the merest documentary hints actually available to the historian. Even G. H. Williams has succumbed to this tendency.[10] To be sure, the epithet "Anabaptist" was freely bandied about to describe Protestant radicals generally. But the term was intended as an insult and, shot through as it was with suggestions of Münsterite fanaticism, as conclusive argument that the persons so described had placed themselves outside the company of reasonable men. It was presumably this polemical, theologically imprecise usage that caused John Hooper, the Edwardian bishop of Gloucester, to claim, in a letter to Heinrich Bullinger, that Kent and Essex were "troubled with the frenzy of the anabaptists more than any other part of the kingdom," and, in an earlier letter, that "anabaptists" flocked to his preaching and "give me much trouble."[11] It was this loose meaning of the term, also, that Lord Riche was using in 1555 when, despite Joan Bocher's apparent silence on baptismal questions, he had occasion to speak of "Joan of Kent and the Anabaptists."[12] The very fact that the term *Anabaptist* was used in such a vague way to denote radicalism generally, should evoke caution about taking such descriptions as accurate theological definitions. Any and every radical opinion could be described as Anabaptist, and every radical was equally anxious to deny the charge. If accusations and denials of Anabaptism have any evidential value at all for the historian, it must be a purely negative one; namely, that a general absence of being labeled "Anabaptist" in the case of a given radical or group of radicals is strong evidence that no Anabaptist influence is present, while (even tacit) admission of such a charge in the face of almost universal execration of the specter of "Anabaptism" is an indicator that such an influence is indeed present.

Whatever the influence of Continental Anabaptist ideas on English radicals may have been, however, it does not seem to have extended to the actual practice of believers' baptism (i.e., to

Anabaptism) itself. John Bale, the Edwardian bishop of Ossory, noted that

> I neuer harde it, that euer any man with in the realme, wente aboute the reiteration of baptisme actually, at any time. What though I hard of manye, which wer of the same sedicious opinion, and of some straungers which wer also executed there, for it.

Only those historians who succeed in unearthing activities that eluded the notice of such contemporaries can hope to overturn this judgment and speak in any meaningful sense of "English Anabaptism."[13] Anyone known to have received such a baptism could not have escaped death, Bale added with perhaps unconscious irony, "vnder king Henry, nor yet vnder kinge Edward, for they both hated that secte."[14] Established, compulsory religion, whether Protestant or Catholic, had been a mainstay of social order in Europe for a millennium; the individual autonomy and voluntarism that were inextricably bound up with Anabaptism were generally considered fatal to royal or hierarchical power. Bale's comment that Henry VIII and Edward VI "hated that secte" that preached such doctrines, is equivalent to an observation that two particular farmyard turkeys are not, on the whole, admirers of the institution of Christmas!

The Conventiclers of Kent and Essex

The first group of English dissenters of the sixteenth century, of whose antipredestinarian views any certain knowledge is extant, are the conventiclers of Bocking in Essex and Faversham in Kent. Members of these groups were arrested in the reigns both of Edward VI and of Mary. They were first discovered at Christmas 1550 when the Faversham group visited their brethren in Bocking and were sufficiently unwise as to crowd into one house to meet. The gathering of some sixty persons thus attracted attention, and a number of the ringleaders were arrested and questioned in front of the Privy Council. M. R. Watts points out that the "conventiclers are not described as Anabaptists" in the depositions recorded by Burrage (a strong indicator that no such influence was present), but even so, when one of them, Thomas Cole, was obliged to preach a sermon of recantation before Archbishop Cranmer in 1553 its published title was *A godly and frutefull sermon, made at Maydstone the fyrste sonday in Lent, by M. Thomas Cole Scholemayster there, against dyuers erronious opinions of the Anabaptistes and others.*[15]

However, another member of the same group, Nicholas Sheterden of Pluckley, who appeared before the Privy Council on February 1550/51, was arrested again in Mary's reign and, in his examination in June 1555 (he was burned at Canterbury on 12 July), rejected the Melchiorite view of the incarnation in terms which made plain the great distance which existed in his own mind between his own theological views in general, and those of the Anabaptists. Before Nicholas Harpsfield, archdeacon of Canterbury, and Robert Collins, commissary of Canterbury, Sheterden answered one of Collins's questions as follows: "then must ye fall into the error of the Anabaptists, which deny that Christ took flesh of the Virgin Mary. . . ."[16]

If at least some of the conventiclers rejected Melchiorite Christology and none advocated an Anabaptist view of baptism, M. M. Knappen is hardly being unjust when he writes that these sectaries "may be called halfway Anabaptists." He justifies this description by pointing out that they

> denounced the doctrine of predestination, and refused to have their children baptized by Roman Catholic clergy, though they did not object to infant baptism as such, or hold many of the other Anabaptist principles of which they were accused.[17]

The accusation of Anabaptism, however, is that of John Strype, the eighteenth-century historian, rather than of a contemporary. The epithet more frequently applied by the conventiclers' Protestant opponents at the time was that of Pelagianism.[18] This charge referred to the belief held by the sectaries that man possesses free will, and that, in the words of Robert Cole of Faversham, "the doctryne of predestynation was meter for divilles than for christian men."[19]

This belief among the Kent and Essex radicals was so pronounced, that both contemporaries and historians have referred to them as "free-willers" or "free-will men."[20] And yet the issue does not appear to have become of crucial importance to them until shortly before their arrest; Henry Hart, one of their leaders, had some of his written works published in both 1548 and 1549, and yet neither book deals with doctrines of predestination and free-will in a polemical way, though their generally Pelagian spirit indicates where his allegiance would lie were such a question to be debated.[21] The subject most likely became a live issue for Hart's group as a result of their contact with strong Reformed teachings concerning predestination as the official attempts to Protestantize the country in Edward VI's reign gathered pace. Perhaps it was the publication of a short tract, *Of predestinacion and election,* written by the Protestant clergyman of Elham and printed at nearby Canterbury in 1550, that finally sparked the debate and drew the conventiclers' fire.[22] Hart was said by his fellow-conventicler John Grey to have taught that "ther was no man so chosen but that he mighte dampne hime selfe Nether yet anye man soo | reprobate but that he mighte kepe goddes Comaundements," and "that Saincte paule mighte haue dampnid hime selfe if he listed." For Hart, a belief in predestination must inevitably lead to moral carelessness; he wrote in 1548 that

> some because they Wolde be hydde from God, mynde them selfes in a folyshe cloke of myare[23] necessyty | sayng in the^m selfes | y^t it can not other wyse be; When in dede they stryve not at all to make resystaûce but doo lette the fleshelye mynde runne whether it lusteth.

Another of the free-will men, George Brodbridge, "saide and affirmed that goddes predestynation is not reteyne but apon condytion &c." Yet another, Humphrey Middleton, was reported as saying, while on a visit to Robert Cole's house at Faversham, "that Adam was elected to be salved And that all men | being then in Adams Loynes were predestynate to be salvid and that ther were no reprobates." It was "a generall affirmation emonge them, that the preachinge of predestynacyon is a dampnable doctryne."[24] The idea that all men were elected to life was known to be a commonly held radical view even before the depositions of 1550/51 brought it to light. Robert Crowley, writing in 1548, had noted that "the freewyl men .'. . crye out . . . to proue Gods vniuersall predestination," pointing to "vniuersal scriptures . . . declarynge that God would haue all men saued." The expression "freewyl men" was used at this period to refer to Catholics on the right, as well as to radicals on the left, and Crowley's writing on that occasion was aimed against Nicholas Shaxton's recantation of Protestant beliefs and relapse into Henrician Catholicism in 1546. However, the fact that Crowley had radical Protestant views in mind, is shown by his admission that, on the subject of predestination, "there be at thys daye manye (and that men of a feruent zeale towardes the trueth) that are of your [Shaxton's] opinion."[25]

The imprisonment of some of the conventiclers seems to have led to that comparitive rarity, the martyrdom of a religious radical under the Protestant Edwardian regime. John Foxe, an admirer of the Edwardian governments, referred to two orthodox Protestants who died, as it were, accidentally, during imprisonment by local officials contrary to government orders, but declared that, apart from these, "during all this time [Edward's reign], neither in Smithfield nor any other quarter of this realm, were any heard to suffer for any matter of religion, either papist or protestant, . . . except only two." These were Joan Bocher and George von Parris, who were actually burned at the stake during this reign, "for certain articles," wrote Foxe, anxious to brush the matter quickly aside, "not much necessary here to be rehearsed."[26] However, one of the Kent free-will men, William Sibley of Lenham, was committed to prison (the record is irritatingly silent about which one) on the orders of the Privy Council early in 1551, and was dead by the following August. That he was probably not an old man at the time would seem to be indicated by the fact that he died intestate (and so perhaps unexpectedly) and that his widow did not die for almost another twenty years.[27] The conclusion that Sibley died as a result of his imprisonment seems unavoidable, and he should therefore be accounted only the third radical martyr under Edward VI to have come to light so far. Although it takes so little space to recount, this fact is significant since Foxe's assurance that Bocher and Parris were the only two to suffer death for their faith in Edward's reign has met with general acceptance by historians.

The activities of the conventiclers were to lead William Sibley to his death; their antipredestinarian opinions were to lead others into sometimes acrimonious debate with more mainstream Protestants when both were imprisoned in the King's Bench in Mary's reign. The free-willers were shocked that their predestinarian brethren, who, like them, looked "every day to suffer for the truth," should be willing to indulge in card games, dice, and such "vain play." The predestinarians retorted that their critics were trusting in salvation by works.[28]

John Careless, a Coventry weaver, told the sectaries that the elect cannot be lost, and he clearly meant what he said, for he had no more compunction about lying than about gaming; indeed his lies were over precisely this debate when his Roman Catholic interrogator questioned him about it (although it might be conjectured that his conscience gave him a special dispensation when telling untruths to the agents of Antichrist!). The reports of schism among the schismatics could only be expected to cheer the Catholics, and the well-named Careless was asked: "of what church art thou of, or what faith? for I hear say that you have divers churches and

faiths in the King's Bench. . . . Dost thou not know one Henry
Hart, or hast thou not heard of him?" The weaver replied, "No
forsooth; I do not know any such, nor have I heard of him, that I
wot of," but explained in his written account of the interview:

> But yet I lied falsely; for I knew him indeed, and his qualities too well.
> And I have heard so much of him, that I dare say it had been good for
> that man if he had never been born; for many a simple soul hath he
> shamefully seduced, beguiled, and deceived with his foul Pelagian opin-
> ion, both in the days of that good king Edward and since his departure.

Careless felt no incongruity in piously remarking, immediately
after this confession, "God convert him, or confound him shortly,
for his name's sake. Amen." When pressed by Dr. Martin on the
subject of disputes among the prisoners Careless again declared,
"Forsooth there is no contention amongst us, that I know of," and
now he was bluntly accused of deceit.

> What! wilt thou lie to me? Is there not great contention between
> thee and one Trew, that was here with me ere while? Yes, that there
> is; and I can tell thee by what token well enough. I hear say one of
> your matters is about predestination. How dost thou believe of
> predestination?

This time Careless simply maintained his denial as best he could.
"Surely we have no contention there, nor ever had but for this
matter of predestination; and that is ended between us, many a
day agone," and explained to his readers that "this I spake to make
the best of the matter; for I was sorry that the papists should hear
of our variance."[29]

Why should John Careless have been sorry that the papists
should hear of disagreements among the inmates of the King's
Bench Prison? He had no time for Hart's "foul Pelagian opinion,"
and thought it better for the man had he never been born. He was
among those who warned John Trew and his companions, that they
were "like to die for it if the Gospel should reign again, affirming
that the true church might shed blood for belief's sake." So what
prevented him from denouncing the free-willers to their common
persecutors, the Roman Catholic interrogators? The answer is
likely to be that there was just sufficient a feeling of being fellow-
Protestants to maintain a front of unanimity in the face of a challenge from this quarter, particularly in view of the Catholics' frequent and telling charge that breaking from Rome led to endless
fission and uncertainty in religion. Had the sectaries really been

explicitly Anabaptist in their theology, the orthodox might well have been more anxious to distance themselves from them. As it was, the conventiclers seem to have occupied a position on the very edge of what the Reformed might have considered tolerable, even under these circumstances of persecution. Even Trew admitted that, at one stage in the dispute, the predestinarians "confessed us to be of the true church and no heretics, and upon the same would have received us to the communion" before trouble flared again over the issue of card-playing and gaming, and then "they did . . . call and report us heretics, cast dust in our faces, and give judgment of damnation on us, and otherways ungodly handled us," following this up with the warning about their likely fate under a future Protestant regime.[30]

John Bradford, the Church of England martyr, was of a more irenic spirit than Careless, more certain than he that the free-willers were in some sense fellow-travelers, however unruly and dangerous they might be. He attempted to win over a number of them to his own predestinarian views in a celebrated correspondence with Henry Hart, John Ledley, Robert Cole, Nicholas Sheterden, Humphrey Middleton, and others, from his cell during the months prior to his execution on 1 July 1555. He told them that he was attempting in his letters "to supply that, which by mouth patiently you cannot abide to hear." The free-willers had claimed "that I am a slander [sic]; which, as far as I know, is only in this to youwards, that I believe and affirm the salvation of God's children to be so certain, that they shall assuredly enjoy the same."[31] For Bradford, the doctrine of predestination, although important, was a secondary consideration when compared to the necessity of repentance and personal faith.

> Know that predestination is too high a matter for you to be disputers of it, until you have been better scholars in the school-house of repentance and justification, which is the grammar-school, wherein we must be conversant and learned, before we go to the university of God's most holy predestination and providence.[32]

Perhaps it was this that enabled him to address Robert Cole and Nicholas Sheterden as "my friends and brethren in the Lord," to write to them all as his "dearly beloved in the Lord," and to refer to Cole as "my good brother" and to the sectaries' leader as "my father Hart."[33]

*   *   *

Radical Theology and a Gathered Church

1. Predestination and Free-Will

Despite his gracious spirit, John Bradford was deeply concerned about the antipredestinarian views of his opponents. In January 1554/55 he wrote, together with Robert Ferrar, Rowland Taylor, and John Philpot, his fellow prisoners, to Cranmer, Ridley, and Latimer in the following terms:

> The effects of salvation they so mingle with the cause, that, if it be not seen to, more hurt will come by them than ever came by the papists; inasmuch as their life commendeth them to the world more than the papists'. God is my witness, that I write not this but because I would God's glory and the good of his people. In free-will they are plain papists, yea, Pelagians: and ye know that *modicum fermenti totam massam corrumpit.*[34]

Enclosed with this letter, Bradford sent the bishops a piece of writing of his own, his reference to which is worth quoting in full, both because it stresses his concern at the activities of the free-willers, and because it gives strong, though not conclusive, evidence as to the identity of the piece in question and of the event that provoked him to produce it. "Herewithal," he wrote,

> I send unto you a little Treatise which I have made, that you might peruse the same, and not only you but also ye my other most dear and reverend fathers in the Lord for ever, to give it to your approbation as ye may think good. All the prisoners hereabouts in manner have seen it and read it: and as therein they agree with me, nay, rather with the truth, so they are ready and will be to signify it as they shall see you give them example. The matter may be thought not so necessary as I seem to make it: but yet, if ye knew the great evil that is like hereafter to come to the posterity by these men, as partly this bringer can signify unto you, surely then could ye not but be most willing to put hereto your helping hands, the which thing I might more occasion you to perceive, I have sent you here a writing of Harry Hart's own hand, whereby ye may see how Christ's glory and grace is like to lose much light, if that your sheep *quondam* be not something holpen by them which love God, and are able to prove that all good is to be attributed only and wholly to God's grace and mercy 'in Christ', without other respect of worthiness than Christ's merits.[35]

The treatise in question is almost certainly Bradford's *Defence of Election,* which is dated 11 October 1554. The context in which he refers to it scarcely makes sense unless the work were on the subject of predestination, and, while it might seem strange that he should wait so long a period before sending it to Cranmer, yet it seems even more unlikely that he would have written another treatise on the same subject within this period. Furthermore, his additional enclosure of "a writing of Harry Hart's own hand" is very likely the work which the *Defence of Election* is designed to refute, namely, *The Enormities proceeding of the opinion, that predestination, calling, and election, is absolute in man as it is in God*. The work cannot be a title for John Trew's denunciation of "enormities," for Trew's work does not contain the sentences cited by Bradford, and, in any case, was not written until 30 January 1555/56, some seven months after Bradford's death.[36] Against the identification of Hart as the author of the work Bradford was attempting to refute, is the argument that sending Hart's work to Cranmer would then have been unnecessary, since Bradford claims not to have left out of his own work "one tittle of every word as he (i. e., Bradford's opponent) hath put it abroad." However, Bradford goes on to mention that it was "sent to me from him, I think; for it was subscribed with his name, and the superscription was to me by name as truly written."[37] The work was, then, either written in the author's own hand, or else printed (this was possible, but unlikely under the circumstances) and signed with a comment by the author. If that author were Hart, it is not unnatural that Bradford should send the original autograph to the bishops along with his own work, notwithstanding his own extensive quotation from it.

Whether or not Hart was the author of this piece, it seems inconceivable, given the context, that it did not, at the very least, come from the pen of one of his circle of free-willers. Ridley replied to Bradford's letter, stating that he had merely glanced through the writings Bradford had sent, since the other prisoners were also anxious to read them. However, Ridley indicated that he had already answered Bradford's antagonist "in a brief letter, and yet he hath replied again: but he must go without any further answer of me for this time." Correspondence was getting more difficult in any case; Ridley complained that "we are so now ordered and straitly watched, that scantly our servants dare do anything for us. . . ."[38] The arguments of both protagonists shed much light on the relationship between antipredestinarian views and the incipient separatism of the free-willers. Bradford quotes the "enormities" attributed by his opponent to the doctrine of predestination.

"The sixth enormity is this," saith he, "that it colourably denieth excommunication to be had and used in the congregation of Christ; for such as they call good they say are predestinate, and those that they call evil may (some say of them) be called. . . ."

The trouble with predestination, then, was what J. W. Martin, in reference to this passage, calls "the doctrine's adverse effect on any effort to maintain a separate religious group that disciplines its members' lives." Even evil-livers might be among those whom God had foreordained to eternal life, and "how they be, nor when they shall be called, say they, that it cannot be known." Excommunication of the ungodly, it was argued, was impossible if the elect could not be identified with any certainty. The predestinarians were charged with holding that it was possible to be sure of one's own election, but not of that of any other person.

For, although they say that predestination is absolute as well towards man, as it is in God himself, which indeed is not true; yet it is not known to any other, but only to them that can so think, or rather imagine: which indeed is called a strong faith in many; but, when the inward eyes of them are truly opened, it will appear either here, or in another place, where it will not be so easy to help a very vain and naughty opinion.[39]

A belief in predestination, the free-willer concluded, brought its adherents in danger of hell-fire. Just as significant as this concern for the purity of the visible church is Bradford's concurrence with his opponent about the ecclesiological effects of a belief in predestination.

As for who be the elect and who be not, because it is God's privilege to know who be his, God's people are not curious in others; but, as in themselves they feel "the earnest" of the Lord, and have God's Spirit in possession by faith, (I speak of those which be of years of discretion;) so do they judge of others by their works, and not further do they enter with God's office.[40]

The elect, in other words, exercised the judgment of charity toward their neighbors, not attempting to discern the election or nonelection of others, and hence the church could continue to embrace all.

The underlying assumptions of the two protagonists in this debate scarcely break surface in their discussion. Both appear to

agree that it is by men's outward works that the church must exercise its jurisdiction of excommunication. Yet Hart accuses the predestinarians of being lax on this point because of their conviction
that some apparent evil-livers may be among those foreordained
to life. Bradford agrees that those of his own conviction "are not
curious in others" in respect to "who be the elect and who be
not." Bradford's assumptions, then, might fairly be described as
inclusivist; God's predestination being secret and past finding out,
God's people "judge of others by their works, and not further do
they enter with God's office." This suggests that the church is to
include all but those who, by their heinous sins, exclude themselves. Hart's assumptions, on the other hand, appear to be exclusivist. His objection to the doctrine of predestination seems to be
that it makes a distinction between true godly living and being in
a state of grace, whereas it appears from his group's refusal "to
Salute a Synner or a man whome they knowe not" that his definition of godly living would exclude most of the population and pinpoint those in a state of grace. As he had noted in 1548, "the
multytude of the ungodlye wyll not repente, for they haue pleasure
to lyue in Synne. . . ."[41] In plain terms, Bradford was assuming
that the purity of the church could be maintained by the excommunication of gross sinners, while his conventicler opponents began,
as it were, from a zero base. The former view assumed that the
wicked would stand out from the crowd and be excluded, while
the latter assumes the ungodliness of the crowd itself, and looks
for the saints to prove themselves to be the exceptions and thus
to constitute the church. It should be emphasized that these appear
to be the underlying assumptions of the protagonists, assumptions
which are nowhere made explicit. But it was the secrecy of God's
predestination that damned it as a doctrine in the eyes of Hart,
and made the visibility of the saints a concomitant of a doctrine
of free-will. The alternative to the shared logic of Bradford and
Hart, namely, the idea that God's predestination might be discernible, does not appear to have a significant history prior to Robert
Browne's teaching on "visible saints" later in the century. This
notion, when it arose, made possible the development of the predestinarian separatist churches of the seventeenth century. But as
long as predestination was seen as a secret affair, a divine mystery
of whose workings one could scarcely be sure even in respect to
oneself, then predestination and separatism were two essentially
opposing ideas. For secret-predestinarians like the Elizabethan Pu-

ritans, the purity or impurity of a church was more to be gauged by reference to its teaching and ceremonies than to its membership.

2. No Communion with Sinners: The Church of "Known Men"

Does the evidence concerning the conventiclers, then, reveal any other traces of separatist principles? Although "thei had refused the communyon aboue ij yeres" when they were questioned by the Privy Council in 1550/51, this fact in itself may only indicate a de facto separation, rather than a principled belief that the church should separate itself from the world. More significant in this regard is the view of Nicholas Young, who "saide that they wolde not comunycate w^t Synners." This again is a statement about their view of the purity of the visible church, not simply in doctrine (the Reformed could have agreed to that), but in membership. Hart, in a sentence that may have been rhetorical but was more likely intended as a call for the excommunication of all evil-livers, had written, "For truly (as saic paul sayth) ye can not be partakers of the lordes table, and of the table of deuels, neyther drynke of the lordes cup and of the cup of deuels. . . ."[42] Furthermore, John Plume of Lenham acknowledged that he had "herde it diuers tymes affirmed as a generall doctryne that they oughte not to Salute a Synner or a man whome they knowe not." This idea is possibly of Lollard origin,[43] but is nevertheless a concept more appropriate to a group who saw themselves as sheep among wolves than to a self-styled "righteous remnant," a state-church-in-waiting. Also consistent with this view of themselves is the response of the free-willers to the taunts of John Careless and his fellows in the King's Bench Prison in Mary's reign; when he told them that they were just as likely to suffer for their beliefs under a Protestant regime as under a Catholic, and that the true church was justified in persecuting misbelievers; they responded by quoting the Sermon on the Mount and other Scriptures, "but it would not serve" to silence the Coventry weaver and his companions. Hart had taught his followers that "we are called . . . to suffer with Chryst, that we might be made partakers w̄ hym in glory," and declared that "blessed and happy are those, (Sayth the spyryte) that love not ther lyves unto the deathe: Truly they shall receaue a Crowne of life."[44] The evidence which has so far been reviewed suggesting the absence of an Anabaptist orientation of the group, should be sufficient to prevent this characteristic (of a "theology of suffering") from being claimed as "evidence" for such a connection. People using the same basic sources for their ideas (in this case primarily the New Testament) will frequently come to similiar conclusions, without the need for postulating the influence of one group upon another. For example, in claiming that true believers "have obtayned not only knowledge and Judgemente to dyscerne and iudge betwyxt the good and ȳ euyl," but are actually "made able through the spyryte whyche lyveth in you whych ye have of God to chose ȳ good & to leave ȳ euyll," Hart was not only taking similar ground to that taken by Melchior Hoffmann, who affirmed that freedom of the will is restored by Christ, but uses the same text (John 8.36) to back up his case: "wher ȳ spirite of ȳ lord is, ther is libertye and throughe hym ye are made stronge, so ye obey. . . ."[45] Yet there is no evidence to suggest a personal link between the two men, nor of direct influence upon Hart by the writings of Hoffmann.

3. The "Stinkyng Floures" of Thomas Cole

At the close of his sermon of recantation preached before Archibishop Cranmer on the first Sunday of Lent, 1552/53, Thomas Cole of Maidstone concluded his remarks on the errors of the sectaries with a confusing mixture of exculpation ("Neither haue I spokē them vnto you in the way of recantacion, neither came I to thys place to retract any doctrine I haue before taught, as some crooked sprites, more apt to contention than to concorde, perhaps either thynke or will hereafter report of me"), lies ("For God is my witnes, before whom I stand, I neuer helde or taught any of these or such lyke erroures"), and denunciation of his fellows ("neither do I knowe any that doth holde or mayntayne any of theym, besydes these two simple men, whiche are here punished for their offences: by whom you may learne to beware of lyke danger").[46] Cole had been obliged to preach "agaynst dyuers erroures of the Anabaptistes and such sectes where soeuer they be, as in christen religion call theym selues Brothers and Systers, and dyuide theym selues from other christian people," and he presented ten such errors.[47] Although I. B. Horst is correct in noting that the sermon "raises many questions about its nature and the intention of the speaker," his claim that "at points he apparently spoke with tongue in cheek, if not with plain double-talk," is stretching the evidence;[48] the sermon reads like the unwilling and embarrassed recantation that it was. Cole had been accused of denying original sin, and it is not insignificant that the opening words of his sermon were as follows:

> Who dooth not meruayle or count it a thing very straunge, that a mortall man, of the generation of Adam, conceyued in synne, borne in wyckednes . . . shuld so boldly speak unto al states and degrees of men, commandynge them to heare.[49]

Furthermore, when listing the "flattering floures of the dyuell" that he was under instructions to denounce, he gave a refutation of each in turn until he came to the eighth, "Namely to deny that children be borne in originall synne, or beynge so fallen, cannot be renewed agayne by repentaunce: or to denye the baptisme of infantes." Here, he merely added, doubtless to the amusement of those in the congregation who knew the true purpose of the sermon,

> Howe the worde of god doth confute these errours, and deface these floures, I woulde declare yf tyme serued: But bycause it is shorte, and I have somewhat more to saye, lette it bee sufficient for you to knowe, that they are pestylent and unwholsom floures.[50]

Cole was not, however, as impenitent as he is claimed to be by Horst, who seriously misquotes him at one point. Horst writes, "At the close he frankly said: 'I haue not spoken of these errours to thys end, that I would haue you to eschew them.'"[51] This is incorrect. Not only was this not the end of Cole's sermon but, more importantly, Cole's words expressed the exact opposite of this sentiment. "I haue not spoken of these errours to thys end, that I woulde haue you to learne them, but that I woulde haue you to eschew them."[52] The eighth opinion which he condemned, "Namely to deny that children be borne in originall synne, or beynge so fallen, cannot be renewed agayne by repentaunce: or to denye the baptisme of infantes," was indeed one that he seems to have held, at least in part, in 1550; in the depositions it was alleged that "Cole of Maidestone saide and affirmed that children were not borne in originall Synne."[53] Bradford believed himself to have detected an implicit denial of the doctrine of original sin in the third of *The Enormities proceeding of the opinion, that predestination, calling, and election, is absolute in man as it is in God.*[54] But Hart, in his *Godly newe short treatyse instructyng every parson, howe they shulde trade theyr lyues in ye imytacyon of vertu and ye shewyng of vyce* of 1548, referred to original sin as if he himself believed in the doctrine. "We were all naturally born ye chyldern of wrath, as wel as al other becaus of orygynall Synne, that reyneth in all fleshe."[55] The denial of original sin, of course, has implications for the validity of pædobaptism, but it is more likely, given that the conventiclers did not reject infant baptism as such, that the denial was but a concomitant of their rejection of predestination.

The second and sixth of Cole's ten points were concerned with those who denied predestination and election.[56] Clearly, the denial of these doctrines was considered an important mark of "such sectes" as dared to "call theym selues Brothers and Systers" and to "dyuide theym selues from other christian people." His argument for predestination is cumbersome and (perhaps deliberately) unconvincing. "If there had been no predestination, then wold not S. Paul have given thanks to God for it," and

> if God bee then displeased at synne (as his word doth declare him to be) than is he not the author of syn, onlesse we shuld grant (as God forbyd) that he is both a mutable god or a dissembling God. . . . For he is the author of nothyng but of that which he aloweth.[57]

Cole denounced "the stinkyng floure of separation or segregation from others as from wycked and damned men, not worthy to communicate the sacraments, or to eate and drynke with them," and advised his hearers, in terms that anticipate the dispute between George Gifford and Henry Barrow nearly forty years later, that if the powers that be "wyl not excommunicate suche as be notorious and manyfest evylworkers, then must the priuate man commit the matter to god . . . and receyue the sacraments without separation."[58] Since it is unreasonable to believe that Cole's sermon was addressing merely hypothetical errors held by unspecified groups of people, then it seems clear that he was describing beliefs held to a large extent by members of the group to which he had belonged. There is no record extant of the Bocking group denying "the baptisme of infantes" as such, but John Trew and his companions denied "that our children might receive a lawful baptism in the church of Antichrist . . . lest we should therein allow and affirm Antichrist to be God's minister. . . ." All of this, Trew claimed, was

> contrary to the Holy Ghost, which affirmeth, that their prayer is sin, and their blessing cursing; and that they should not take God's word in their mouths; and that we should have nothing to do with them, but separate ourselves from them, lest we be partakers of their sins, and so to receive of their plagues. . . .[59]

This denial of the validity of Catholic baptism is essentially Catabaptist (i.e., the willingness to rebaptize on the basis of rejecting the validity of baptisms administered by a false church), rather than an espousal of believers' baptism. And even here, it is not known whether the radicals ever translated their theory into practice. Probably they did no more than withhold their infants from baptism by the Catholic clergy. However, those arrested in 1550 had most certainly refused to "communicate with sinners," and had absented themselves from their parish churches for two years. By their actions they had also upheld the view, later denounced by Cole in his sermon, "that it is lawfull to be a publyke preacher in a christen common welth, without the authoritie of the christen magistrates."[60] All of these actions point toward the conclusion that the general direction of their ecclesiology was separatist.

4. Not Many Wise: Egalitarianism and the Errors of the Learned

In addition to all of this, there are some hints about the kind of spirituality that prevailed among the Kent and Essex free-willers, and these, too, point in the separatist direction. Upchard of Bocking gave an account before the Privy Council on 27 January 1550/51 of a meeting that had taken place in his house. He related that

> thei fell in argument of thinges of the Scripture, speciallie wheather it were necessarie to stande or kneele, barehedde, or covered at prayer, whiche at length was concluded in ceremonie not to be materiall, but the hartes before God was it that imported, and no thing els. . . ."[61]

The freedom of debate is significant in itself, anticipating later separatism and the debates among the General Baptists at Thomas Lambe's church in Bell Alley, Coleman Street, in the 1640s. But it is important to note also the conclusion, namely, that "the hartes before God" were the prime consideration. The whole spiritual impetus behind the Reformation had been the internalization of religion, but none of the magisterial Protestant churches had gone so far as to make matters of ceremony immaterial; in general, they had satisfied themselves with some degree of simplification. Some standard form of ceremonial was a sine qua non of any official church; for the magisterials, if a thing were among the *adiaphora,* this meant that it was worthy of uniform acceptance for order's sake, not that it was the legitimate subject of approval or rejection by private men.

Hart and his companions went further, however: Laurence Ramsey told his captors in 1550/51 that "harte saide that/ Learned men were the cause of grete Errors," while William Forstall confirmed this report. "Henry harte saide the same tyme that his faithe was not growndid apon Lernyd men for all errors were broughte in by Lernyd men."[62] Antiintellectualism certainly figures in Hart's writing; he spoke of "a fayned ryghtuousenes grounded upō naturall wysdome and carnall reason." "Truly knowledge is daungerous," he wrote, "where loue and obedyence is lackynge | for it tyckelyth the mynde of foles, and lefteth them up w^t vanyty."[63] Nicholas Sheterden wrote to his brother Walter in 1555 that if his captors "had studied God's word, the Author of truth, as they have done logic and Duns [Scotus], with the legend of lies, they should have been as expert in the truth, as they be now in bald reasons," and a shocked John Bradford told Cranmer, perhaps with some exaggeration, that the free-willers "utterly contemn all learning."[64] In his 1564 edition of the *Letters of the Martyrs,* Coverdale added, in a side-note to this comment of Bradford's, that "thys is well knowen to all those which haue had to do wyth them in disputations or otherwyse: for the wrytyngs and authority of the learned, they haue vtterly reiected & despised."[65] Such a reaction by the free-will men to the learning of their antagonists would hardly be surprising if the attitude of John Philpot was at all typical of the predestinarian side. He dismissed the radicals as people who would not "submit their judgment to be tried . . . by the godly learned pastors . . . but . . . take upon themselves to be teachers, before they have learned, . . ." and thus could hardly be as surprised as Bradford seems to have been if they did "utterly condemn all learning" in response; Philpot's attack, after all was not on any lack of experience in learning from the Scriptures—Hart had been active for some two decades—but on the fact that they had no formal theological education.[66] Philpot sneered at their lack of sophistication; although they cried for "the scripture, the scripture," "it cometh like a beggar's cloak out of their mouth, full of patches and all out of fashion," and he wished that they would "leave bogging of heresies . . . and fall to their own occupation, every man according to his own calling, and learn to eat with the sweat of their own brows their bread. . . ."[67] In the eyes of some on the predestinarian side, then, there seems to have been a close link between clericalism and the upholding of learning, just as the free-will men tended to connect their own egalitarianism with the rejection of learning.

John Laurence and John Barre, free-willers writing in reply to Latimer's Swiss servant Augustin Bernhere on the subject of predestination, exhibited a more moderate tone; they mistrusted those who took refuge in their scholarly status and knowledge of "the tongues," even if they did not "contemn all learning." They claimed that Bernhere could not produce any text of the scripture to support his belief in a supralapsarian reprobation of the damned, but suspected that he would "make one yoᵣ self & say it is in yᵉ greek tonnge: as youᵘ have used the same shift wher in yoᵣ booke & youᵘ cōdeme all yᵉ englishe translations: wᶜʰ new translated, of all well lerned mē as yō be"; their apparent approval of the English translations and the scholarly work that went into making them, suggests that they did not condemn all learning as such, but profoundly mistrusted the reasonings of learned men.[68] They complained of Bernhere's attempt to "exalt yoᵣ selfes & yoᵣ owne cōpany calling some of them: most godly lerned as though neither yᵉ pʳᵒphettes nor apostles were to be cōpared wᵗʰ them," and a note in the margin directed readers to Paul's observation that "not many wise mē aftᵣ yᵉ flesh, & but yᵉ folishe before yᵉ world hath god chosē 2.Cor.2."[69]

Antiintellectualism, or the decrying of learning, was, of course, to become a separatist commonplace in the years ahead. One of the few English Anabaptists of whom we know anything (and even he is known to us only by his initials!), the mysterious "S.B." who was imprisoned in Newgate in the 1570s, claimed, presumably as a virtue, that he had "not bene at Universitie to studie Aristotles divinity," and the most famous sermon of Samuel How, the separatist pastor of the pre-Civil War years, was a plea for *The sufficiencie of the Spirits Teaching, without Humane Learning.*[70] Barry Reay, the seventeenth-century specialist, feels that the elevation of the Spirit above the Scriptures "was the uneducated man's and woman's way of rejecting the hegemony of a learned elite," and the same can be said of the antiintellectual enterprise as a whole.[71] Hart told his readers in 1548:

Brethern [*sic*], youre mindes are now lightned by grace, and ye have now receyved the spyryte of God | whych bryngethe, knowledge and a perfecte willinge obedyent mynde to do the wyll of God; But whosoever hath not the Spyryte, the same is none of hys.[72]

Such sentiments pointed to a high degree of spiritual independence in the converted, and are pregnant with George Fox's later dictum to the convinced. "Ye need not that any man should teach you." The rejection of a learned ministry is liable to be a long step toward the rejection of an officially imposed ministry (since few have ever advocated an officially imposed, unlearned ministry); it is a call for leadership to be based upon a measure of spiritual endowment, and hence a call for voluntarism. If the Spirit's teaching sufficed, then official edifices and ecclesiastical hierarchies were redundant. It is not necessary (nor is it possible) to demonstrate that the men of Kent and Essex had thought through their rejection of a learned ministry to its logical conclusion. By the nature of the case, a theology whose premise was the rejection of learning, was likely to lack the intellectual rigor to pursue that premise to its full conclusions. But this way of thinking is certainly pregnant with separatism.

*   *   *

The religious vision of the free-willers was essentially egalitarian, a declaration of the common man's spiritual independence. The doctrine of predestination was seen as elitist, for "they affirm, that Christ hath not died for all men. Whereby they make Christ inferior to Adam and grace to sin, . . ." the radicals saw the potential for salvation in all people, since any man might "truly repent, unfeignedly believe with a lively faith, and persevere therein to the end of this mortal life" and thus be saved, since there was "no decree of God to the contrary."[73] Trew and his company

> saw in it [i.e., in predestination] that they did hold and affirm, that none but great learned men could have the true understanding of the word of God; and in that they would not nor could not answer us how they approved their doctrine . . . they do jointly agree with the Papists, that do the like to maintain their superstition. . . .

Trew also listed as the "23d Enormity" of predestination the charge that

> in racking, and washing away the holy Scriptures, and in affirming, that no simple man without the tongues can truly understand them, it doth not only agree with the Papists, but also it doth cause all such as believe it to neglect reading of the holy Scriptures. . . .[74]

Clearly, the free-willers saw themselves as more consistent in their biblicism and in their rejection of Catholic-style churchly authority than the predestinarians. If the orthodox Protestants were more vigorous in adhering to that aspect of Reformation teaching which denied to man any ability to contribute to the soterial transaction, then the free-willers were more consistent in adhering to that aspect which stressed the importance of the individual's ability to commune with God independently of church or scholarly authority.

* * *

Evidence of Conversion: An Incomplete Letter

The disputes which the free-willers had in prison with their predestinarian opponents were not without their effects; members of the one party were converted by those of the other. John Philpot, after being moved from the King's Bench to the bishop of London's coal-house, wrote to Careless expressing his sorrow at "thy great trouble which these schismatics do daily put thee to," and urging him to be content "if there come not such fruit of your good labours as you would wish, . . . and know that a stony ground cannot fructify . . . let not care eat out your heart."[75] Indeed, the upholders of predestination even expressed concern that they might lose adherents to the party of free-will.[76] Nevertheless, it was the free-willers who eventually lost out in this struggle. The somewhat equivocal capitulation of Thomas Cole in 1553 has already been noted, but it appears that several more of the radicals came to possess genuinely predestinarian convictions in the process of debate with their opponents. John Careless, writing to Bradford, claimed his prayer to be that God would "work in the hearts of Trew and his company, as he hath done in the rest of them that were with them"; clearly Trew's losses had been considerable.[77]

The most significant document in this regard is an incomplete letter from a former free-willer to his erstwhile colleagues, urging them to do as he had done and to accept the doctrines of election. The author of this letter blamed the calamities that had fallen on the Protestant cause in England—presumably a reference to the persecution under Mary—upon "the sins of us all that have professed the gospel here in England of late." "And one cause was," he informed them, "because we were not sound in the predestination of God; but we were rather enemies unto it." He then expounded his new understanding of the doctrine of divine Providence, and added a word concerning himself.

I, for my part, repent that ever I was so bitter unto them that were teachers of this undoubted truth. . . . I went about by all means to persuade others, wherby they might be one with me in that error of freewil; albeit that God in his good time will revele his truth unto you, as it pleased him to open it unto me . . .[78]

The author of the letter indicates that Hart's confused ideas on the place of good works in salvation had permeated the whole group of the free-willers.

> My dearly beloved brethren, herein was I deceived, with many mo besides me, because we could not discern the truth in good works. . . . For I myself could not understand S. Paul and S. James, to make them agree together, til our good preachers, which were my prison fellows, did open them to me. . . . First, Paul saith, Faith only justifieth, and not the deeds of the law. And S. James saith, Faith without deeds is dead. Here are contraries to the carnal man. . . . And thus they were opened unto me, that faith doth only justify before God, and the good deeds that S. James speaketh of, justify before the world.[79]

The antiintellectualism of the free-willers, it appears, made them unable to look favorably on attempts to harmonize James and Paul, and thus left them in a position of ambivalence toward the doctrine of justification by faith.

The letter makes it plain that its author was not the only casualty upon the free-willers' side.

> I also se how mercifully he hath dealt with many of our brethren, whom you do know wel enough, as wel as though I did recite them by name, God forbid that I should doubt you, seeing that it hath pleased God to revele himself in these days, to them that heretofore were deceived with that error of the Pelagians; yea, and suffered imprisonment in the defence of that which now they detest and abhor.[80]

As to the identity of these converted brethren, the letter names only two: "I thank God, that they, whom I thought would have been mine enemies, are become my friends in the truth: as in sample, by our brethren Ledley and Cole, and such like."[81] There can be no doubt that the Cole referred to here is Robert Cole; Thomas Cole, as has been noted, had recanted the radical cause in 1553 and does not figure at all in the prison debates in any capacity, being in exile in Germany at this time, while Robert Cole is noted in a letter of 1557 from the informant priest Stephen Morris to Bishop Bonner as working closely together with John Ledley.[82]

The Defectors

Robert Cole had, however, been converted to the orthodox Protestant cause some considerable time before 1557; in a letter of 1555 from Bradford to John Philpot, Cole is mentioned as "my good brother" who "hath written to me in this matter, to labour to persuade them with my letters. Therefore I purpose to write something to Trew and Abyngton thereabouts, which you shall see."[83] If Cole's eagerness gives the impression that his conversion to predestination is still fairly recent (another letter of the previous February had been addressed to Cole along with Hart and other free-willers), Bradford speaks of it here as an established fact. Cole is mentioned again just before the text of the anonymous/unfinished letter breaks off: "for my brother Robert Cole did give you a good report to me and to my prison-fellows. . . ."[84] Clearly, the author of that letter was himself a prisoner, and not one of the "extramural" participants in the debates, as Hart, Kemp, Gibson, Ledley, and Cole were. Indeed, his belief "that God wil receive me home unto himself shortly" suggests that he anticipated martyrdom.[85] This is a problem; of the free-willers who are known to have been martyred, no records exist of any having abandoned their radical opinions. Sheterden, although clearly portrayed by Foxe in a favorable light, was still exuding antiintellectual rhetoric of a kind typical of the group at a very late stage in his particular day; J. W. Martin's conjecture that Sheterden had been converted to predestinarian opinions by the time of his martyrdom is not supported by any evidence, and that which Martin offers proves nothing.[86] The safest assumption is that he remained a free-willer. The information given by Foxe on Middleton and Brodbridge is, as usual, circumspect, but does not indicate any drastic change of view by either man.[87] John Careless's silence about the martyrdoms of Thomas Avington and Thomas Read, two members of Trew's group in the King's Bench, in a letter in which he mentioned the two men burned with them, is sufficient testimony that they, too, must have remained radical to the end.[88] It could be, of course, that the writer of the incomplete letter was mistaken in anticipating martyrdom.

Apart from Thomas Cole, the radicals who are known to have abandoned their heterodox stance at some stage are Robert Cole, John Ledley, Thomas Upchard (Upchear), John Kempe, Cornelius Stevenson, and one Skelthrop.[89] Clearly, neither Robert Cole nor John Ledley can be the author of the incomplete letter, since they are mentioned in it as third persons.

There is no evidence to prove that John Kempe was ever imprisoned, and although he appears later to have conformed to the Elizabethan establishment and to have accepted a benefice in the Isle of Wight, this may not represent a deep-seated change in his

convictions as much as a simple pragmatism on his part after the
death of Hart; as late as 1557, the year of Hart's death, he was
sharing lodgings with the free-willers' leader in London as a base
for evangelizing Kent. Wilkinson, the polemical writer against the
Family of Love in 1579, referred to the mention of Kempe in a
letter by Bishop Bonner's informant, Stephen Morris, and commented, "This Kempe is now liuing and is preacher in the Yle of
wight, and is by this popish priest slaūdered, the sayd Kemp being
a very Godly man."[90] The addressees of a letter from Bradford to
the free-willers include Kempe's name, however; the autograph
manuscript leaves a blank for his first name, but in Coverdale's
1564 edition of the letters of the Marian martyrs the first name
was given—whether in error or as a favor to Kempe's newfound
respectability—as William. Although Morris had professed himself
ignorant of Kempe's doctrine in 1557, Careless had had no doubts
the previous year that he remained a free-will man.[91] The reputation continued to cling to Kempe, and in the 1576 edition of his
Acts and Monuments of the English Martyrs, Foxe included an
account of several pages concerning him, which was based on a
"report . . . written by his own hands." He had been

> requested therunto by his frends . . . to purge hym selfe of such reports
> as haue ben geuen out hurtful to his good name, by one Morys & Tye
> a priest to B. Boner. Wherfore the said John Kempe desireth thee the
> christiã reader . . . to remoue that infamie which . . . Morys, Tye, &
> also Carles by report of others, dyd take as a truth.[92]

As papists and Marian persecutors, Morris and Tye could easily
be branded as liars, but the reputation of John Careless could not
be allowed to be besmirched by this exculpation of Kempe! Foxe
then gives a statement of Kempe's doctrines, which he said he
taught during Mary's reign, and continued to teach. This statement
is, to say the least, a little cagey on the vital issues of predestation
and free-will. He states that "the elect shall neuer perish" and
"the reprobate shall neuer be saued," but adds that election is "in
Christe" and that reprobation is for sin. He also insists that "Christ
by his merits is the only cause of saluation and euery part therof"
while "the Deuyll & mans sinne" is "the only cause of damnation."
Furthermore, "God neither ordeyneth, wylleth, nor commaundeth
sinne to be done of man," and, though he has a secret will, this is
not contrary to his will expressed in the Scriptures, which was
what John Trew had said in his *Cause of Contention in the King's
Bench.*[93] Here, it seems, is a summary, albeit very carefully

worded, of most of the concerns which the free-will men had contended for more than twenty years. Neither Morris, Tye, nor Careless had made any mistake in their identification of John Kempe; if he was ever a truly convinced deserter from the radical camp, it does not appear to have been as a result of the prison disputes.

The "Vpcharde of Bocking" examined by the Privy Council on 27 January 1550/51 is almost certainly the "Upchear" whom Trew mentioned as one of those "that were delivered out of prison" on 18 December 1555.[94] By June 1557 Thomas Upcher, weaver of Bocking in Essex, was settled in Frankfurt with his wife and children. On 25 April 1560, he was ordained deacon by Grindal, and later became rector of Fordham before moving on to be rector of St. Leonard's, Colchester. In 1582 he resigned this last post, having joined the Classical Movement.[95] His conversion to the more orthodox Protestantism of his subsequent career seems to have taken place in prison, however. John Careless wrote at least two letters to his "dear Brother, T.V." in terms which are so warm and intimate as virtually to preclude the possibility that writer and recipient were engaged in acrimonious debate with one another.[96] The copies of these letters held by Emmanuel College, Cambridge, read "Thomas Upcher" for Foxe's circumspect "T.V.,"[97] and, if this identification is correct, then the conclusion must be that Upchard was among those free-willers won over to predestinarian theology at the time of the prison dispute. From the extant evidence, therefore, it remains possible that "Upcher" was the author of the letter to his former comrades.

Two other free-willers converted during this period were Cornelius Stevenson and someone by the name of Skelthrop. The former had signed Trew's confession of faith in January 1555/56, while Bradford, in a letter to John Careless, mentions the latter as follows:

> Commend me to our good brother Skelthrop, for whom I heartily praise my God, which hath given him to see his truth at the length, and to give place to it. I doubt not but that he will be so heedy in all his conversation, that his old acquaintance may ever thereby think themselves astray. Woe and woe again should be unto us, if we by our example should make men to stumble at the truth. Forget not salutations in Christ, as you shall think good, to Trew and his fellows. The Lord hath his time, I hope, for them also, although we perchance think otherwise.[98]

On this evidence, Skelthrop would appear to have been one of Trew's group, but the absence of more information precludes any further conclusions being drawn about the significance of his conversion. Similarly, Cornelius Stevenson, who signed Trew's confession of faith at the end of January 1555/56, seems to have gone over to the predestinarian side at some point during the next four or five months; John Careless mentions as much in a letter to the remaining free-will men.[99]

Two other possible free-willers who at some stage seem to have adhered to more orthodox views were William Porrege and Richard Prowde. Both are among the addressees of Bradford's letter of 16 February 1554/55 to Hart, Sheterden, Middleton, and other leaders of the free-willers.[100] Yet both men are mentioned in another letter of Bradford's, written the previous August to Joyce Hales, from which it is clear that they acted as messengers between writer and recipient.[101] Several explanations for this state of affairs suggest themselves: either the barriers between the parties were not always so absolute as to preclude mutual assistance of the kind which Porrege and Prowde provided for Bradford in bringing him news and letters, or else the two had been converted from the orthodox to the radical party during the period August 1554 to February 1554/55. It is also just possible—though unlikely given its contents—that Bradford's letter of February is addressed to a mixture of free-will men and others. Neither Porrege nor Prowde seems to have been imprisoned, given that they were at liberty to deliver messages, and, indeed, Foxe recounts Porrege's narrow escape from arrest, on his way back after a trip to Calais, in about 1556 or 1557.[102] Porrege's and Prowde's radicalism—if that is what it was—did not, however, prevent them from accepting ordination to the priesthood at the hands of Bishop Grindal, Porrege in January 1559/60, and Prowde two months later.[103] It is also worth noting that Porrege's will was witnessed at Faversham in 1569 by Thomas Cole, who was by then a respectable—and predestinarian—clergyman.[104] The definite allegiance of both Prowde and Porrege cannot be pinpointed with certainty, and this, together with the more significant fact that they were not imprisoned, would eliminate them from the number of those likely to have been the author of the partly lost letter.

Master Gibson

There is only one candidate known to posterity who, on the basis of the letter's internal evidence, fulfills all the necessary criteria to be its author. Bradford, in a letter written shortly before his martyrdom, reports that

> Master Gibson is here in prison upon an action of thousands pounds; I say not of a thousand but of thousands. Who knoweth whether God hath sent him hither to me (for I may twice a day speak with him), to turn him yet afore my death?[105]

Bradford assumes that his correspondent (it was John Philpot) knew who this Master Gibson was. Foxe gives an account of the sufferings and martyrdom (on 18 November 1557) of Richard Gibson,

> who was first cast into the Compter in the Poultry (where he had been a prisoner by the space of two years for suretyship in a matter of debt, and then stood upon his deliverance), then upon suspicion and evil will was accused to Bonner, for that in the prison he was never confessed, nor received at the popish altar.[106]

The Compter in the Poultry was Bradford's prison in 1555,[107] and so Foxe's martyr is undoubtedly the debt-laden Gibson mentioned in Bradford's letter. The Gibson whose articles of belief and responses under examination appear in Foxe is, needless to say, impeccably orthodox, so that, if Foxe's account is to be believed, then Bradford's hopes for Gibson were indeed realized, and Gibson died in the same faith as his fellow-prisoner.[108] John Careless had mentioned, in his account of his own first examination how "Hart, Kemp, and M. Gybson, would have persuaded" twelve condemned prisoners of the orthodox party to change their allegiances, "but, thanks be unto God, the serpent prevailed not," and Wilkinson, the scourge of the Familists, probably using the same source for his information, speaks of "one M. Gibson who sought to peruert & turne frō the truth xij. godly Christiãs which were Martyred."[109] On this evidence, the case seems clear-cut: there was one Master Gibson who worked with Hart and Kemp to persuade Protestant prisoners to accept the doctrines of human free-will, thus becoming known to figures such as Bradford and Philpot. This Gibson was later imprisoned for debt in the same prison as Bradford, was converted to predestinarian views and died as a martyr in 1557. On this view, Gibson is the only person whose name is known to history who could have been responsible for the letter to other free-will men seeking to persuade them to recant their opinions.

There are, however, two problems with this explanation, although neither of them, perhaps, is insuperable. The first is that

Careless's examination, just mentioned, occurred on 25 April 1556, a date by which, as Bradford's letter (mentioning Gibson's first imprisonment) and Foxe's account of Gibson's martyrdom both agree, Gibson would have been in prison for about a year. However, it is not impossible that Gibson could have acted in concert with Hart and Kemp from his prison-cell. The second problem is that Bradford's letter of February 1555 is addressed to, among other free-willers, John Gibson, while the martyr described by Foxe is named Richard.[110] However, either the single reference to "John Gibson" in Bradford's letter, or the name "Richard Gibson" in Foxe's account may be incorrect; if this is so, then Bradford's reference could be a slip, but Foxe's references to "Richard" are so manifold that, if incorrect, they could only be understood as an attempt to conceal the identity of a onetime radical. The alternative to all of this is to insist that there were two Masters Gibson, one named John who was a free-will man, and the other a debtor named Richard who was converted in prison and martyred. This is the interpretation of the evidence favored by J. W. Martin, but it would seem to have the effect of leaving the authorship of the incomplete letter unresolved.[111] But, if this is so, then Bradford's reference to the imprisonment of the second Gibson in the context of a short letter concerning the dispute with the free-willers, a letter in which Trew and Avington are mentioned by name, is a very strange coincidence indeed!

The most likely conclusion, then, must be that "John" is a mistake for "Richard," and that Richard Gibson was converted from his radicalism while in prison for debt, albeit this conversion was effected after the death of Bradford, who went to the stake in June 1555. This Richard Gibson would very likely have been the author of the incomplete letter.

As will be apparent from the foregoing, conclusions on this subject are best preceded by epithets such as "tentative" and "probable," but what is clear, is that the prison disputes, despite degenerating at times to the level of a shouting match, did not thereby leave all of the participants unmoved by the arguments of the other side. The losses of Trew and his company to the predestinarian side were, it seems, considerable. After the martyrdoms of Avington and Read and the escape of Trew in 1556, it may even be that the free-will party within prison walls was extinguished altogether. It also remains just possible, on the evidence of the correspondence referred to in this chapter, that William Porrege and Richard Prowde were converted in the opposite direction. If the generalities of this theme may be stated with that confidence which attaches itself to certainty, the details must, alas, be consigned to varying degrees of mere likelihood.

*   *   *

The Extent of the Free-Will Group and Its Contacts

In assessing the importance of the free-willers as an expression of popular religious enthusiasm, it is just as well to consider the actual extent of their operations, in terms of numbers of people involved, geographical distribution, and their relationships with other religious groupings. The picture that thus emerges is of a fairly widespread phenomenon with well-established links both to more conservative Protestants on their right, and with more radical groupings to their left.

The meeting in Upchard's house at Bocking over Christmas 1550 was described as "an assembly being of lx persons or moo," and the depositions and extracts from the Privy Council Register give the names of thirty-three individuals who, whether present at the meeting in question or not, were undoubtedly connected with the group at this time.[112] Those names, with place of residence and occupation if known, are in the table on p. 52.

All of those mentioned are males. It may be that the authorities on this occasion took no notice of women conventiclers, and it is therefore possible, if the womenfolk of most of these were also present, that the names recorded represent an exhaustive account, of the men at least, who were at the meeting in Upchard's house, since this would agree with the statement that the attendance was a little above sixty.

None of these individuals are among the signatories of Trew's *Cause of Contention,* of whom there were twelve: John Trewe, Thomas Avington, Richard Harman, John Jackson, Henry Wickham, Cornelius Stevenson, John Guelle, Thomas Arede (or Read), John Saxby, Robert Hitcherst, Matthew Hitcherst, and Margery Russell.[116] Avington and Arede were from Sussex, as Trew seems to have been.

In addition to those mentioned in the depositions of 1550/51 and the signatories of John Trew's document, perhaps a dozen or so other names may be counted as sometime free-will men, though in one or two cases the evidence is very ambiguous. Skelthrop is known to posterity only by the fact of his defection to the predestinarian cause. John Kempe was said by Morris, the informant priest, to be a great traveler into Kent, presumably for the purpose

Surname	First Name	Residence	Essex/Kent	Descript
Bagge/Blagge,	Richard	Bocking	E	
Barrett,	John	"Stamphorde"	E	Cowher
Barrey[113]				
Boughtell			E	
Brodebridge,	George	Broomfield	K	
Broke,	Thomas		(K)[114]	"Mr."
Chidderton		Ashford	K	
Cole,	Robert	Faversham	K	Student
Cole,	Thomas	Maidstone	K	Schoolm
Cooke,	Robert	Bocking	E	Clothier
Dynestake,	Richard		(K)	"Clarke"
Eglise/Eglins,	John	Bocking	E	Clothier
Forshall/Forstall,	William	Adisham	K	
Grenelande,	William		(K)	
Grey,	John	Wingham	K	
Hart,	Henry	Pluckley	K	
King,	John	Bocking	E	
Lydley,	John	Ashford	K	
Lynsey,	Roger		K	
Middleton,	Humphrey		(K)	
Morres,	Edmonde	Adisham	K	
Myxsto/Myxer,	Thomas	Bocking	E	
Plume,	John	Lenham	K	
Pygrinde/Piggerell	Thomas	Bocking	E	
Ramsey,	Laurence	Adisham	K	
Sharpe,	Thomas	Pluckley	K	
Sheterden,	Nicholas	Pluckley	K	
Sibley,	William	"lannams" (Lenham)	K	
Sympson[115]				
Upchard	Thomas	Bocking	E	Weaver
Wolmere,	Robert		E	
Yonge,	Nicholas	Lenham	K	
Yonge,	Thomas	Lenham	K	

of evangelizing; he may well have been from the county.[117] The scale of the capital with which Gibson was dealing when arrested for debt in 1555 might lead one to conjecture that he was a London businessman, but hard evidence is lacking. Several other addressees of Bradford's letter of 16 February 1554/55 are also possible free-willers.[118] As has been said, a question mark hangs over the allegiances of Richard Prowde and William Porrege, but if Prowde came from Faversham in Kent (a town closely connected with free-willer activity) as Christina Garrett suggested,[119] then his link with the group may be partly explained. Christina Garrett, in

The Marian Exiles, appears to have believed that William Porrege hailed from Sandwich in the same county; a Faversham will of 1569, however, is of one "William Poredge," and this mentions Thomas Cole—perhaps the archdeacon of Essex and former Maidstone schoolmaster who had been arrested with the free-will men in 1550—as a witness, and speaks in tones consistent with strong personal Protestant conviction of Christ "by whose pᵉcyous deathe and passyon I surely trust and hope to be saved."[120] Nothing is known of Roger Newman, another addressee of a letter by Bradford to the free-willers; indeed, even his first name is uncertain, since it did not appear in the autograph manuscript of the letter, and Emmanuel College's manuscript copy erroneously gives John Kempe's name, in the same letter, as William, while Bishop Coverdale's *Letters of Martyrs* of 1564 names none of the addressees at all.[121]

This leaves William Lawrence, who may well have been the "master Laurence of Barnhall" mentioned in close conjunction with Robert Cole, Ledley, Hart, and Kemp by Stephen Morris; John Barr, also addressed in Bradford's letter, is spelled Barre in some copies of the manuscript, and was probably the John Barre (or Barry) described by Morris as Laurence's servant.[122] Laurence and Barre wrote a reply to a treatise on predestination by Augustine Bernhere, Latimer's Swiss servant, in which they made clear their own opposition to the doctrine.[123] They also implied a rejection of belief in hell understood as everlasting torment, which would have made them very radical indeed by the standards of the day. They told Bernhere that "yoᵘ say mē be not Destroyed, though they be damned & in hell" and asked: "what is destruction if hell & dañacion be not?"[124] If Laurence and Barre really meant what they implied here, then they must be considered an exception to D. P. Walker's contention that, although during "the 17th century a few attacks on it [the doctrine of eternal torment], mostly anonymous, had appeared," "this is not true of the preceding centuries."[125] In view of this, J. W. Martin's description of Laurence and Barre as "fully orthodox Protestants" seems very strange indeed, and seems to indicate his unawareness of their intimate connection with the radical free-willers; presumably this accounts for the failure of the "Biographical Register of Freewillers," in his book on sixteenth-century religious radicalism in England, to include details about the pair.[126] John Jeffrey, stated by Morris to be Laurence's brother-in-law, and who stayed with Laurence and Barre at John Dudman's alehouse in Cornhill, London, assisted them "in persuading the people."[127]

The evangelistic activities of George Eagles, or Egles, known as Trudgeover, may also have served to widen the circle of the free-willers if, and only if, there is any substance in M. R. Watts's speculation that he was related to, or even identical with, the John Eglins, or Eglise, who was among those detained in Bocking after the meeting there at Christmas 1550.[128] The occupation of the Bocking man was that of "clothier," while Foxe described Trudge-over, who was hunted by the Marian authorities in Kent, Essex, Suffolk, and Norfolk, as a tailor.[129] As Watts points out, if the latter was indeed connected with the Bocking conventiclers, then his convert, John Johnson, must presumably also be counted as a radical. Johnson, a widowed, thirty-four-year-old laborer and father of three from Thorpe-le-Soken in Essex, was burned at Colchester on 2 August 1557, while his mentor was hanged, drawn, and quartered at Chelmsford the same year for allegedly praying that God would "turn queen Mary's heart, or else take her away."[130] This line of inquiry trails off into speculation, however. On the one hand, the connection between the Bocking conventicler and the notorious evangelist cannot be proven while, on the other hand, if there were a close connection, then there would very likely have been many unrecorded converts from Trudgeover's preaching who espoused radical views.

The foregoing is an exhaustive account of all those names known to have been attached to the free-will cause, and yet it amounts at the most to just over fifty known persons. Only one of these names is of a woman, Margery Russell, although the extant records make passing references to the wives of Robert Cooke, Robert Cole, and John Lidley.[131] If allowance is made for the womenfolk of those known to have been involved (and the estimate of sixty or more present at the Bocking meeting in 1550, over against the thirty-three names given, invites the historian to use a similar ratio for the free-willers as a whole), then this still amounts to little more than a hundred persons. This is, of course, to build one supposition upon another. However, both suppositions seeming to be entirely reasonable, the resultant figure of just over a hundred, if treated as the merely provisional estimate that it is, seems not unreasonable either.

Was this the sum total of free-willer strength? The question is probably not answerable; those who neither wrote nor came to the attention of the authorities have, by the same token, eluded the historian's grasp, and even those who failed to avoid leaving traces on official documentation did nothing to implicate their fellows. Neither did they, like Joan Bocher, claim a thousand (or any other number) of followers. Indeed, the question of free-willer strength may not even be meaningful if the free-will men were not a sharply distinguishable sectarian organization, but merely a conspicuous and distinctive manifestation of wider currents of religious radicalism—a radicalism which could and did merge at some points with what was coming to be defined as Protestant orthodoxy. The conventiclers at Bocking in 1550 certainly appeared to observe certain practices—not greeting those unknown to them, absenting themselves consistently from parish worship under a Protestant regime, mutual help and meeting together between brethren of different towns and even counties—that are consistent with the beginnings of a formal sectarian organization. Stephen Morris also noted of Henry Hart that "he hath drawn out thirteen articles to be observed amongst his company, and, as far as I do learn, there come none into their brotherhood except he be sworn."[132]

John Bland and the Radical Connection

However, the free-willers enjoyed contacts with Protestants who were part of the official church, as evidenced, for example, by the support which John Bland, parson of Adisham, enjoyed from Grey, Forstall, Ramsey, and Morres, four of his neighbors arrested at Bocking in 1550. John Grey, William Forstall (or Forshall), Laurence Ramsey, and Edmonde Morres, the four first-mentioned conventiclers in the depositions of 1550/51, appear to have come from the district of Adisham, a village near Canterbury a dozen or so miles distant from the Ashford-Maidstone-Faversham triangle which was the home of most of the Kentish conventiclers. Forstall and Edmund Mores (presumably the same person as the Edmonde Morres whose name appears in the depositions) were both signatories as witnesses to the behavior of John Bland, parson of Adisham, who was burned with Sheterden and Middleton at Canterbury on 12 July 1555. This paper, published by Foxe, relates to events which took place in December 1553 at Adisham; and to have been eyewitnesses of the whole proceedings there related, Forstall and Mores would probably have had to be parishioners.[133] In another document published by Foxe, Bland recounts his arrest as follows:

Thus they brought me out of the church, and without the door they railed on me, without pity or mercy: but anon the priest came out of the church, and Ramsey, that of late was clerk, said unto him, "Sir,

where dwell you?" And therewith Thomas Austen took him by the
arm, and said, "Come on, sirra, you are of his opinion:" and took his
dagger from him, and said he should go with him. "I am content," said
he, and a little mocked them in their envious talk. By this time there
came in at the church-style, one John Gray, of Wingham, servant to
John Smith, and seeing them hold Ramsey by the arms, said to him,
"How now, Ramsey, have you offended the queen's laws?" "No," quoth
he. "Then there is no transgression." Therewith Thomas Austen took
him, and said, "Ye are one of their opinion; ye shall be with them for
company:" and took his dagger from him, and then demanded what
he did there? but after, I think, for very shame they let him go again;
but they carried me and Ramsey to Canterbury with eighteen persons weaponed.[134]

John Grey (or Gray) is, of course, likely to have been quite a
common name, and this account does not so much as give Ramsey's first name. However, the conjunction of the names in this
fashion appears to be more than merely circumstantial evidence;
"Iohn Grey william Forshall Laurence Ramsey and Edmonde Morres" are listed together in the depositions of 1550/51, and the testi-
monies of the first three are treated as a separate grouping within
the evidence there listed.[135] The fact that the parson of Adisham,
John Bland, was martyred at the same time and place as Nicholas
Sheterden and Humphrey Middleton, two of the leading spirits
among the free-willers, suggests a possible link with them, and the
natural appearance of the four local men in the events surrounding
Bland's arrest—not to mention the fact that Gray and Ramsey
were obviously generally known as Protestants—leads to the almost irresistible conclusion that they were the conventiclers arrested in the time of Edward VI. Wingham, the place in which
John Gray is stated by Foxe to have lived, is a village some three
miles to the north of Adisham.[136]

Already minister at Adisham in 1542, Bland had preached a
forcefully antitraditional sermon at Faversham, another area fruitful for the free-willers, which got him into trouble.[137] The fact that
Sheterden and Middleton were martyred alongside Bland is a further indication that the latter's status as a minister of the Edwardian church establishment had not hindered him from contact with
the wider circle of the conventiclers, as well as with those living
near or within his parish.

Indeed, it is through Bland that the group can be connected with
groups more radical than theirs. One John Toftes, who "was noted
as a common maintainer of persons accused of heresies," protected
Joan Bocher in his house after she was accused. "His house,"

noted Cranmer, "has been the resort of Bland. . . ."[138] Perhaps
it was Bland's connection with the Bocher circle, hovering as it
did on the fringes of Anabaptism, that led him to claim, in the
Northgate Parish, "that in the christening of children priests be
murderers."[139] Thomas Dawby, parson of Wycheling in 1543, but
formerly curate of Lenham and thus very possibly a contact of the
earliest conventiclers, was also a likely contact of Joan Bocher's
radicals. J. F. Davis, using wisely tentative language, claims only
that he was "in circles in which Joan Bocher moved"; in point of
fact Dawby is mentioned within a few paragraphs of Bocher in
Cranmer's records of proceedings against heresy in Kent.[140] But
the inference that there was a connection is a fair one, especially
in view of Dawby's apparently Melchiorite Christology (the heresy
for which Joan Bocher was finally to be burned in 1550): "Our
Lady," he was accused of teaching in 1539, "was no better than
another woman," and "she was but a sack to put Christ in."[141]
Possibly through Thomas Dawby, then, and certainly through John
Bland, the free-willers had connections with very radical groups
indeed.

And yet they also had undoubted connections with more orthodox Protestantism, a fact illustrated by the attempts of some of
their antagonists in the prison debates to speak softly to them, and
even to attempt to maintain a united front against their Catholic
oppressors, an attempt which, as has already been noted, would
certainly not have been made had the free-willers clearly been a
rigidly delimited sectarian organization on the verge of Anabaptism. But there seems to have been sufficient open-endedness to
allow the orthodox to treat them with at least some degree of
fellow-feeling. The very question mark hanging over the loyalties
of William Porrege and Richard Prowde underlines the fact of the
"fuzzy edges" of the group when two such individuals could apparently enjoy relationships of trust with the circles of both Hart
and Bradford.

A Red Herring: Robert Cooke and Robert Cooche

Robert Cooke and Robert Cooche have sometimes been held to
be the same person. The former was a conventicler at Bocking in
1550/51, while the latter was a maintainer of Anabaptist opinions
whose views were attacked by William Turner in his *Preseruatiue,
or triacle, agaynst the poyson of Pelagius, lately reneued, &
styrred vp agayn, by the furious secte of the Annabaptistes.*[142] If

it could be demonstrated that the two were, in fact, identical, then the connection, which a number of historians have alleged to exist, between the free-willers and Anabaptism would be at least partly vindicated.[143]

Cooke was a clothier of whom Doris Witard has claimed that

> Cooke's house, easily identified by its Tudor archway, still stands in Bradford Street, Bocking. As a clothier, he must have been a person of wealth and influence, Richard Upchard and John Sympson were among the witnesses of his will.[144]

Although her book provides no references of documentary evidence, she seems to have been referring to the copy of the will and probate in the Public Record Office which refers to Cooke's "two tenementes . . . in the strete called Bredford Strete" in Bocking.[145] The Richard Upchard mentioned in the will was presumably a relative of Thomas Upchard the conventicler. John Sympson who also witnessed the will may have been the husbandman of Great Wigborough, or the "one Sympson of the same sorte" mentioned in the depositions of 1550/51, or a relative of Cooke's servant and apprentice Thomas Sympson; in this shadow-world of patchy evidence, nothing prevents all three identities converging upon one individual.[146]

Robert Cooche was steward of Queen Catherine Parr's wine cellar, according to a 1574 letter of Bishop Parkhurst to Rudolph Gualter, the Zürich reformer. He had been the object of William Turner's literary abilities in 1552 by disputing the doctrine of original sin, but had abandoned his beliefs a few years before 1574. He was a long-serving singer in the queen's chapel.[147]

Doris Witard has raised the question as to whether Robert Cooke, clothier of Bocking, is one and the same with Robert Cooche, steward of Catherine Parr's wine cellar and singer in Elizabeth I's chapel: "name, date, and doctrine coincide, but until positive proof is available, the problem remains unsolved."[148] This suggests that she had no firsthand acquaintance with her sources, for the date of the probate granted on Robert Cooke's will is 1553, which precludes the possibility that he was active in the 1570s. In any case, in refuting Cooche's arguments in 1551, Turner had made fun of his opponent's demands for explicit biblical warrants for pædobaptism by saying that "God neuer in his worde expressedly commaūded his Apostelles to suffer suche tal men as you bee to lyue syngle: ther fore your curate doth wroug [sic] to suffer you to lyue syngle."[149] Burrage cited the remark about the curate as evidence that Cooche was not part of an Anabaptist congregation.[150] But the jibe also demonstrates that Cooche can hardly be Robert Cooke, the Bocking clothier and conventicler, for the Bocking man's house was to have been the venue for the meeting at Christmas 1550 until his wife went into labor![151] Cooke's wife, Agnes, was still alive in 1552, when Cooke made his will.[152] Witard's suggestion, though attractive, is a red herring; Cooke and Cooche cannot possibly be the same man.

The Free-Willers and the Wider World of English Radicalism

The Lollard-like utterances of some free-willers, and the expressions of hostility to intellectualism, to worldly clerics, and to the enforcement of belief: all give an impression of being radical commonplaces rather than components of a coherent sectarian ideology. And the absence of a coherent sectarian ideology suggests the absence of a coherent sect. As far as sectarian structure is concerned, the state of affairs in 1550, whereby one congregation could act as support for another, may well have represented a high point. Thomas Cole had already recanted in 1553 and, during Mary's reign, Sheterden, Middleton, and Brodbridge were martyred and Upchard was imprisoned. Although the free-will party in prison held together to some extent, Henry Hart appears to have based himself in London in order to give the prisoners his chief attention, which suggests that his pastoral concerns in Kent and Essex were less extensive than hitherto. However, the fact that the Marian authorities were looking for Hart in Pluckley in 1557, shows that he could not have spent all his time in the capital. Bradford's letter of 16 February 1554/55 to the free-willers, is addressed likewise to "all other that fear the Lord and love his truth, abiding in Kent, Essex, Sussex and thereabout," which may indicate that the named addressees, of whom Hart was the principal, continued to reside occasionally in those counties, and certainly that they continued to be in regular contact with their brethren there.[153] It also, incidentally, demonstrates that free-willer activity was not confined to Kent and the area of Essex around Bocking, but also took in Sussex, as the martyrdoms of Thomas Avington and Thomas Arede at Lewes confirm. Morris's comment about none coming "into their brotherhood except he be sworn," might arguably be interpreted as meaning that Hart had formed the rudiments of a congregation in London outside the prison walls, though, if he had, the work escaped all disruption by the persecutors and all comment by the Protestants.[154]

In sum, the free-will men whose activities, in 1550/51 and again in the reign of Mary, brought them to the attention of the authorities seem to be, not the tip of a large sectarian iceberg of free-willers, but rather a particular manifestation of broader radical undercurrents that embraced Lollard survivals, tendencies to Melchiorite views, and, during Mary's reign, Protestantism itself. The constituent parts of this radical underground were not, on this evidence, each mutually exclusive worlds unto themselves, but rather differentiated, though somewhat open-ended, groupings within a continuous spectrum. The free-willers were one such grouping, possessing its own identity, and yet with contacts among radicals like Joan Bocher, who lived at the very doorway to Anabaptism, and state-church Protestants alike.

*   *   *

What is the significance of the points which have here been considered relative to these radicals of the 1550s? It is possible to interpret each of their distinctive beliefs in a sense which makes the conventiclers separating in practice without being completely separatist in principle, rather in the manner of the church founded by Henry Jacob in London in the following century. But, taken cumulatively, the evidence for an incipient separatism is overwhelming, and in this regard their rejection of a learned ministry is of particular importance. The plea for a spiritually endowed, rather than an academically trained, leadership amounts to a cry for a nonofficial church. This conviction was carried through into their denial of the right of the true church to enforce itself by persecution. Their most generally held distinctive was a belief in human free-will, and it was this conviction that attracted the attention, and aroused the opposition, of other Protestants. This repudiation of predestination was integrally connected to their belief in the necessity of a pure church, as the author of *The enormities proceeding of the opinion, that predestination, calling, and election, is absolute in man as it is in God* (which author it has here been argued was Hart) makes plain. In making this connection, his opponent Bradford concurs; by rejecting Hart's premise (free-will), he makes it clear that a pure church in the sense that Hart wants, is neither attainable nor desirable. For Bradford, God's secret predestination makes the continuation of an all-embracing church justifiable even after it has been accepted that the godly can be certain of their salvation here and now. For the free-willers, predestination must be repudiated for precisely this reason. Hence the doctrine of human free-will becomes the "motor" of their separatism.

Incipient, or implicit, separatism is really the most accurate way of describing the free-willers' position. Burrage was overstating the case when he claimed that the evidence was insufficient to make them separatists.[155] And yet the free-willers themselves were hardly conscious of the full implications of their own position; John Trew, concluding his *Cause of Contention* with a confession of faith, wrote that "we do heartily acknowledge . . . that our Saviour Jesus Christ his pure religion, and secret will revealed in his word, sufficient for man's salvation, was in this realm declared and known in good King Edward the VIth his days; which word of God was then truly preached, and sufficiently taught, and his sacraments duly ministered, and of some followed. . . ."[156] This statement alone should serve to stress that the theology of the free-willers was inchoate in many respects, and that their separatism was neither explicit nor consistent. They initiated no tradition or denomination, and the separatists of the later sixteenth century, and of the early seventeenth, showed no signs of indebtedness to them, or even an awareness of them. The Laudians, far from seeing them as an important precedent for their own views on free-will, would have contemplated them (if they did so at all) with horror at their unlearned, evangelical radicalism. Their significance lies in the fact that they represent an example of a popular response to the relocation of the sources of religious authority that the Reformation had brought about in people's consciousness. The priesthood of all believers, the supreme authority of the Scriptures, the ability to know one's salvation here and now, and to have a personal experience of God: these things could not but find an outlet in popular religious expression and ecclesiological experimentation, and they were to do so increasingly as time passed by. With or without an Anabaptist presence in England, the gathered church was an organization whose time was fast coming. The free-willers were moving just a little faster than most.

2

Three Leaders: Henry Hart, John Trew, and Joan Bocher

HAVING considered the nature of the free-will grouping which centered around Henry Hart and John Trew, it seems appropriate to focus on the personalities of its leaders and also to look at another leader who created an even greater impact on the public consciousness, both at the time and since, Joan Bocher. The apparent connections between the free-willers and Bocher have already been noticed here; certainly, Bocher and Henry Hart carried on activities in very close geographic and temporal proximity to one another, and both seem to have emerged from a Lollard-type background. As will be seen in the following pages, Hart may even have been influenced by the radical Christology for which Joan Bocher suffered martyrdom. Given that Joan died in 1550, sometime before the disputes in Mary's reign which are so crucial in assessing the careers of Hart and Trew, it might have been thought more logical to consider her first. However, the free-willers have been the focus of attention up to this point, and so it seems wiser here to set aside chronological considerations and to examine first the careers of the free-willers' leaders, Henry Hart and John Trew.

Henry Hart: His Life and Writings

Little about Hart's life is known with certainty; a Henry Harte of Pluckley (which was the home of Nicholas Sheterden and Thomas Sharpe, two of those arrested in February, 1550/51) was mentioned in a letter of 29 April 1538 from Archbishop Cranmer to Thomas Cromwell as being a holder of conventicles.[1] Common though the name might be, the identity of the location and activity makes it difficult to resist the conclusion that the Henry Harte in question was the leader of the free-willers in the reigns of Edward VI and Mary. If this is so, it may well be significant that Hart's name is the first in the list of six men, two from Pluckley and four from the neighboring village of Smarden, indicted "for unlawful assemblies" (none of the other five appear in the depositions of 1550/51); perhaps, even then, he had a certain preeminence within his group.

The immediate vicinity seems to have been a fertile seedbed for Protestant ideas. The village of Smarden was "celebrated for the manufacture of broad-cloth" and the textile trade, being international, was certainly closely associated with the spread of Protestantism, as it had earlier been associated with the spread of Lollardy. One of the Smarden men indicted with Hart, Gervis Golde, appears to have been related by marriage to the parson of Smarden, Osmund Chubbe, who had been collated parson by Cranmer on 23 June 1533. In his will, dated 1550, Chubbe left legacies to John Golde, Robert, Bedgeamyn, and Rabedge Golde whom he described as "my wyeffe's children."[2] If Chubbe was married, he was presumably of Protestant sympathies! Pluckley, too, had a Protestant parson by the name of Lancaster who was reported in 1543 to use no holy water in the church porch and

> in going on procession he does not rehearse *Sancta Maria* or any other Saints' names. When told that Stephen Giles . . . blessed himself daily and nightly *In Nomine Patris,* &c. and that he said a *Paternoster,* an *Ave* and a Creed in honor of God and Our Lady, &c., the parson said that if he knew Giles had used that form of prayer he would never accompany him or drink with him."[3]

The assemblers indicted in 1538 are described as "fauters [i.e., fautors, supporters] of the new doctrine, as they call it," and Cranmer makes it cleare that they "favour God's word."[4] J. W. Martin appears to believe that the "they" whom Cranmer claimed were referring to the teachings of the Church of England as "new doctrine", were the local conservative gentry who had caused the men of Pluckley and Smarden to be indicted.[5] But this is not at all a natural reading of Cranmer's letter; rather, it indicates that the conventiclers themselves counted the teaching of the Church of England as in some sense "new," which of course raises the question of the antiquity of the tradition in which the dissenters stood. Such a reference to "new doctrine" certainly suggests a link with older radicalism, perhaps Lollardy, which is also reflected in the Lollard-like remark of John Plume of Lenham in 1550/51 about not saluting "a man whome they knowe not."[6] Watts, in his discussion of the free-willers of the early 1550s, posits such a pedigree for both the Kent and Essex groups, and points out that Bocking is

only eleven miles from Steeple Bumpstead, which had been the
home of Joan Bocher and a center of Lollardy in the 1520s.[7] In
1538 Cranmer clearly sympathized with the indicted men and urged
clemency on Cromwell. This incident may also account for Ridley's
statement in a letter of 1555 to Austin Bernhere that "my lord of
Canterbury knoweth him [i.e., Hart] best of all us."[8]

The Father of the Free-Will Party

Bradford's affectionate reference to "my father Hart" may indicate something of Hart's age, as well as Bradford's goodwill, and
also perhaps reflects his preeminence among the free-willers.[9] Several of those arrested in 1550/51 mentioned Hart as the source of
their heretical ideas.[10] It is not apparent, however, that Hart was
ever arrested, either in Edward VI's reign or in Mary's, although
by the latter period he was clearly well-known, both to prominent
Anglicans such as Bradford, and to ordinary Protestants like the
Coventry weaver John Careless. Hart's apparent immunity from
arrest is worthy of remark. Cranmer had pleaded for lenient treat-
ment for him in 1538. He does not appear to have been among
those arrested in 1550/51, and the letter of 27 January 1550/51 from
the Privy Council, asking Sir Edward Wootton and Sir Thomas
Wyatt to apprehend certain of the Kentish conventiclers who had
escaped the net, does not include Hart's name.[11] J. W. Martin comments on his ability, during Mary's reign, "to move in and out of
the prisons with some degree of unexplained liberty."[12] I. B. Horst,
in his article on "Anabaptism in England" in *The Mennonite Encyclopedia,* claimed that Hart was imprisoned under Mary.[13] He per-
sisted in this unsubstantiated belief in Hart's imprisonment in his
later book, *Radical Brethren,* which states that "Hart's name heads
the list of nonconformist prisoners addressed by Bradford" in that
martyr's letter of 16 February 1555.[14] In point of fact, although the
addressees of the letter did include Sheterden and Middleton, none
of the others are known to have been in prison, and Bradford
followed the list of names with: "and to all other that fear the Lord
and love his truth, abiding in Kent, Essex, Sussex and thereabout"
and presumably not, therefore, in prison![15] Hart may have made
the acquaintance of Careless through visits to the King's Bench
prison to see members of his own group. Stephen Morris, the informant priest, told Bishop Bonner that

> John Kempe and Henry Hart: these two do lie at the bridge-foot, in a
> cutler's house whose name is Curle; and namely Henry Hart, is the

principal of all those that are called free-will men; for so they are termed of the Predestinators. And he hath drawn out thirteen articles to be observed amongst his company, and, as far as I do learn, there come none into their brotherhood except he be sworn.[16]

This was in 1557. Nothing is known of Hart's career after this, but by later that same year he was dead. The visitation records of Nicholas Harpsfield, archdeacon of Canterbury and Chancellor to the bishop of London, show that the order was given to arrest Hart and some others at Pluckley. However, a note made next to this entry in the same hand lists Hart as *"iam mortuus,"* now dead, while the date of probate recorded in the Archdeaconry Act Book for Henry Harte of Pluckley was the early months of 1558 (new style).[17] The full entry in Harpsfield's visitation records reads as follows:

Also it is commanded that the bosholder doe apprehend the wife of John Hart and others whoise names are conteyned in a bill and beinge suspected of heresie and also to bring them to Crambrok apon Satterdaie next.
Also it is commanded that thies persones following beinge suspected of heresie be secretlie apprehended and brought to the Kings and Queens comissioners

Henrie Hart	*iam mortuus*
Johannes Anowre	*abiit*
Nicholas Hugge	*abiit*
and one Hatche	*abiit*

Hart died intestate, and his son John was named, on 16 March 1557/58, as the administrator of his property.[18] It seems to have been this John Hart who himself died little more than a year later; his will is dated 7 June 1559, and indicates that the son was likeminded with his father.[19] Wills of this period frequently provide, in addition to the almost perfunctory religious references, some additional comments indicative by their choice of terminology of the heartfelt religious convictions, whether Catholic/traditionalist or Protestant, of the person concerned. John Hart's will gives a veritable sermon, expressing convictions identical with those of Henry Hart, and expressed in a style every bit as disjointed and confusing as his.

I comytt my soule into the handes of all mightye god mye lovinge father, whiche I knowe beleve and confesse hathe of verye love bye

thobedyence and bloude of ower savior Jesus Christe, ordayned me
And all man kynde from Synne. It is from the bondage of Sathan o^r mortall enemye, as many as will here his holye word that is to saye
obey to the wyll of god and labor to do the same, to the same god
which onlye is wyse bye [*sic;* = be?] p̄yse honor domynyon & glory
for Aver and Aver amen.

Hart named his wife Lettes as his sole executor, and expressed
concern about the "bringinge vpp of mye children godlye and hon-
estlye." He had three sons, and his words indicate that they were
still young, which seems to confirm that this John Harte was identical with the son of Henry named as his father's administrator and
not, say, a brother of similar age to Henry Hart himself. John
Hart's will mentions Joshuah and Thomas Hart as his brothers,
and a (presumably unmarried) sister, Patience Hart. A Paul Hart
is also mentioned as a witness to the will, but the relationship is
not specified. To Lettes, John Hart left his house and tenement,
and to Joshuah Hart he left £40, so the family was not poor.

The Letter to Newgate and the Christological Question

Hart's last known piece of writing is a letter written probably
sometime in April 1556. It was intended as a response to certain
articles of faith circulated by John Careless. Careless and John
Trew had, just before Christmas 1555, reached some kind of truce
in their disputes, and Trew claimed that a confession of faith agree-
able to both parties had at one stage been considered, but that
agreement had broken down.[20] If this is so, then Careless's confession, on which Hart chose to make his own comments, may
be the result of this final breakdown in relations between predestinarians and free-willers. Careless reported that his interrogator,
Dr. Martin,

> read Hart's most blasphemous articles against those which I had writ-
> ten and sent to Newgate, whereunto all those twelve godly men that
> were last condemned had set to their hands, whom Hart, Kemp, and
> M. Gybson, would have persuaded from the same again; but, thanks
> be unto God, the serpent prevailed not.[21]

The chief of the martyrs in question was William Tyms, curate of
Hockley in Essex, who had previously been imprisoned in the
King's Bench, and so presumably took part in the disputes there,
before being transferred to Newgate and finally burned on 24 April

1556.[22] Hart's writing survives (though Careless's confession of faith to which it was a reply does not) in a copy at Emmanuel College, Cambridge, which describes itself as

> A true coppye of letter wch Henrye Harte sent to | newgate to ye prysoners ther condemned to dy for ye conffessyone of chrystes verytye Agaynst sertayne Artycles wch they Alowed y^t were sette furth by sertayn prysoners in ye kyngsbench to appeace ye contencyon y^t theyr felowe prysoners had w^t them.[23]

In it, Hart questioned what he saw as his opponents' dismissive attitude toward the value of good works ("Though ye confese all y^t chryst hath done & beleve it as an undouted verytye as it is in dede yet if ye leave y^t undone wch ye shuld do yet shall ye perysh") and, in an unmistakable reference to John Careless, warned them, "Frynds I feare ye eccepte a carles mane to be yor teacher and he hath tawght ye as carles a fayth."

This letter, like his other writings, reveals Hart as a poor theologian, from whom a degree of antiintellectualism would naturally be expected, if only as a defense of his own failings. In his comments on Christology he confuses the ideas of "person" and "nature."

> In ye ij article ye saye y^t god and mane were joyned to gether in christ into one persone nev^{er} to be devyded | and and [sic] in ye fyrst ye saye y^t god was iij persons w^{t}out begynnynge and ending so y^t ye make quaternytye in god if ye holde the humanytye wch our savyour christ toke of ye blessed virgyne marye for a persone and is not . . . ye hold and affyrme in yor fyrst artycle that god is iij persons and then ye sayd in ye second that he is made one persone forever | I pray you lett me knowe wch of these ye entend to hold for ye truth when ye have well wayed ye matter Amongst your selves.

Although the articles to which Hart's comments refer are not extant, it seems on this evidence overwhelmingly probable that Hart had confused orthodox teaching on the two natures in Christ, with the doctrine of the three persons in God, and thus thought himself to have detected in his opponents teaching which indicated quaternity in God. It hardly seems possible that Careless and the circles in which he moved in the King's Bench would have been either doctrinally illiterate or heretical on the points in question. So either Hart genuinely failed to understand orthodox doctrine on this point, or else he was, unlike Sheterden and Trew, influenced by the Christology of ultraradical groups which tended to a form of

Monophysitism (the idea that Christ took no flesh of the virgin but "passed through her as water through a pipe"). Monophysite Christology was closely associated at the time with the name of Melchior Hoffmann, who had taught that

> if redemption emerged and took effect from the same seed of Adam it would logically follow that sinners were redeemed by sin . . . that filthy people were cleansed and purified by filth. . . . If redemption had been achieved by Mary's flesh and blood God would have wronged Satan. . . .[24]

This rejection of the two-nature doctrine of Christ was part of a concern to emphasize the unity of God, and it may be that it was this current of thought, which spread to English radicals such as Joan Bocher (though it had been present in England—and the Netherlands—from at least the turn of the century), that had influenced Hart and led him to quibble at the two natures in Christ.[25] It was the stress on Christ's human nature that appears to have offended Hart: "ye holde the humanytye wch our savyour christ toke of ye blessed virgyne marye for a persone and is not." Admittedly, a passing comment made eight years earlier in his *Godly newe short treatyse* indicates that he was orthodox on the point at that time. "Yf the sonne of God, takyng oure nature upon hym, myghte not escape [suffering]. . . . Thynke not ye to escape | my Brethern. . . ."[26] It is possible, of course that Hart had changed his mind in the interim, but more likely, as with Hart's other views, that consistency is not so much to be looked for as an overall direction of thought. Hart certainly had contacts, albeit perhaps indirectly, with those who held Melchiorite views,[27] and other aspects of his thought point in a somewhat spiritualizing direction consonant with an aversion to the idea that "redemption had been achieved by Mary's flesh and blood." The evidence that Hart did hold Melchiorite opinion, while circumstantial, seems quite strong. John Trew's group in the King's Bench angrily rejected the accusations of their opponents that they held to a Melchiorite Christology; the question still remains as to why they should have been accused of it in the first place, and the answer is perhaps that Hart held it.[28]

Hart's constant denigration, in his other writings, of the flesh and of natural reason is consistent with his holding a Melchiorite Christology, because both emphasize the New Testament distinction between flesh and spirit to an almost Gnostic degree. "Reason was blynd and nature corrupte," said Hart in his *Godly newe short treatyse* of 1548, "therfore coulde it not obeye to the wyll of GOD." "Chryste had no felycytye in thys presente worlde whych is now corrupte," he taught, and urged all to "labour earnestly by the helpe of the spyryt to kepe your selues unspotted of the worlde, that ye may be saued . . . ."[29] In rhetoric of this sort, the physical world becomes understood as evil in and of itself. "Hate the filthy vesture of the flesshe," Hart told his readers the following year, "for doubtles it is subject to corruption, it is also, the very gate and meane whereby Sathan . . . corrupteth both bodie & soule, and draweth man to utter distruction." "Our god," he claimed, "hath taken part againste fleshe and bloud, because it is become his verie enemy."[30]

Hart concluded his letter to the prisoners in Newgate with his usual, and distinctive, mode of expression: "by yor frynd what so ev^{er} ye say or judge henrye hart | as far as charytye byndeth me as knoweth god." (He had concluded his *Consultorie for all Christians. To beware least they beare the name of christians in vayne* [H. iii^r] with "yours as charitie byndeth me. H. H."). After this conclusion were added responses by the letter's several recipients, beginning with William Tyms. "Be fore god and mane I protest this doctryne of henrye hart to be most blasfemose to chrystes [?] death and passyon by me willyame tyms the xxjth day of apryll comdemned to dy [?] for chrystes verytye." Other prisoners at Newgate who added further derogatory comments included Christopher Lister, Robert Drake, George Ambrose, Thomas and Richard Spurge, Richard Gratwyke (who in 1557 signed the same submission as John Saxby, who was one of John Trew's companions, and was released) Richard Nicholl, John Spenser, John Herman, and Simon Fen.[31] The date given by Tyms, 21 April, is just four days before the first interrogation of John Careless, in which Dr. Martin showed himself in possession of the document, and only three days before Tyms, Drake, the Spurges, Ambrose, and one John Cavel were burned at Smithfield.[32] Interestingly, Richard Spurge (and Foxe implies the same of Thomas Spurge, George Ambrose, and John Cavel) came from Bocking in Essex, and so may well have been known to Hart from his activities there in Edward VI's time.[33]

The Pelagian Tendency

Hart's writing is characterized by a rambling, sometimes almost incoherent style. His two short books do not possess any obvious

structure of argument or ordering of subject matter. Both are ex-
hortatory in intent and, after brief introductions, plunge into their
subject material and simply wallow around in it, urging their readers to godly living for the sake of their souls. This raises perhaps
the most serious point about the actual content of Hart's writings.
By his opponents he stood accused of Pelagianism,[34] and if such a
charge might often be no more than mere name-calling directed at
free-willers by predestinarians (who might insist that any doctrine
of human free-will made faith a "work"), then an examination of
Hart's writings indicates that there does seem to be some real
substance in the charges in Hart's case. Perhaps the kindest interpretation that could be placed upon Hart's insistence that good
works are vital for salvation, is that he was simply stressing the
idea propounded in the Epistle of James, namely, that faith without
works is dead, and that a true faith will always bear a harvest
of good deeds. "Trewe faithe," he told his readers in 1549, "is
accoumpanyed with godly loue."[35] Godly living was for Hart the
infallible mark of those who were of the true church: he wrote of
those who considered themselves "the trewe churche and espouse
of God upon earth, as al that lyue godly doubtles be," by way of
contrast with "all them that call themselues of the congregation of
god, and yet are not because they lyue ungodly, and are the bond
seruauntes of syn."[36] He urged his readers to

> stryue daily against your lustes, and mortyfie your affections, compell
> your fleshe to be ruled and ordered, by the rules of Christe, prescrybed
> in the sacred worde of god, unto you. Then doubtles our heauenlye
> father wyll not onelye loue us, & take us for hys dear children, but
> also for Christes sake . . . clearelye forgeue and forget our synnes.[37]

This is harder to interpret in a merely Jamesian sense, and makes
the accusations of Pelagianism against Hart appear more fully justified. Hart sometimes appears to teach that moral virtue enabled
one truly to believe. "Repent & turne frō your euill waies with
your whole hertes, that ye maie beleue, & set your faithe on a sure
ground, build it on yᵉ sure foundacion of gods holy worde."[38] But
a moment later he seems to assert that faith, as long as it is uncontaminated by human reasoning, does indeed make righteous.

> For true fayth is liuely, & no uncertayne thynge, it is surelye grounded
> and stablished upon the sure rocke of Gods woorde and promise, as it
> is written, Abraham beleued God in hys promise, and none opinion of
> his own imaginacion, & it was counted to hym for righteousnes, but

yf your faith bee without the word, then is it carnall and fleshely, beyng builte upon naturall reason, and therefore it is vayne.[39]

It seems that, for Hart, the objection to the old Pelagianism of Rome was not that it was Pelagianism, but that its authority depended upon the pronouncements of the great and the learned. Although, as this last quotation shows, he could sometimes appear to endorse justification by faith, he does not seem to have had a consistent soteriology at all, but rather seems (most of the time!) to have viewed a correct faith as a condition of, but not of itself sufficient for, salvation.

For him, the idea that faith justified completely smacked of philosophical speculation of a kind that naturally aroused his suspicion. As he warned the prisoners in Newgate in 1556,

In your fowrth article you saye yo^u do beleve all your salvaiyon redempyon and & [sic] remyssyon of syns comethe unto you holye and solye by ye meryt & faver of god in chryst purchased unto you through his most p^{re}cyous death & blod-shedyng onlye | & in no parte or pece by or through any of your owne meryts workes or deservyng howe manye or good so ever they be and yet ye saye ye do not denye nor destroy good workes | but ye acknowledge & confese y^t all mene are bounde to do them and to knowe and kepe gods comandement:

yet "all though ye Alowe good workes in worde yet if ye declare no benefytte to be towards them wch do them | ye wer allmost as good to deny theme."[40] The expressions used here of the orthodox party's beliefs concerning the cause of salvation probably come close to the *ipsissima verba* of Careless's confession and their other statements of the matter; as J. W. Martin points out of some of the free-willers' own expressions, they have about them "a certain tone of oral debate."[41] In addition, the unidentified former free-willer who wrote to his erstwhile comrades urging them to abandon their beliefs used almost identical expressions. "Al salvation, justification, redemption, and remission of sins, cometh to us wholly and solely by the mere mercy and free grace of God in Jesus Christ, and not for any of our own works, merits, or deservings."[42]

Hart leaned heavily on Col. 1.24 in his letter to the prisoners at Newgate, in order to demonstrate what he saw as the necessity for good works in addition to reliance on the merits and passion of Christ; he pointed them to "Colosy i. ye shall fynd some what also for you to do in ye flesh besyds all y^t christ hath done wch if ye do not ye shall perysh not w^t standynge all his doinges,' and another admonition to them relies on the same text.

> ye were best to folowe saynt pall who thought it no derogayon to
> christes death nor passyone to saye | nowe joye I in my sufferynge w^ch
> suffer for you and fullfyll y^t wch is be hind or lackynge of ye passyone
> of chryst in my flesh for his bodyes sake wch is the congregayones."

In fairness to Hart, it should be pointed out that his earliest
extant piece of writing, *A godly newe short treatyse* of 1548, does
not exhibit these Pelagian tendencies to quite the same degree. He
appears relaxed in quoting Eph. 2.8–9 early on in the treatise,
without apparently so much as feeling the need to immediately
"balance it up" with verse 10 (which states that we are created in
Christ Jesus for good works); instead, he adds a quotation from
John 1.12–13 as a supporting text.

> But by grace are ye saved through faythe, (sayeth paule) and not of
> youre selfes nor throught workes, leaste any man shuld boast hym
> selfe: but by Chryst are we saved and made the beloved sonnes of the
> hyghest: As Wytnessethe sayncte John sayinge: He gave them power
> to be the Sonnes of GOD, as many as beleve in hys name . . . .[43]

At one point in his *Consultorie,* however, Hart seemed to imply
that even unbelievers might be saved by their works: "hate the
euill, & chose ye good, so shal ye lyue for euer, for thei that do
these thynges are born of god, and are made the belouing sonnes
of the highest, of what relygion, tong or nacion soeuer thei be."[44]
The explanation follows a moment later: "yf an infidell turne in his
hert frō his infidelitie, and do ye thynge that is equall & right, although he neuer receiue christen name nor outward sacrament,
thinke ye that he shal not be saued?"[45] The Spiritualist Sebastian
Franck had said something similar in his celebrated letter to John
Campanus, and Anabaptist radicals on the Continent, such as Michael Sattler, had sometimes made shockingly favorable references
to the Turks, though there is no evidence to suggest that Hart had
read their writings.[46] Although he does not here actually say that
unbelievers who remain such will be saved by their works, he
certainly implies it.

If Hart really believed that good pagans would be saved by their
works, one might be tempted to speculate that his insistence elsewhere that false belief brought damnation was a mere polemical
device to be used against his adversaries. But this is unlikely, and
indeed there is probably no answer to this conundrum; Hart's theology simply is not consistent enough, in this or in any other area,
to allow of more precise analysis than that of noting the general
direction of his thought. The judgment of his adversaries, that in

the area of soteriology that direction was essentially Pelagian, does not seem unjust.

*   *   *

John Trew and His Group

John Trew was a leader among a group of free-willers in the King's Bench who were in dispute with the predestinarians. In his *Cause of Contention,* Trew gives a partisan account of the progress of this argument. Precisely what the nature of the relationship between his group and that of the Bocking and Faversham conventiclers was, or whether they were one and the same group, it is not possible to say with certainty. Although Trew does mention in his account "Simson, Upchear and Wodman, with other that were delivered out of prison"; "Simson" cannot have been the "Sympson" who was committed to the Marshalsea in January 1550/51, but "Upchear" is almost certainly the "Vpcharde" of Bocking committed with him at that time.[47] None of the cosignatories of his *Cause of Contention* were among those named in the proceedings against the conventiclers at Bocking in 1550.[48] William Wilkinson, writing in 1579, assumed that Trew's group and Hart's were one and the same.

> Of this ungracious cōpany also was one Trewe of Kente, who albeit before for the truthes sake he lost his eares (for perswaydyng the people from goyng to Masse,) yet afterward happenyng into the cōpany of Pelagians he became deadly enemy to good Iohn Careles, as appeareth by Careles his examination, whiche he . . . penned before he dyed in prison as in this booke of Martyrs is to be sene at large.[49]

Although Wilkinson claimed that Trew was "of Kente," one of Trew's own statements seems to indicate that he was, in fact, from Sussex. By way of illustration of one of his polemical points, he wrote that "we have in Sussex very many iron mills."[50] At least two other members of Trew's group, Thomas Avington and Thomas Arede (Read) were also from this county. Foxe, who was careful to make no more than passing references to the antipredestinarian radicals who impinge upon his narratives, seems to have been the source of so much of Wilkinson's information[51] that it is difficult to know what value to place upon Wilkinson's testimony when his information becomes, for the modern reader, an independent source in its own right. Certainly his polemical interests—he connected the group with the Family of Love—took priority over his concern for strict historical accuracy, hence his assumption that Trew's group was one and the same with Hart's, while very likely correct, does not settle the argument.

Indeed, there are indications of marked differences in opinion between Trew and Hart which, while they do not demonstrate any desire on the part of the two men to disassociate themselves from one another, nevertheless do indicate a degree of independence of thought. Trew's writing is innocent of Hart's reticence about the doctrine of justification by faith. "Because we did use abstinence and prayer," he complained, his opponents in the King's Bench

> reported us to be justifiers of ourselves, and such like; to the which we answered that our justification came by faith in Christ's death, but that we did, we did it, that God might make us able to bear his cross . . . .[52]

"We do by the holy Scriptures satisfy every man that doth repent and unfeignedly believe with a lively faith," he claimed, that he

> is in a state of salvation, and one of God's elect children, and shall certainly be saved, if he do not with malice of heart, utterly forsake God, and despise his word and ordinance, and become a persecutor of his children . . . .[53]

This is no Pelagianism; even the qualification about what the believer must not do is no more than a free-will gloss on the phenomenon of falling away from faith exactly parallel to the predestinarian explanation (i.e., that the person falling away was never of the elect in the first place). The confession of faith at the close of Trew's *Cause of Contention* uses the conventional phraseology concerning justification that echoes that of his predestinarian opponents and is in flat contradiction to Hart's misgivings about the doctrine.

> Also we confess and believe and faithfully acknowledge, that all salvation, justification, redemption, and remission of sins cometh unto us wholly and solely through the mere mercy and free favour of God in Jesus Christ, purchased unto us through his most precious death and blood-shedding, and in no part or piece through any of our own merit, works or deservings, how many or how good soever they be.[54]

Nor is this the sum of the doctrinal differences between the two men. In his letter of early 1556 to the prisoners in Newgate, Hart had queried the Christology of Careless and his party in a way

which implied that Hart himself leaned toward a Monophysite view
of the nature of Christ. The most usual form of this heresy among
English radicals was like that of the Melchiorites, and it was for
this that John Bocher had been burned in 1550. Although Trew
was accused by his opponents of holding such views, he angrily
repudiated the charge. He complained that his predestinarian
opponents

> raised up new slanders on us, reporting us that we should deny that
> Christ was come in the flesh, and that he passed through the blessed
> Virgin Mary, as saffron doth through a bag: which detestable opinion
> we hate and utterly abhor . . . .

In his confession of faith, Trew made clear the orthodoxy of his
own position.

> And we confess and believe, that the second person in trinity, which
> is Jesus Christ . . . took so much flesh and blood and nourishment of
> the blessed Virgin Mary, as any child doth of his mother, as St. Paul
> saith; forasmuch then as children are partakers of their mother's flesh
> and blood, he also took part with them, and so became very man in
> all points, sin only excepted, so that two perfect natures, the Godhead
> and manhood, were perfectly joined together in one Christ, never to
> be divided . . . .[55]

Trew himself absconded from prison in 1556, as John Careless
explained in a letter to Harry Adlington, a Protestant prisoner in
the Lollards' Tower, "bragging John T. hath beguiled his keepers
(who trusted him too well), and is run away from them . . . . Thus
you may see the fruits of our free-will men, that made so much
boast of their own strenth."[56] Since Trew was evidently still in
prison on 25 April 1556, when he was mentioned in a discussion
at the examination of Careless by Dr. Martin, he must have made
his escape some time between that date and Careless's death on
1 July.[57] By thus escaping at once the grasp of both his captors and
historians, Trew disappears from the story of the free-willers.

Fellow Free-Willers in the King's Bench

It remains to consider the circle of Protestant prisoners who
followed Trew's lead in the "contention." The martyrdoms of two
men, Thomas Harland and John Oswald, are mentioned in the same
letter of John Careless as that in which he refers to Trew's escape.

Careless calls them "sweet brethren," and it is perhaps significant of the gulf that had opened between orthodox and free-willers as a result of the prison dispute that Careless says nothing of the two others who suffered with Harland and Oswald. These were Thomas Avington, turner of Ardingley, and Thomas Read. Both were signatories of Trew's *Cause of Contention,* and Avington appears to have been Trew's lieutenant among the prisoners. Thomas Read is certainly the man who signed himself "Thomas Arede" at the end of Trew's account, for the information later given to John Foxe by Roger Hall calls him "Thomas A Reed who was burned at Lewes," and the *A* has been crossed through.[58] Avington and Arede, with Harland and Oswald, were burned at Lewes on 6 June 1556.[59]

Two other of Trew's cosignatories, John Saxby and John Jackson, would seem to be among those mentioned by Foxe. The name of John Saxby is included in a list of twenty-eight signatories to a Submission to the doctrine of transubstantiation. This document hardly amounts to a full recantation of Protestant beliefs, but includes a promise

> to live as it becometh good christian men, and here in this realm to use ourselves as it becometh faithful subjects unto our most gracious king and queen, and to all other superiors both spiritual and temporal, according to our bounden duties.

Twenty-two of the signatories were prisoners arrested in Colchester and sent to London in August 1556; John Saxby was not one of these, so it is likely that he was already a prisoner in London before the arrival of the group from Colchester, and thus very possibly the same John Saxby who had been part of Trew's group in the King's Bench. All twenty-eight signatories to the Submission were released.[60] Foxe also gives a brief account of the examination of John Jackson before Dr. William Cook, the recorder of London, on 11 March 1555/56, but this account provides no hard information other than identifying Jackson as, in his captor's opinion, "the rankest heretic of all them in the King's Bench." Foxe concluded his brief entry by claiming that, "Of this John Jackson, besides these his foresaid answers and examination before Dr. Cook, one of the commissioners, no more as yet came unto our hands."[61] If Foxe was being his usual circumspect self in respect to the free-will radicals, then this may reflect a happy absence of more embarrassing documentation, but is more likely the result of judicious editing on Foxe's part; certainly Thomas Bryce, the author of the doggerel poem *The Regester,* written in celebration of the Marian martyrs and lauding the coming of Elizabeth to the throne, knew of a Jackson who died for his faith in June 1556, just three months after the interview mentioned by Foxe.[62]

In any case, further documentation likely to embarrass Foxe certainly existed, whether or not Dr. John Fines is correct in his certainty that the martyrologist saw it.[63] A letter of John Careless to "my deare brother Jackesoñe" and "the Rest of youre cõpanye," pointed out, at tedious length, the more likely intended meaning of Paul's words to the Corinthians about being saved "as through fire," as against the free-will men's tendentiously literal interpretation that

> yf a mān holde never so many Errours; yett yf he be burned for a truthe; all hys Eresyes be they never so greate shall not hurte hym; but that . . . the partye yᵗ holdethe theñ shalbe saved thrughe the fyer.[64]

The letter's manner of address implies what later comments make plain, namely, that it was Jackson who had written to Careless requesting to answer to various points. Careless hoped that his work would "provoke you to Repentaunce as yt hathe done my deare brother cornelis and dyvers other; most worthy mēbres of christes churche."[65] The "cornelis" mentioned was presumably Cornelius Stevenson, one of the signators of Trew's confession. Since Stevenson had been of the free-will party at that time, that is, on 30 January 1555/56, the letter must have been written sometime after this. Though it might be tempting to conjecture that the singling out of Jackson as a principal recipient implies that it was sent after Trew's escape and that Jackson had assumed the leadership of the party remaining, this is improbable; even if Jackson did have some kind of leading role among the free-willers in the King's Bench, it is almost inconceivable that Careless would have failed to mention such a significant event, perhaps (if his feelings expressed to Adlington are anything to go by) as a taunt.

Woodman, Simson and the *Cause of Contention*

John Trew's *Cause of Contention* dates itself as "the 30th of January, Anno Dom. 1555" (i.e., falling within 1556 by modern reckoning).[66] Bradford would then have been dead since the previous June, which accounts for Trew's lack of any reference to him as a participant in the "contention." The discussion between the

Catholic interrogator Dr. Martin and John Careless on 25 April 1556 seems to take for granted that the events described in the *Cause of Contention* are relatively recent.[67] The work is an account of the disputes between Trew's party of free-willers in the King's Bench, whom Trew refers to simply as "we," and the predestinarians. This dispute, according to Trew, was near to being resolved, or at least patched up, "three or four times, but most likest at Christmas last,"[68] and the account gives most attention to this attempt at an amicable settlement, which at the time of writing appears to have been the most recent. When the attempt broke down, Trew recorded, "we gave them over, and meddled as little with them as we could, until Simson, Upchear, and Wodman, with other . . . were delivered out of prison . . . ." The allegiances of these prisoners at the time of their release seem, in each case, to have been on the predestinarian side. The identification of "Upchear" with the Upcharde of Bocking in whose house the meeting at Christmas 1550 had been held, and who later went into exile seems conclusive. As has been argued in the previous chapter, his change of sides seems to have been effected before his release.[69] But the identity of "Wodman" with the Richard Woodman who was martyred with nine others at Lewes on 22 June 1557 is more probable than certain, and the identity of "Simson" is the most difficult of all.

Richard Woodman, while in his final imprisonment, wrote that

> since I was delivered out of the bishop of London's hands, which was in the year of our Lord 1555, and the same day that master Philpot was burned, which was the 18the of December, I lay in his coalhouse eight weeks lacking but one day; and, before that, I was a year and a half almost in the King's Bench after my first apprehension, for reproving a preacher in the pulpit, in the parish of Warbleton, where I dwelt. . . . And it pleased God to deliver me with four more out of the butcher's hands, requiring nothing else of us but that we should be honest men, and members of the true catholic church . . . the which all we affirmed that we were members of the true church . . . .[70]

If Woodman had been imprisoned for nearly eighteen months before his release in December 1555, then he must have been arrested in the summer of 1554. His release from the King's Bench with four others just before Christmas 1555 ties in precisely with Trew's account, since "Christmas last" would be that of 1555.

Woodman has been quoted by Champlin Burrage as saying that he had been a "prisoner in ye kinges benche" "one whole yere the sixt daye of Iune laste paste, for ye Testimonye of Iesus Christe. 1552."[71] Burrage's purpose in quoting Woodman's views, stated in his "Confession," on the subject of baptism was to demonstrate that he could not have been a possible Baptist, as some "over-zealous historians" had claimed.[72] However, this dating of the "Confession" suggests that Woodman had a history of radicalism, since he would then have seen the inside of the King's Bench under the Protestant, and relatively tolerant, regime of Edward VI, thus making Woodman a possible candidate for allegiance to the free-will party. Alas, such an analysis falls down on the actual contents of the "Confession" itself, which are even more conservative than Burrage indicated. In the first place, the Confession makes it clear that its author was writing during Mary's reign, and not during that of Edward VI.

> And this salvacyon, Justificacōn and Redempcion is apprehended and receved of vs by only faithe in Jesus Christe, in yᵉ sence as it is declared in yᵉ homely of Justificacōn moste godlie, wᶜʰ was apoynted to be redd in this pecūliar churche of Englande in Good Kynge Edwardes daies yᵉ syxt, wᶜʰ homilie wᵗʰ all yᵉ reste I beleve & affyrme to be a moste certayne and wholsome doctryne for all christian men. . . . But alas, for oʳ unthankfulnes this plague of popery ys come amonge vs. God delyver England frome it shortley for his names sake.[73]

The 1552 dating is thus incorrect; 1555 would be more natural, and, since Burrage's citation of the original is correct, the mistake must be attributed to a scribal error in the manuscript.[74] In the second place, Woodman clearly aligned his own views with the official Protestant orthodoxy of the Edwardian church. Speaking of the glories of the Gospel, he claimed that

> it was moste truly and syncerely preached of Mʳ Tailoʳ byshop of lyncolne, Mʳ hoper, Mʳ Rogers, Mʳ Farrowe bishop of S Davides, Mʳ Tailor of hadley, Mʳ Bradforde, Mʳ Cardmaker, and Mʳ Saunders wᵗʰ a great sorte mooe of learned, godlie christian pʳᵉchers . . . .[75]

If Woodman endorsed Bradford, then his allegiance to the predesti-narian side in the contention in the King's Bench can safely be assumed. His praise for men of learning, also, was hardly likely to have come from the pen of one of the free-will party.

The problem of identifying the "Simson" who was released with Woodman and Upchard remains, however. Since A. G. Dickens cast doubt upon the traditional identification of "one Sympson" mentioned in the depositions of 1550/51 with Cuthbert Simson, the deacon of the underground Protestant church martyred on 28 March 1558, it has been supposed that the former was John Simson

of Great Wigborough in Essex. This remains probable, but John
Simson, since he went to the stake at Rochford in June 1555, following a brief imprisonment in London, cannot be the Simson
referred to by Trew as being released just before the following
Christmas.[76]

If John Simson of Great Wigborough is ruled out of the reckoning, then the two most likely candidates must surely be Thomas
and Cuthbert Simson, who may have been brothers, and who were
both deacons of the London underground church pastored by John
Rough.[77] In the case of Cuthbert, at least, it would be necessary to
posit a release and rearrest, since he was arrested in December
1557 and martyred on 28 March 1558, though Foxe does not mention any earlier imprisonment.[78] If the "Simson" mentioned by
Trew was one of these two, then he would hardly have been of
Trew's party in the King's Bench, since Rough's congregation was
a survival of Edwardian Protestantism in close contact with Reformed churches and English exiles on the Continent. Trew's further reference to him implies as much.

> (for Simson came to us, and desired us to be at unity in the truth,) we
> answered, that it was our desire . . . . And the order of the unity was
> of both the parties put into Simson's and others, that were of that
> sect's, hands . . . .[79]

Admittedly, the expression "Simson's and others, that were of that
sect's, hands" might be taken to imply that the process was even-
handed, Simson balancing those of "that sect," and that Simson
was therefore one of Trew's party. But more compelling are the
statements that "Simson came to us, and desired us to be at unity
in the truth" and "we answered, that it was our desire." These
strongly imply that Simson was not one of "us," but of "that sect."
This is consistent with "Simson" being either Cuthbert or Thomas.
Bradford's statment, in a letter of 1554 to a free-willer, that he had
received "three letters, one from my brother Simson, another from
Henry Hart, and another from you" gives no clear indication as to
the likely allegiance of "Simson."[80]

Trew's escape, along with the martyrdoms of several of his group
and the defection of some others to the predestinarian cause,
seems to have reduced the numbers of the free-will party in the
King's Bench considerably, and the submission later in 1556 of
John Saxby, just mentioned, to the Catholic authorities, is all the
more understandable in the light of these events. Nevertheless, the
significance of John Trew's free-will party in the King's Bench in

casting light upon the seedbed of radical ideas in mid-Tudor England is considerable. The *Cause of Contention,* in particular, remains one of the prime sources of information on the nature of that radicalism and its response to contact with what was coming to be understood as Protestant orthodoxy.

* * *

A Wayward Virago: The Life and Heresies of Joan Bocher

Joan Bocher's activities and martyrdom have been related by J. F. Davis in his article "Joan of Kent, Lollardy and the English Reformation,"[81] and the general outline of her story is in any case well-known. The function of this account is as much to reassess as to retell, and to shed as much doubt, as any further light, on parts of previous accounts. Active as a Lollard conventicler in Steeple Bumpstead, Essex in the late 1520s, Bocher abjured sacramentarian heresies in Colchester, perhaps as a result of the major drive against Lollardy in Essex by Bishop Tunstall in 1528. Several of the conventicles appear to have taken place in her house. On 11 May, a "Joan Bocher, widow" was identified as being "of the same sect" with Richard Fox, the curate of Steeple Bumpstead who doubled as one of the leaders of the Lollard congregation.[82] The other two leaders were John Tyball and William Gardyner, who was one of three Augustine friars belonging to the group. On this occasion the recorded abjurers, including "William Bocher, of Steeple Bumpstead, ploughwright," recanted sacramentarian heresies and the opinion that pardons were of no effect.[83] William Bocher was noted to be of tainted stock, since his father had been burned as a heretic, so, if Joan Bocher was a relation, it seems that she was part of a radical family. She is sometimes referred to in these records as "Mother Bocher,"[84] so she was presumably not a young widow; indeed, she may even have been the mother of William, which would mean that she had been widowed by a previous prosecution of heresy. If this were so—and it is only speculation, of course—it may help to account for her own determination and steadfastness later, in contrast to her willingness at this stage, quite usual among Lollards, to recant when apprehended.

Two things should be noted about the Steeple Bumpstead group in this context. The first is the evident and typically Lollard attachment, of some members at least, to the Epistle of James. Thomas Hilles deposed on 15 October 1528 that he had learned the first two chapters of that work by heart, the first having been taught

him by a girl from Finchingfield to whom he had engaged to be
married but who had since died, and the second by a Lollard
butcher of Coggeshall.[85] A similar group in Colchester showed a
tendency to emphasize the same epistle.

> John Pykas, of the parish of St. Nicholas, Colchester, . . . had commu-
> nication with Best . . . concerning the epistles [sic] of James, which
> Best could say by heart, Best had been taken as a known man and a
> brother in Christ for a year. . . . Spoke also to Gyrlyng about a chapter
> of James . . . . Has talked with William Raylond about the Lord's
> Prayer and the Apostles' Creed in English, about the Epistles of James
> and John, and about the eight Beatitudes.[86]

As E. G. Rupp has pointed out, "the Epistle of James with its
simple, practical piety and its emphasis on brotherhood was the
handbook of the "known men."[87] He claimed that "the references
[by Lollards] to this Epistle are more numerous than to any
other" and cited Foxe's record of the heresy-hunt in Amersham,
in the diocese of Lincoln, in 1521 and the 1527/28 proceedings
against heresy.[88] A. G. Dickens concurs with Rupp's view: "Lollardy," he says, "apotheosized the simple and practical Epistle of
St. James."[89] The tendency toward Pelagianism observable in
Henry Hart may be explicable in such terms; it would naturally
be spawned in such an environment, and it is noteworthy that Joan
Bocher shared this background. Neither Rupp nor Dickens has
been slow to note the potential created by this Jamesian emphasis
for conflict with doctrines of justification by faith. "The lack of
theological leadership and the failure of the movement to produce
any living theology," claimed Rupp, "marks it off from the later
Reformation. . . . 'Justification by only Faith' was to touch heights
and depths unsounded by what we know of later Lollardy."[90] Dickens notes that "Lutheranism deprecated [the Epistle of James],
concentrating upon Romans and the intellectual emphasis upon
Justification by Faith."[91]

The second point of note is that the Steeple Bumpstead congregation seems to have had at least some contacts in Bocking, where
the free-will men were to be arrested more than two decades later.
John Tyball had taken Richard Fox and another member of the
group, John Smyth, on a trip to Colchester, staying the first night
on the way with Mother Beckwith at Braintree, before being joined
next day after dinner by "Old Christmas" of nearby Bocking, and
confessed on 28 April 1528 that he had discussed heresy with him.[92]
Neither does the meeting with "Old Christmas" seem to have been

a chance encounter, for when Margaret Cowbridge and Margaret Bowgas purged themselves on 17 July at St. John's monastery, Colchester, the former produced the names of eight compurgators, including that of "Ann Christmas," while the latter named six including "Catharine Cristmas" [sic].[93] Christmas (or Cristmas) being the unusual name that it is, and Lollards being the small minority that they were, Ann and Catharine are very likely to have been relations of "Old Christmas" of Bocking. The fact that the Steeple Bumpstead congregation of Lollards had at least this contact in the later Essex center of free-willer activity might perhaps be placed alongside another geographical coincidence: Joan Bocher's next known place of abode was Frittenden in Kent, which lies only seven miles from Henry Hart's home village of Pluckley, and she was accused of breaking the Easter fast of 1541 by eating a calf's head at the house of John Clerke of Headcorn, which is only four miles from Pluckley.[94] These facts on their own prove nothing, and simply illustrate the receptivity of both the Weald of Kent and north Essex to Protestantism in general and to radicalism in particular, but it nevertheless seems highly unlikely that Henry Hart and Joan Bocher, both radicals who had been previously apprehended but remained active in the early 1540s, did not meet.

The Disturbances in Kent

By 1543, Bocher had clearly emerged as an influential propagator of radical views: John Milles opined in a letter to Cranmer that "most of the vulgar people think the foundation of . . . errors in these parts cometh by the fault of heresies not punished set forth by Joan Baron, sometimes called Joan Bucher of Westgate [Canterbury]."[95] She had been arrested again after the incident of the calf's head breakfast but, remaining in prison "for 2 years, more or less, no evidence was brought against her, though she manifestly denied the Sacrament of the Altar with many slanderous words."[96] She also said that "matins and evensong was no better than rumbling of tubs," an outburst which Cranmer described as "offensive."[97] She had remarried by this time, for the parson of Westbere (a village about four miles northeast of Canterbury) and two of his parishioners claimed that "they heard her husband say that she was abjured at Colchester."[98] The identity of the husband is not apparent from surviving records, but the allegation just mentioned suggests that he was living in or near Westbere at this time, rather than at Frittenden, nearly thirty miles away. If so, he may, of course, have moved to be nearer Bocher's place of imprisonment, but the extant records are silent on the matter. By 1543, however, Bocher was staying at John Toftes's house at Westgate, in Canterbury, Toftes having pleaded her defense in the Consistory court where, as John Milles complained, "before he never was proctor in that court, nother sythe."[99]

Toftes was notorious as a maintainer of heretics; he had acted as surety for Bocher's codefendant John Clerke of Headcorn, and his house was the resort of other radicals, including Giles Barham, who acted as a priest without actually having been ordained, John Bland, the parson of Adisham, one Jonas, a married priest (his wedding had been performed by the unordained Barham!), and the unnamed parson of Hothfield (a village between Pluckley and Ashford), who not only denied transubstantiation, but likened the mother of Christ "to a saffron bag," an expression usually connected with Monophysite Christology.[100] It may have been in Toftes's house, then, that Joan first encountered and began to adopt Monophysite views herself. Toftes was something of an iconoclast. On 17 November 1538, together with two accomplices, he pulled down most of the pictures in the church of Northgate, Canterbury; just over four years later, he came back for one he had spared on the previous occasion: taking the picture of Our Lady home with him, he "did hew her all in pieces".[101] His family were like-minded in their blunt opposition to Catholic traditionalism: his daughter-in-law was reported as saying "that her daughter could piss as good holy water as the priest could make any."[102]

The state of Bocher's second marriage seems to have been questionable, to say the least. Referred to as "Joan Bocher, widow" in 1528,[103] she continued to be known as Joan Bocher or Butcher, though other names were used of her less frequently: Joan Knel,[104] Joan Baron or Barnes,[105] and simply Joan of Kent.[106] This seems unusual, given the references in 1543 to a husband as still alive, indicating that she had remarried; normally, she might be presumed to have taken, and become generally known by, his name. But even if that name were Knel or Baron (and at least one of these must have been simply an alias), she was not usually referred to by it. Furthermore, her husband does not appear to have been arrested with her, and he apparently supplied hostile witnesses with the information that she had previously abjured heresy in Colchester,[107] though this may have been only careless talk on his part rather than an attempt to do her harm. Nevertheless, it seems strange that she broke the fast on Easter morning with John Clerke (and apparently without her husband) at Clerke's house, and that she stayed with John Toftes and his wife in Canterbury after her release, rather than returning to her husband. Perhaps her radical activities had placed a strain upon their marriage and led them to have a rather distant relationship.

Even if Cranmer felt Bocher's views to be offensive, both he and his officials seem to have been prepared to tolerate her at this time. The conservative Edmund Shether complained that "I have heard men say many things, as that my lord [Cranmer] did know . . . of Joan Barnes' opinon, . . . and other things which were not reformed . . . . "[108] Miles Hogarde, in his 1556 work, *The Displaying of the Protestantes & Sondry their practices, with a description of divers their abuses of late frequented,* claimed that in the earlier stage of her career (i.e., prior to her final arrest and subseqent execution) Joan was actually encouraged by Cranmer, and implied that the latter saw her as a useful disseminator of Protestantism.

Marciō to prepare the mindes of the people in Rome to fauour his heresy sent a woman before muche lyke Joane Butcher, which in the beginnyng of our newfound [*sic*] opinions was greatly maintayned by Cranmer in Cantorbury, & other places of Kent.[109]

Certainly Cranmer had sought to protect Henry Hart and his friends from conservative local officials in 1538, but he could not always be relied upon to act in this fashion; the conservatives' hands were strengthened by the Six Articles Act of the following year, and Cranmer appears by his letters of 1539 to Lord Lisle to have been an eager participant in persecuting the Protestants Thomas Broke, customer of Calais, and Raaf Hare.[110] There is no need to postulate the direct protection of Cranmer in seeking to explain why, despite her own confession to sacramentarianism, Bocher remained unconvicted and was finally released after having been supplied with a royal pardon by dubious means; the man responsible for shielding her from the rigors of the law was Cranmer's commissary, Dr. Nevinson. Nevinson appears to have been determined to prevent Bocher's conviction for heresy; Robert Serles, the conservative prebendary, complained that the commissary "would have delivered her by proclamation as a 'gynteles' person," and that he attempted to keep her written confession from the hands of her opponents.[111] By Serles's account, Nevinson did later declare in court that Bocher was a heretic, but added, "You have a thing to stick to which may do you good. I advise you to stick to it," which seems to have been a cue line for her to produce a pardon document.[112] This she did, and was released. John Milles seems to have understood the events in this light, for he told Cranmer that Bocher, "having a pardon in her bosom, was bid deliver it (as she did) and thereby was delivered."[113] Serles lamented that, despite having "as it is said, abjured of heresy at Colchester for opinions sustained against the Sacrament of the Altar," Bocher had "since spoken and defended openly her erroneous opinions in Canterbury before many, and yet she is quit by a pardon."[114] Nevinson seems to have engaged in these subterfuges as a matter of policy; Serles noted that, when Mr. Sponer, vicar of Boughton north of Ashford, told Nevinson he had obtained from John Bland a written denial of auricular confession, "the Commissary desired Mr. Sponer to let him see, swearing he would not keep it, but when he had got it he put it in his purse."[115]

Monophysite Christology and Joan Bocher

It is important to note that, at this stage, apart from the usual Lollard and Protestant vilification of traditional ceremonies and religious observances, Bocher had been charged with nothing more theologically radical than sacramentarianism, the same heresy which she had abjured in Colchester some years before. She is best known, of course, for her unyielding defense of Monophysite Christology and her ultimate martyrdom for refusing to recant. Had she been converted to Monophysite views by the time of her second arrest in 1541, however, the fact would certainly have emerged during the proceedings against her at that time, and would probably have taken prime place in the charges which she faced. It would also have been far more difficult for Nevinson to protect her, even on the assumption that he would still have been inclined to do so under those circumstances. It seems overwhelmingly likely, therefore, that the Monophysite views for which she was tried in 1549 and burned in 1550, which were distinctive features of Melchiorite Anabaptism and may well intimate direct or indirect connections with that movement, were adopted by Bocher during the 1540s. As has been mentioned, the parson of Hothfield who frequented John Toftes's house in Canterbury is one possible source of influence in this direction, though the members of Toftes's circle were generally so radical that others besides him may have held similar views. Whence these, in their turn, may have come by their opinions is not clear. Between the arguments of I. B. Horst, who seems inclined to argue for a very strong

Anabaptist influence, and even a direct presence, in English radicalism, and to take contemporary accusations of "Anabaptism" at their face value,[116] and of J. F. Davis, who ascribes much of English Protestantism, let alone radicalism, to developments from indigenous Lollardy,[117] there is simply insufficient evidence to adjudicate in many cases. Simon Piers, of "Waldershare" (Walderslade?) in Kent, taught Monophysitism in the years before the Reformation, but there were more instances in the 1530s and 1540s.[118] Either these were an outgrowth of the earlier—and perhaps tiny—indigenous base, or they resulted from subsequent contacts with Dutch Anabaptism. The latter explanation seems the more likely; persecution in the Netherlands in the wake of the Münster debacle created a significant influx of Anabaptists into England in the mid–1530s. About twenty were arrested in London, of whom perhaps a dozen were burned, in 1535.[119] Not long before, in 1532, six Englishmen and two Flemish Anabaptists, who met at the house of one John Raulinges in London, were discovered importing and distributing "the books of the Anabaptists' Confession."[120] At least one Englishman and one Fleming of this group held "strange" and "damnable opinions concerning Christ's humanity."[121] In November of that year, three Dutch Anabaptists were burned, including the twenty-two-year-old Peter Franke at Colchester, of whom John Bale, writing seven years later with a surprising degree of sympathy, noted, "This lerned I in Colchestre of them which were by his onlye deathe or pacient sufferaūce | coüerted from . . . papisme vnto true repentaunce."[122] But John Huntington, the Catholic poetaster against whom Bale wrote on that occasion, had no doubt at all that Franke's chief error was "that Christ and God, Toke not manhode, Of Marye the Virgine," so if the onlookers at his death were converted to that, as well as to his confession of Christ as "his onlye sauer and redemer," then Monophysite views presumably gained some kind of a following in radical Colchester.[123] Bale claimed that Franke "dyed in no soche wycked opinion as manye haue crediblye reported" but, given the agreement on all sides that the martyr was both Dutch and Anabaptist, he would have been an unusual specimen had he not held Monophysite views.[124] Bale, with typical immoderation, was making a point of finding some lie or heresy in literally every phrase of Huntington's ditty (four short lines of doggerel to every three pages of repudiation is about the average); of the charge of Monophysitism against Franke made by Huntington and the rejection of it by Bale, the former is the more likely to be true. If Colchester was indeed affected by Franke's witness, London and Kent were unlikely to have been left untouched, either by the ripple effects of the Franke affair, or by similar events in those other areas. It seems likely that the distinctive Anabaptist Christology found fertile ground. By 1549, John Hooper was worrying that "thys ungodlye opynyon," by which he meant Monophysitism, "is goten into the hartes of manye" in England.[125] Though he did not specifically mention Anabaptists, Martin Micronius wrote from London on 20 May 1550 to Heinrich Bullinger expressing his concern at imported heresy transmitted by fugitive radicals coming into England.

> An indeed it is a matter of the first importance that the word of God should be preached here in German, to guard against the heresies which are introduced by our countrymen. There are Arians, Marcionists, Libertines, Danists, and the like monstrosities, in great numbers. A few days since, namely, on the 2nd of May, a certain woman was burnt alive for denying the incarnation of Christ.[126]

Micronius seems to have assumed a link between the Germanic radicalism he feared, and the burning of the indigenous heretic Joan Bocher. The influx of Anabaptists into England continued in any case; in 1551 Sir Thomas Chamberlain complained that "too many [of the Ghent Anabaptists] run into England."[127]

Bale noted during Mary's reign that, even if these foreign Anabaptists had apparently failed to draw Englishmen into the actual practice of believers' baptism, some had been converted to a mental endorsement of it, or at least to antipaedobaptist beliefs.[128] Robert Cooche endorsed the baptism of believers, and Michael Thombe argued "that the Baptyme of infantes is not profitable because it goith w'hout faith," which implies that he believed the baptism of believers was profitable.[129] John Bland had stated that "in the christening of children, priests be murderers," which certainly indicates an antipathy to paedobaptism.[130] Of these, the last two combined baptismal unorthodoxy with Christological heresy. Michael Thombe asserted the same Monophysite view, that "Christ toke no flesshe of o^r lady," for which Joan Bocher was condemned, though he recanted on 11 May 1549.[131] Bland may have been even more radical, since he was accused of preaching in March 1542 "that the image of the Trinity is not to be suffered and he cannot find *Trinitas* throughout Scripture, but that Athanasius put it in his *Symbolum*."[132] While this last does not necessarily amount to a Socinianism of the kind abjured by John Assheton, parson of Shiltelington in the diocese of Lincoln, in December 1548,[133] it does suggest a biblicism sufficiently radical to call ortho-

dox Christology into question. The nature of Bland's alleged statements convey an impression of Lollard-rooted rationalism, while
Thombe's heresies touch on some of the central concerns of Melchiorite Anabaptism. Bocher seems to have had some connection
with both men; she and Bland were both frequenters of John Toftes's house in Canterbury, while she was examined at the same
time and place, and on one of the same heresies (the records are
silent about her beliefs on baptism) as Thombe.[134]

Indeed, it has been conjectured by some modern historians that
Thombe may have been Bocher's husband, though the only apparent basis for this is the use of the word *Bocher* to describe the trade
of the former, which led James Gairdner to coin the speculation in
the early part of the present century; A. G. Dickens repeats the
speculation, but cites no evidence as support for the idea.[135] I. B.
Horst is guiltless of this error; he describes Thombe as a tailor![136]
In point of fact, Thombe was almost certainly an example of Dutch
influence within English radicalism, and of the transmission of Monophysite Christology in particular. Though described as an "Englishman" in an official document of 1571, he seems to have been
either Dutch or of immediate Dutch descent. His history is trace-
able to some extent through his employees. He was definitely present in London as early as 1541 (when a Dutchman, William Orton,
had been his servant), but more than a quarter of a century later,
in 1568, three Dutchmen were listed as being servants to Michaell
Thombe, butcher, and three different men, again all Dutch, in
1571.[137] Of these, all but Orton were recorded as attending their
parish church of St. Mary Magdalen in Queenhithe Ward so, unless
Thombe practiced Nicodemism, his household does not appear to
have retained its radicalism as it clearly retained its connections
with the Low Countries. Johannes Thombe, the hatmaker, who
had been born in Flanders, who came to England in the 1540s and
was naturalized in 1549, may have been a relative.[138]

Bocher is reported by Miles Hogarde to have claimed at her
trial "that a M. in Londō were of her sect."[139] She can hardly, under
the circumstances, have been speaking of Lollardy, for the claim
would have meant little by the middle of Edward's reign; Lollardy
was becoming increasingly diffuse and had been for some time,
and was now merging with the new official Protestantism on the
right and mutating into different kinds of radicalism (of which Joan
herself was an example) on the left. Whatever the accuracy or
hyperbole entailed in the numerical estimate of a thousand, if Hogarde's report of Bocher's claim is correct, then she must have

been alluding to supporters of the view for which she was on trial,
namely, Monophysite Christology.

In what sense were Bocher's views Monophysite? She was accused in April 1549 of believing

> that the worde was made flesshe in the virgins Belly But that Christ
> toke flesshe of the virgin you beleve not because the flesshe of the
> virgin being outwarde man was sinfully gotton, and bo'ne in Synne |
> But the wo'de by the consent of the inwarde man of the virgin was
> made flesshe.[140]

In such beliefs as this, Cranmer felt, the "detestanda annabaptist-
arū Secta" was manifesting itself, though, like the chronicler of the
Grey Friars of London who called Thombe, Joan Bocher, and a
Colchester tanner named Putto "ante-baptystes," he may have
been using the term in its wonted loose fashion to refer to radicals generally.[141] Bocher's objection to more orthodox Christology
seems to have lain in her response to the Lollard (and Protestant)
debunking of Mariolatry; the reduction of Mary to the status of
normal womanhood seems to have been perceived as a threat to
the deity of Christ. At least that is the implication behind Bocher's
defense of her views to Roger Hutchinson, Thomas Lever, and
other Protestant clerics sent to convert her. According to Hutchinson's report in his *Image of God,* published in London on 26 June
1550, some eight weeks after Joan's execution, her argument ran
as follows:

> I deny not that Christ is Mary's seed, or the woman's seed; nor I deny
> him not to be a man; but Mary had two seeds, one seed of her faith,
> and another seed of her flesh and in her body. There is a natural and
> corporal seed, and there is a spiritual and an heavenly seed, as we may
> gather of St. John, where he saith [I Jn.3.9], "the seed of God remaineth
> in him, and he cannot sin". And Christ is her seed; but he is become
> man of the seed of her faith and belief; of spiritual seed, not of natural
> seed; for her seed and flesh was sinful, as the flesh and seed of others.[142]

If the contrast between the seed of faith and the natural seed was
a very common motif in the circles in which Bocher moved, it is
even possible that she may have shared something of John Champneys' convictions about the entire sanctification of believers, according to which "the ynwarde man could not synne,"[143] whatever
the outward man might do. According to a sermon preached by
Bishop Hugh Latimer at Grimsthorpe, on St. John Evangelist's
Day, 1552, however, Bocher's opinion was not nearly so subtly

expressed as Hutchinson indicated. "The Son of God, said she, penetrated through her, as through a glass, taking no substance of her. . . . this foolish woman . . . said that our Saviour had a phantastical body."[144] On the ordinary principle that those accounts most damaging to those relating them (or most favorable to their opponents) are the most likely to be true, Hutchinson's account may, perhaps, be preferred to Latimer's. But in this case it is very possible that Bocher adopted both lines of argument during the course of her trial and the subsequent extensive attempts to persuade her to recant and thus save herself from burning.

Martyrdom

But she did not recant. Michael Thombe abjured his Monophysite and antipædobaptist opinions, as did Putto his unknown, but probably similar, heresies. Bocher, however, remained firm. Condemned in April 1549, she was kept alive by a government unwilling to be seen to enforce the death penalty for heresy. In the following reign, when Protestants of all shades were facing persecution, a strange conversation took place between Lord Riche and John Philpot, during the examination of the latter by the former for heresy, in the course of which it emerged that both men had been employed in attempts to reclaim Joan Bocher. Riche spoke of her as one of the "Anabaptists."

> I had myself Joan of Kent a seven-night in my house, after the writ was out for her to be burnt, where my lord of Canterbury and bishop Ridley resorted almost daily unto her. But . . . they could do nothing with her for all their learning . . . .[145]

Philpot responded that "she was a vain woman (I knew her well), and a heretic indeed, well worthy to be burnt."[146] It is comforting to know that Philpot was in such hearty agreement with the principle by which he himself was to suffer! By April of the following year, with the tolerant Somerset regime removed from power and replaced by that of Northumberland, the Council determined to enforce the condemnation of Joan with a death warrant. The terse report from the minutes of the Privy Council at "Grenewiche, the xxvij[th] of Aprile, 1550" reads: "A warraunt to the Lord Chauncellour to make out a writt to the Shirrefes of London for thexecucion of Johan of Kent, comdempned to be burned for certein detestable opinions of heresie."[147] According to Foxe's account, Edward VI was fortified in his refusal to burn anyone for their conscience (a tolerance presumably gleaned from his uncle . . . rather than from his father!) by Sir John Cheke.[148] The historian Gilbert Burnet, writing early in the eighteenth century, appears to have had access to further information of the same sort.[149] According to him, Cranmer argued that repudiation of points of the Apostles' Creed constituted blasphemy, which kings, as God's deputies were bound to punish, just as the king's own deputies were obliged to punish treason. An unwilling and tearful king is then said to have signed, laying the responsibility upon Cranmer. In a slight variation from Lord Riche's recall in 1555, Cranmer and Ridley then took Bocher into their own houses in their final attempts to persuade her before the burning. As Burnet commented,

> People had generally believed, that all the statutes for burning heretics had been repealed; but now . . . the burning of heretics was done by the common law; . . . and the repealing the statutes did not take away that which was grounded on a writ at common-law.

This version of events remained more or less unchallenged until the editors of the Parker Society volumes in the midnineteenth century decided to rescue one of their principal heroes from this smear upon his character. Cranmer, it was argued by J. Brude, perhaps on the basis of a statement made by Strype to this effect, had not even been present at the Council meeting in question, and no action by him or the king would have been necessary to carry out the execution.[150] Josiah Pratt, editing Foxe some years after this new explanation had been mooted, was in full agreement; he added an editorial footnote, "No such thing!" to this section of Foxe's account.[151] Positive proof seems to be lacking, but in favor of the nineteenth-century churchmen it should be pointed out that Foxe had to blame someone for this lapse of charity toward a heretic for whose opinions he had no sympathy; Cranmer was dead, while Edward's half-sister, from whom support for the cause of the godly was hoped for even as Foxe wrote, was very much alive. Cranmer could be more safely blamed than Edward, especially if Foxe hoped to forestall any recurrence of such events in the new reign. A passage immediately following Foxe's relation of these events, which was included in the Latin but omitted from English editions of the *Acts and Monuments,* indicates Foxe's general approval of the notion of religious toleration.[152] By including abhorrence at persecution as part of his idealized characterization of the king, Foxe may originally have intended to suggest similar policies to future Protestant monarchs. The real, nonidealized boy-king, however, betrayed no emotions in the account of the execution in his journal.

> May, 2. *Joan Boucher,* otherways called *Joan of Kent,* was burnt for holding, *that Christ was not incarnate of the Virgin* Mary; being condemned the Year before, but kept in hope of Conversion; and the 30*th* of *April,* the Bishop of *London,* and the Bishop of *Ely,* were to persuade her, but she withstood them, and reviled the Preacher that preached at her Death.[153]

Bocher's vilification of Scory at her execution is also attested by Hogarde. The defiant remark about the number of her followers, attributed to her by Hogarde, has been noted already. His account relates further that Bocher "reuyled and spytted" at Scory, "makyng the sygne of the gallowes towardes him, boldly affirming that all they that were not of her opinion shuld be dampned."[154] Edmund Becke referred to Bocher's obstinacy to the last when he described her as "the wayward Virago, that wold not repent The deuils Eldest doughter, which lately was brent" in his polemical poem, *A brefe coñfutation of this most detestable, & Anabaptistical opinion, that Christ dyd not take hys flesh of the blessed Vyrgyn Mary nor any corporal substaunce of her body. For the maintenaunce whereof Johne Bucher otherwise called Jhone of Kēt most obstinately suffered and was burned in Smythfyelde, the. ii. day of May,* printed later that year.[155]

Robert Parsons and the Death of Joan Bocher

The aspect of Bocher's final defiance which has been most often repeated, and perhaps most easily captures the imagination, is the final speech attributed to her by historians from John Strype to J. F. Davis. Davis is so certain about its genuineness that he seems quite relaxed in closing his account of Joan Bocher with the claim that "her last words were: 'Go, read the Scriptures.'"[156] Strype, whose information on the period has generally been allowed to fill the gaps at those points where the original sources now fail modern historians, was reliant in this case, however, upon the accounts of Robert Parsons, the Elizabethan and Jacobean leader of the English Jesuits.[157] The speech itself is given by Parsons in two versions: one in his *Temperate VVard-vvord to the Tvrbulent and Seditiovs VVach-word of Sir Francis Hastinges knight, vvho inde-*

voreth to slaunder the vvhole catholique cause, & all professors therof, both at home and abrode, and a shorter, simpler one in his *Third Part Of A Treatise Intituled: of three Conuersions of England.*[158] The former was published in 1599, and purports to be "by N. D. Imprinted vvith licence," though no place of publication was named. The latter identified itself in the same way, though the date of publication was given as 1604. Nicholas Doleman was an assumed name of Robert Parsons, and there is a portrait of Parsons on the page next to the title-page of the similarly ascribed *Treatise of Three Conversions of England from Paganisme to Christian Religion* of 1603.[159] In the fuller version of the speech, quoted by Strype and subsequent historians, Parsons reports Joan Bocher as saying:

> *It is a goodly mattter* [sic!] *to consider your ignorance; it is not long agoe since you burned Ann Askew for a peece of bread, and yet came your selues soon after to beleeue and professe the same doctryne, for which you burned her: & now (forsooth) you wil needs burne me for a peece of fleshe, & in the end you will come to beleeue this also, when you have red the scriptures and vnderstand them,* and when she came to dye in Smithfield and D. Story endeuored to conuert her she skoffed at him, saying, *he lyed like, &c.* and bad him *goe read Scriptures.*[160]

This speech, apart from making impressive oratory, is extremely significant if it is genuine, representing the vast majority of her own words which the records have preserved.

Parsons is also the earliest known source for the story that Bocher had helped to distribute Tyndale's New Testaments in court and became a close friend of Ann Askew, who was burned as a sacramentary in 1546. Parsons's chronology is very vague; her activities as colporteur may, on his account, have taken place only over the period immediately before Ann's martyrdom, or over a much longer time. Her residence in Frittenden, Kent, and imprisonment at Canterbury in the early 1540s create problems for either scenario. Unfortunately for admirers of Bocher's supposed speech at the stake, however, the authenticity of Parsons's information seems highly suspect. In the first place, even he admitted in 1602 that his source was the reminiscence of a personal witness rather than any contemporary document,[161] though, in *A Treatise of Three Conversions of England,* he gave accurate information about the place and date of the trial which he may well have gleaned from the *Chronicle of the Grey Friars:* he spoke of Bocher as being with "her fellowes [Putto, Thombe, and perhaps others] in our Ladyes chappell of *S. Paules* Church in London vpon the 27. of Aprill,

when he [Cranmer] gaue sentence of death against her."[162] Parsons
was writing, of course, more than fifty years after the events he
described, and there is certainly a possibility, if the eyewitness
who gave him other details was a fellow-Catholic, and therefore
antagonistic to Protestants in general and to radicals such as
Bocher in particular, that the account may have borne an impressionistic relationship to the actual events. Moreover, Parsons was
himself apparently recalling the story from some time before he
first wrote it in 1599; when giving her name as "Ioan knell alias
Burcher" he added "if I forget not."[163]

All of this, of course, is merely circumstantial evidence against
Parsons's testimony; what really brings it into disrepute is, on the
one hand, an obvious untruth, and on the other, the way in which
the account is moulded to serve Parsons's polemical interests. In
effect, he accused Joan of sexual immorality: he described her as
"a certayn foul fusteluggs, dishonest of her body with base fellows,
as was openly reported."[164] "Which I charitably suppose," commented Strype, drawing a limit to his own credulity, "might be
but a calumny, too common with Parsons."[165] The contemporary
sources show no evidence of libertinism by Joan Bocher, which
would hardly have been ignored by her persecutors in 1549/50, nor
of personal hypocrisy, which would have given them an opportunity to hold her up to ridicule. Parsons's remark comes in the same
sentence in which he speaks of her supposed friendship with Ann
Askew. On the reasonable assumption that this cannot refer to a
period before the mid–1540s, both by reason of Ann's age (only
twenty-five at her death in 1546) and Bocher's imprisonment from
1541 to 1543, then Bocher would have been too old for such behavior to be very likely in any case. It is possible that she had been
widowed young, of course, but the expression "Mother Bocher"
used in the accounts of the Lollard trials of 1528, would hardly
have been appropriate descriptions of a woman much younger than
forty, in which case she would have been at least in her late fifties
during the period to which Parsons claimed to be referring. His
veracity thus impugned, it must also be pointed out that both the
supposed friendship with Ann Askew and Bocher's reputed final
speech are presented in such a way as to serve Parsons's anti-
Protestant polemic. A few memorable phrases apart ("you burned
Ann Askew for a peece of bread"; "And now you vvill burne me
for a peece of flesh"), there is no close verbal resemblance between
the two accounts of Bocher's speech given in *A Temperate VVard-
vvord* and *The Third Part Of A Treatise*.[166] Of course, the resonant
phrases may constitute an authentic core, to which Parsons chose

to add material suitable to his purposes; what seems certain is that he did add to the speech, if he did not fabricate it entirely. Its main point seems to be the parallel between the two women, the fact that the establishment of the Church of England came to share Askew's sacramentarianism shortly after her death, and the implied logic that it should proceed to hold Monophysite beliefs as well. In the fomer account only, Bocher is portrayed as laying great stress on the fact that it is the study of the Scriptures which will bring the Protestant leaders to this, and it is very significant that this version of the speech forms part of a longer passage in which Parsons was at pains to argue the calamitous effects of allowing the vernacular Bible to circulate freely among the unlearned, with Bocher as a prime case in point. Seen in this light, her supposed "neerest frēdship" with Ann Askew may simply be a fiction designed to sharpen the effect of Parsons's "slippery slope" argument against vernacular Bibles and Protestantism. Joan Bocher of course, would have been unfavorably looked upon by public opinion fifty years after her death as she had been at the time, and Parsons's account looks suspiciously like an attempt to blacken the name of the respectable Protestant martyr Ann Askew by association with the decidedly unrespectable sectarian radical as "her deare syster, disciple & handmayd . . . . Whome she vsed most confidently in sendinge hereticall books hither and thither, but especially into the court."[167] Only one contemporary source suggests any link at all between the two women, and even that is more likely to be a rhetorical expression than a statement of fact: in speaking of Ann Askew, Miles Hogarde described Joan Bocher as "her pure fellowe & syster in Christ."[168] This may, of course, be a contemporary reference to an association about which others were well aware, in which case at least some of Parsons's account is vindicated. More likely, however, Hogarde's remark is a mere rhetorical flourish by a Catholic pamphleteer, lumping all Protestants together as equally corrupt. If so, then any connection between Ann Askew and Joan Bocher, and with it what J. F. Davis describes as "a glimpse of lowly Lollardy influencing women at court," are without basis in extant contemporary documents.[169] While his account cannot be considered definitely fictitious, Parsons as a source of information on Joan Bocher certainly looks unreliable.

The view taken of Bocher and her beliefs by the established Protestant church was as harsh as the sentence imposed upon her. Roger Hutchinson, in his *Image of God,* published less than two months after her burning, included a passage that reflects his own arguments with her.

Brethren be of one nature and substance, touching their flesh and body. Therefore she that denieth Christ to have taken his flesh of his mother, is not the sister of Christ, but the eldest and firstborn daughter of antichrist. Yet she pretended that she believed that Christ was a true and natural man; but indeed she denieth his manhood.[170]

As a trained theologian, he asked questions of Bocher's radical beliefs to which there were no apparent answers.

If he had it [his humanity] not of his mother, define and shew from whence he had it. Yea, they say, it is unknown and undefined in the scriptures. How then can we warrant Christ's humanity against heretics, if we make it uncertain whereof he took it, and if it be unknown whereof it was shapen?[171]

The radicals' various theologies were not, in general, as watertight as Hutchinson demanded. As in the case of Hart's free-will men, they did not constitute an overall ideology, but merely highlighted some particular theological or practical concerns of the group or individuals in question. Joan's concerns, insofar as the extant records provide a picture of them, seem to have included a desire for a vernacular Bible, a rejection of traditional Catholic beliefs and practices in general, and of the Real Presence at communion in particular, and, later, an espousal of Melchiorite Christology. Unlike Hart's beliefs, these do not point in an inevitably sectarian direction; her essential sectarianism is seen in her actions, and in the theological company she kept, rather than in her actual opinions, which might conceivably have been adopted by an official church.

*   *   *

The extant information concerning these three leaders differs greatly in its nature in each case. Henry Hart published two small books, and composed two other writings which have survived. His opinions were also recorded in the depositions of his followers. John Trew wrote only one surviving piece, and most of the other information concerning him consists of the hostile comments of Protestant prisoners, and the records of correspondence, interrogation, or punishment of his fellow free-willers. Joan Bocher is not known to have written anything at all; posterity is fortunate that angry contemporaries wrote so much about her which almost compensates for this omission. All three succeeded in arousing the spokesmen of magisterial Protestantism to fury, provoking genuine fears about the amount of support these mavericks might succeed in attracting. It is small wonder that the machinery of official repression and the weight of scholarly refutation were mobilized against them to ensure that those fears were not realized.

3

Radical Writers

Having considered three leaders who are known to have had a definite personal following, attention will now be focused on the ideas of those radicals who came to public notice solely on the basis of their writings, but about whose followers, if they had them, little or nothing is known. John Champneys and Robert Cooche are obvious candidates for consideration under this heading, but a writing by "S.B.," an English Anabaptist imprisoned in 1575, is also examined, as are two anonymous pieces: *The cōfutation of the errors of the careles by necessitie,* whose author may or may not have been Cooche, and *The copie of an answere,* often wrongly ascribed to Champneys.

The Vain Elijah: John Champneys

John Champneys was, by his own account, "an vnlearned laye mane borne in the countie of Somerset, alytyl [*sic*] besydes brystowe."[1] In 1548, being now a resident in "Stratford on the Bowe,"[2] he published a small book designed "to put such men in remēbrance as be of god, and yet dothe not muche exercyse thē selfues [*sic*] neither in readyng nor hereyng of the holy scriptures. . . ." Its contents were to bring him into serious trouble, both for the radical views which the book expressed, and perhaps also because he chose to play the Elijah.

If it may please the kynges maiestee, to graunt and permit like libertie to some one of them being of small reputaciō & learnyng, which be now regenerate with the spirit of Christ: as was granted to Elias, in the tyme of Ahab. . . . That lyke tryall as was beetwene the sayde Elias, and all Baals prophetes . . . may be now openly and only by the holy scriptures written, after the trew litterall sence: betwene one suche of the elect in Christ & the whole multitude of our markt ministers. . . .[3]

By "markt ministers," Champneys meant "the mynisters of the deuyll and the Beast, whose marke thei beare," under which description he seems to have included virtually the whole of the national ministry.[4] If he was victorious in the debate, he proposed, then the ministry should be despised and forsaken by the people, but

> on yᵉ other side if the cōpiler hereof, a poore lay man, & of small litterature, be not able by gods assistaũce, only by the power of the Spirite of Christ, to shew the word of God writtē in the true literal sence, both for the cleare discharge of his owne conscience & conuersacion, & also of all other that be regenerate in Christ, let it bee death vnto him.[5]

Alas for frantic boast and foolish word! Champneys was arrested and forced to abjure the errors "presumptiously in my booke sette fourth in my name," to bear a faggot at Pauls Cross while Miles Coverdale preached, and then to do all he could to recover the copies of his book so that they could be destroyed.[6] The fact that two sureties, Reginald Mohun of Cornwall, and Lawrence Clerke, a barber of Whitechapel, were bound for five hundred pounds until his penance was performed seems to indicate that he had fairly wealthy connections. Since his abjuration was on 27 April 1548, the publication of his book can be dated to within a month, since the new year had begun, under the old style of dating, only on 25 March. Champneys was required to recant six "hereseis and dampnable opinions" gleaned from his writings by his inquisitors. The first of these was "that A man after he is Regenerate in xpe [Christ] cannot synne" and, while *The Harvest is at Hand* had not claimed this in so many words, it had stressed the idea of the Johannine epistles that the regenerate are manifested by their deeds and love, and had stated that "they shal haue . . . power in spirite to lyue alway accordyng to the trewe professyon of the Ghospell."[7]

Sanctification

This last statement suggests a belief in *posse non peccare,* rather than in *non posse peccare,* and this would seem to be confirmed by an amazing passage in the latter part of his book which teaches a Wesleyan-type doctrine of sanctification or holiness distinct from, and subsequent to, conversion.

Faythe of it selfe hathe neither perfecte knowledge of the holy Scriptures, neither power to doo that whiche the Scripture cōmaundeth: for that cōmeth onely by the gyfte of the holye ghost after fayth, sometime immediatly, as we reade. Act .x.g And of the good theife, Luke .xxiii.d. and some tyme longe after. For there were dyuerse congregacions in the Apostles tyme whiche were baptised and receyued faythe in Christ, long before they receyued the gyfte of the holy gost, as we reade in the Actes the .vii. chapiter.c. the xix.a. Howe be it, their knoweledge was alwayes vnperfecte vntyll that tyme they were regenerate wyth the Spirite of Christ, i.cor.iii.a.viii.a.[8]

Although this passage stresses knowledge as a gift of the Holy Spirit subsequent to faith, it also includes "power to doo that whiche the Scripture cōmaundeth," and this idea is stated again in the fifth article which Champneys was required to abjure. This fifth article, read from the record of Champneys's abjuration alone, seems at first very confusing as to what views Champneys stood accused of holding, and makes sense only when compared with the text of *The Harvest is at Hand,* from which it is all (except the first two words) a rough quotation.

Fifthly that that was the most principall of oᵣ markid mans doctryne to make the people beleve that their was no such spirite geven vnto man wherby he shuld Remayne Righteouse alwaies in Christ which is a most develishe errour.[9]

The view rejected by Champneys, then, had been "that their was no such spirite geven vnto man wherby he shuld Remayne Righteouse alwaies in Christ," and the abjuration presumably amounted to a confession, not that the clergy did not make this denial, but that such a denial was not, after all, "a most develishe errour." J. F. Davis thinks the "use of the term marked men . . . suggests Lollardy," but Champneys had certainly not used the expression "markid man" to denote himself; he consistently employed the term throughout the work in an idiosyncratic sense to describe "our fayned speritualtie, whome I doo most comonly name in the proces here of markt mene or marckt mōsters, not onely because they are marcked in their bodies & somtimes weare disgysed mōstrus garmētes, but because their doctrine is marked also."[10]

Despite the fact that his book stressed the *posse non peccare* rather than *non posse peccare,* there may well have been no clear distinction in Champneys's own mind. When accused of holding the latter view, he appears to have defended it anyway, for the second article of his abjuration, "that I haue defended the said first article graunting That the outwarde man might synne and the ynwarde man cold not synne," does not reflect any explicit teaching in the book itself.[11] Nevertheless, an antinomian note consistent with such a view is occasionally struck in *The Harvest is at Hand;* Champneys stressed that the elect "haue a new hert geuen them of God, which is always obediēt to the spirite of Christ. Ezechiel.xi.d. & the .xxxvi.f. & the Ebrues the viii.c. and the .x.c."[12] The empowering of the Holy Spirit made the law redundant.

> All people whiche be regenerate in chryst, are no lenger [*sic*] vnder the lawe, galath.iii.d. for the lawe is not gyuen to no personne which is made righteous in chryste, by a true faith, hauyng the power in spirite by the gyfte of the holy ghost, to loue al the elect people of god. . . .[13]

The idea that truly regenerate persons will always love their brothers and sisters in Christ is a recurrent theme in Champneys, and is reflected in the fourth article abjured by him, namely, "That godly love falleth never away from them which be Regenerate in Christ."[14] Champneys believed that

> euery one which loueth Christ, loueth also all people whiche be regenerate in Christ. Jhon.v.a not only in wordes, but in actuall deedes. ep.Jhon.iii.c. for all people which doth the contrary be the children of the deuyll. ep.Jhon.iii.b.[15]

The fourth article itself is a quotation from Champneys's book and, in context, can be seen to reflect his conviction that "ye people of god & ye people of ye deuil, are perfitly knowen," since "all the elect people of god, are knowen by godly loue" and could not be infected with the sins of envy and malice.[16] This was, perhaps, a test of visible sainthood at least as exacting as the self-examinations later to be required among Puritan radicals, for it involved a weighing of the attitudes of the heart, not only in God-directed matters of faith, but also in respect to "horizontal," this-worldly relationships with others. Even so, Champneys was not entirely confident that the ungodly would concur with the godly in demarcating the distinction between the two; he explained that, even bearing the inevitable fruit of hatred of sin, "the electe be not perfectly knowen but only to them selues, neuerthelesse by doyng of the contrary . . . the people of the world ar plainly knowen to be the subiectes of the deuil. . . ."[17] The logic of this, as well as his other statements, seems to indicate that, by "knowen . . . to them selues," Champneys meant that the godly would be known to one another, and not merely each individual to himself alone. The ungodly, presumably, could not discern anything! This combined stress upon the identifiability of the truly regenerate and the importance of heart attitudes is, of course, implicity separatist, and it was this aspect of Champneys's teaching with which the third article he was required to recant seems to have been attempting to deal.

Identifying the Godly and Separating from the Wicked

This third item of the abjuration concerns a quotation from *The Harvest is at Hand:* "that the Gospell hath been much persecuted, and hated ever sythins the apostelles tyme, that no man might be suffred openly to followe hit."[18] Such a view would not, of course, have been acceptable to Reformed admirers of the post-Constantinian church. However, much though Champneys's view might have been objected to as an observation about matters of fact, it was also pregnant with an idea far more revolutionary, namely, that the massive and highly visible structure of the institutional church was not God's intention for His people.[19] Champneys's conviction that the saved would, in any case, be "but a small nombre in comparison to the multitude" is entirely in keeping with an outlook that would, in sociological terminology, be considered "sect-type" as opposed to "church-type."[20] Throughout the work, Champneys attacked the clergy as "clouds without water & trees withoute fruyte at gatherying tyme, beīg twise dead;" they were "lyke the ragynge waues of the sea, fomynge oute their owne shame," "the people whom god hath appointed to his wrath," whose "abhominacion & crafty delusion, doth farre excede, and is much more then hath ben found in any maner of people, synce the begynnyng of the worlde."[21] The clergy, he claimed, preached lies, "for now that they perceiue y^t the highe powers, wyll not suffer them to vse their old abhominacions, they set foorth newe Ipochritish doctrin," and he may have been attacking the continuing use of Latin, as well as "clerkly lernynge" when, citing Isa. 33, he argued that the godly "shall not se people of astrange [sic] tonge, to haue so diffuse alangauge [sic] that it may not be vnderstand neyther so strange aspeche [sic] but that it shalbe perceued."[22] One of his main objections to the national clergy, then, was their lingering attachment to Catholic ways and doctrines. Indeed, they were the very men who had

procured and sougth [*sic*] the death of all maner of people which pro-
feste ye true religyon in christ . . . and yet dayly doth so fare forth as
thei dare for fere of the temporall power . . . and yet wold stil be naēd
to be the ministers of christ. . . .[23]

Such criticisms are very similar in tone and nature to those made
by the returning exiles who were to form the nascent Puritan party
early in Elizabeth's reign. They, too, denounced the fact that many
of the clergy were crypto-papists who had assisted in the persecution under Mary and yet continued in office. Also like the Puritans,
Champneys further bemoaned the fact that they "delite in habōn-
dance of temporal possessiones, hauynge names of dignitie lyke
tēporall Princes and rulers, cleane contrary to the doctrine of
christe. math xx.d. & .xxii.b. mark.x.f. Luke.xxii.c John.xiii.b.
Pet.v.a."[24] No informed Christian, Champneys believed, could
"name thē to be any of ye people of god," but his confidence that
"all they whiche hath bene of the marke, and be nowe truly
cōuerted, perceiueth this to be true," was an implicit recognition
that not all of the clergy were children of the devil.[25] Nevertheless,
those clergy—the vast majority—who were "deceyuers of the people" were to be separated from entirely.

who so euer fauoreth any of you [the marked men], which blasphemeth
the spirit of christ, is a partaker of your yll .ii.Epist. of Jhon.c. where-
fore God cōmaundeth all his electe people to departe out of your company, & to seperate them selues clearely from you, and not to touche
any of youre vnclennesse. Esaie.lii.c. ii.Cor.vi.c. the first Timo.vi.b.
Apo.xviii.b.[26]

It is surprising that this call for separation was not among the
articles which the authorities insisted Champneys recant. Admittedly, separation is implicit in the third article, but the failure to
seize upon this yet more radical passage can probably only be
attributed to an oversight.

The "True Literal Sence" of the Scripture

The Harvest is at Hand is marked by a profound mistrust of
learning in general, and of what Champneys perceived to be the
tendency among the clergy to do less than justice to the literal
meaning of the text of the Scripture. The "true literal sence," applied to the Scripture, is a recurring expression in his book.[27] He
complained that the clergy "wold haue the people to beleue part

of the holy scriptur as it was spoken and writtē vnto vs, and som other partes therof they wolde not haue them to beleue in the true litterall sence, but wolde haue the people to beleue it & receiue it, only as they do marke it & appoynt it out vnto thē."[28] This last, one suspects, is the real cause for complaint; the monoply of religious authority by a learned elite excluded the unlearned from full participation. It was only natural that men such as Champneys should resent such "shameles mōsters" who "wolde haue men to beleue, that their clerkly sophistical doctrīe should sufficiently instructe the people, in the knowlage of the holy scriptures;" unlike Champneys, "they them selues know not what the regeneracion of yᵉ spirite of christ is, but what the subtilitie of mans wit by outwarde lernynge knoweth, yᵗ many of thē be perfect in."[29] True ministers, Champneys argued, would not rely on their education even if they were learned themselves, but would

dispise their out warde holynes and clerkly lernynge as saint paul did, philipp.iii.b. for sainct paul beynge lerned wold in no wise precahe [sic] or wryte any thynge cōsernynge the gosple of christ, after yᵉ maner of outward lernynge. 1,cor.ii.b. and gala.i.c.[30]

Medieval allegorization of the Bible, and the fourfold method of exegesis, had robbed scripture of much of its force. Nicholas of Lyra, in the fourteenth century, had pleaded for a greater emphasis upon the literal meaning of the words of the text, but it was not until the Reformation that this cause had become a powerful force. The reformers, of course, had perceived the difficulties for their own position of too rigorous an application of this rule, while some of the evangelical Anabaptists on the Continent had attempted to be more consistent in their literalism. A general pattern was to emerge during the course of the sixteenth century; by and large, the more radical the churchmanship and the more complete the departure from Catholicism, the greater the emphasis upon biblical literalism. This phenomenon was recognized by contemporaries; thus Jean Veron could speak of "these smatteryng Anabaptistes, whyche vnderstande not the letter of the scriptures, wherin (I meane, in the bare letter) they do truste moste."[31] Only on the spiritualist fringe that marked the leftward boundary, it seems, does this generalization begin to break down. The advantage of literalism, of course, was that it then lay within the capacity of almost anyone who could read to expound the Word. The idea naturally went together with an egalitarian type of churchmanship. Thus Champneys could claim that "all the electe people of God

haue power to knowe & to declare whose synnes GOD hath for-
geuen in Christ, & also whose synnes he dothe retayne to iudgement."[32] He did not take the rationalist view that any person could
understand the Scripture in "the true literall sence," but that such
knowledge was a gift of the Holy Spirit. Such a combination of
plain-speaking literalism, devoid of "crafty delusion,"[33] with the
necessity of spiritual enlightenment contains, of course, an element
of paradox; the authority to expound is taken from one elite, the
learned, and given, not to all people indiscriminately, but to a different elite of the spiritually initiated. Seeming to equate the elect
with the unlearned, he claimed that "al the electe vnlearned people . . . woulde learne by hert . . . the true literall sence of the
holy scriptures as they be written. For the true vnderstanding is
geuē them of god. Esa.liiii.d Jhon.vi.e. and x.a."[34] Such a view
was, of course, potentially subversive of the official church; if true
ministers were charismatically inspired rather than trained and
educated for the purpose, then the basis for an officially imposed
ministry looked slender indeed.

If Champneys called for a separation from the godless ministry
of the established church, he nevertheless shared with many of his
radical contemporaries—and with later Elizabethan separatists for
that matter—a lingering, ultimately inconsistent willingness for the
true church to be ordered by a godly magistracy. He considered
that

> our most bounden duty is, to pray, for the preseruatyon of the moste
> Royall estate of the kinges maieste, my Lord protectors grace and
> all other of yᵉ kinges most honorable Coūsell that the kynges highnes
> procedynges maye prosperusly take good effect . . . to the encrease of
> all godlynes, in yᵉ vtter dystrucciō of yᵉ whole Incorporatiō and power
> of all marckt presthod, and to restore the people of god within all his
> realmes and dominions, again frely in to the true lebertie of yᵉ gosple
> of christe, like as the godly kyng Josias. . . .[35]

Champneys's appeal to the king for an opportunity to debate with
the learned divines is itself an indication of his acceptance of royal
jurisdiction in ecclesiastical affairs. His work closes with a loyal
"God saue the kyng. my Lord Protector, the Nobilitie, and all
those, which vnfainedly loueth the gospel," though whether this
was a precautionary addition by Humfrey Powell, who had printed
it "Cum priuilegio" and also published Jean Veron's translation of

one of Bullinger's anti-Anabaptist works that year, is impossible to ascertain.[36]

Binding the Tares: Millenarianism

One aspect of Champneys's teaching which must have disturbed the authorities as much as its implicit—and occasionally explicit—separatism, was its occasionally millenarian tone. The complete title of his book—*The Harvest is at Hand, VVherin the Tares Shall Be Bovnd. and cast into the fyre and brent. Math.xiii. D.G.*—suggests as much. True, the apocalyptic note does not dominate the work, but it crops up continually as a kind of backdrop, or context, for the other points made by his writing. His use of apocalyptic language is generally vague, but if, like Melchior Hoffmann's, it did not exactly amount to an incitement to violence in itself, it was certainly capable of being used as an excuse for such had he ever gained a sufficiently large and excitable audience.

> For the tyme is come that whatsoeuer wil not receyue the trewe doctrine of Christ shalbe destroyed from among the people. Actes.iii.d. And the vngodly transgressors & suche as are become vnfaithfull vnto the Lorde, must all together be vtterly destroyed. Esa.i.g. for the Lorde Jhesus shal shew himselfe from Heavē with the Angeles of his power with flamyng fyer, which shall render vengeaunce vnto theim that knowe not God. . . .[37]

Such rhetoric could not be dismissed as referring to some distant Second Advent; Champneys declared that "the tyme is come," and he spoke of "this present tyme, in the appearaunce of the second comyng of Christ."[38] Champneys envisaged an imminent triumph of the saints; since the apostles' time they had been persecuted, but "now God wyll glorifye all theim that loue it [the Gospel], for euer and euer, thoroughoute all posterities. Esai.1x.c. And wyl clerely destroy the whole power of all the enemyes therof. Esay.1x.b."[39] Pointing to the eleventh chapter of the book of Rev., he announced that "the Temple of God shalbe open, and the Arke of his Testament seene therin," and that this signified that "the people shall conuerte to the Gospell," "for the power only of the spirite of Christ shall reigne ouer al the earth. . . . And as for all rule, power, and myght that is vnder heauen, it shall bee geuen to the holye people of the moste hyghest."[40] Whether or not Champneys saw this triumph as being delivered through the instrumentality of the secular authorities in thoroughly reforming the church, and doing away with the "marked men" who had served under the tainted Henrician regime, is not immediately apparent, and one suspects that the scenario was not entirely clear in Champneys's own mind.

The sixth article which he abjured, "that god doth permitte to all his electe people their bodilie necessities of all worldly thinges," sounds more subversive than in fact it was.[41] The words were taken from Champneys's book, but probably amounted to no more than a careless use of words on his part and certainly did not, in context, amount to "Libertine heresy" as claimed by J. F. Davis.[42] Cranmer and the ecclesiastical authorities would understandably have been in dread of any suggestion of libertinism, or of revolutionary spiritualism which might, like Thomas Müntzer, have declared the rich expropriated—and worse—by the godly. Champneys's apocalyticism would, perhaps, have furnished ample grounds for such fears. But in reality, the expression seized upon was an isolated phrase balancing his immediately preceding statement that "God doth forbyd all men from the louyng & inordinate vsyng of worldly things."[43] His protestations of loyalty to, and prayer for, the king and his council were evidently insufficient to dispel suspicions of anarchism, and he was obliged to confess that God did not permit the elect to take anything, except by means of the law and order approved by the civil policy."[44]

The Standard-Bearer of the Free-Will Men

Finally, the question of Champneys's position on the subjects of free-will and predestination at the time of the publication of *The Harvest is at Hand* in 1548 deserves consideration, both because of his later opposition to reformed doctrines in this regard, and because some have taken him to be supporting them at this juncture. The term *the elect* occurs very frequently in *The Harvest is at Hand,* but its usage seems to be more in the style of late medieval apocalyptic than in the measured, clinical tones of Reformed theology. Similarly, the fourth article of his abjuration, "That godly love falleth never away from them which be Regenerate in Christ," relates to his teaching on entire sanctification by the Holy Spirit, and should not be viewed in some anachronistic, post-Dortian sense as an indication of belief in the inevitable perseverance of those chosen before the foundation of the earth.[45] That said, Champneys does give some indication of leaning toward predestinarian views, but it is equivocal, to say the least. I. B. Horst, anxious to demonstrate the "anabaptist connection" of Champneys (and of everybody else!), is certain that "it is not correct to claim that Champneys before his recantation held certain predestinarian views" as claimed by the *Dictionary of National Biography*.[46] The relevant passages from *The Harvest is at Hand* are almost all capable, like the biblical quotations which they largely reflect, of being pulled by partisans in either direction. The sentences which seem to bear the aspect of free-will are as follows: "all true ministers of the gospell of Christ, seketh with most diligence to haue all people to come to Christ: that is, to beleue all the promyses made in Christ;" "at this present tyme god is so mercyfull too offre it [salvation] to all people . . . and yet but a small nombre in comparison to the multitude do receyue it, wherfore his wrathe wyll shortly be knowen."[47] Bearing the aspect of predestination are sentences that tell the "marked men" that they are "the people whom god hath appointed to his wrath," the reference to the "new song" in Revelation which "onely the nombre appoynted" could learn, and the citation from the eleventh chapter of Romans to the effect that "God hath wrapped all nacions in vnbeliefe, that he might only haue mercy on all his electe" (the words *only* and *his electe* are not in the Great Bible, and appear to be exclusivist additions made by Champneys himself).[48] Perhaps most telling is the apparently predestinarian gloss on Philippians 2.10: "it is God which worketh al goodnesse in vs. bothe the wyll, and also the deede. . . . Wherfore, the onely trewe & perfect remedy is for all reasonable people to seeke of God in prayer, the regenaciō [*sic*] promysed in Christ."[49] If this is predestinarianism, it certainly seems to have been linked in Champneys's own mind with his robust solafidianism, which is in such marked contrast to Henry Hart's embarrasment with the doctrine and with the Jamesian emphasis upon works of some of the radicals of Lollard origin. Despite his antiintellectual bent, Champneys clearly had no difficulty with so theoretical a doctrine, and emphasized it repeatedly: "all people which shalbe saued in Christ, & receyue euerlastyng lyfe, shall receiue it only by grace geuē of God, in the mercifull promyse made in Christ, without any assystance thervnto of any of our owne workes. Eph.ii.b."[50] It is certainly not possible to claim, as it is with Henry Hart, that there was at this juncture any connection, implicit or otherwise, between Champneys's doctrines of free-will, or of predestination, and his separatism.

If Champneys was relatively uncommitted in, or (perhaps more likely) unaware of, debates about predestination and free-will in

1548, by 1561 he was firmly committed to the free-will cause, and went into print again, this time to combat the views of the Frenchman, Jean Veron. Perhaps the debates of the 1550s had made Champneys aware of the issues at stake, but in any case, he retained his radicalism and combined it with a determined opposition to reformed doctrines of predestination. Veron had published his *Fruteful treatise of predestination* and *A moste necessary treatise of free wil* earlier in the year, and it was evidently one of these that became the object of Champneys's attack.[51] On this occasion, Champneys published anonymously, but the printer was identified and caught, which was presumably how Veron came to know the identity of his assailant.[52] Champneys, however, had purchased all the copies from the printer in order to "send thē vnto his priuy frendes abrode whom belyke he suspected to be of his affinitye."[53] The use of the word *suspected* seems to indicate that Champneys belonged to no organized sectarian grouping that Veron was aware of. Unfortunately, the work has not survived, but according to the very jaundiced account of his opponent, Champneys argued that God's predestination was based upon His foreknowledge.[54] Veron twice described his opponent as a "sectarie," and as one of the "free wyll men, whose standard-bearer Champneyes would fayne be."[55] The Frenchman claimed that

> he doeth . . . studye laboure and trauayll all that in him lieth, to bring the godly learned ministres of this our time, as he did them yᵗ were in kiuge [*sic*] Edwarde the sexts dayes, in to the obloquie & hatred of the world.

And if this was not mere abuse, then it seems likely that Champneys had again indulged in antiintellectual rhetoric and attacks upon the institution of a learned ministry.[56] "For," explained Veron,

> ther be non so greate enemies vnto learninge, as they yᵗ be altogether vnlerned, & withoute godly knowledge, as this valyaunt champion of the free wyll men is, who is so rude and ignoraunt, that he can not construe 2 lines of Saint Augustine, nor of any other godlye writer.[57]

Veron mocked his arguments. "Who would haue thought so muche dyuinitye to be in Champenyes?" and derisively called him "thys hyghe deuyne."[58] Evidently, Champneys remained unlearned still.

By appealing in his arguments to the Book of Wisdom and to 4 Esdras, which Veron, of course, rejected as uncanonical and therefore not authoritative in matters of dispute, Champneys betrays the origins of his ideas in the older, passing world of native

English radicalism.[59] Already, Thomas Matthew's translation of the Bible published in 1537, listed these books as "Apochripha," and the Great Bible of 1539 as "hagiographa."[60] Champneys seems to have been a maverick in any terms; his publication of 1548 gives no evidence that he was part of an organized radical group, and—however orthodox on evangelical essentials—his ideas were still far too radical, and his station in life too lowly, for him to have been sponsored by a group of zealous-reforming Protestants. The conclusion seems unavoidable, for *The Harvest is at Hand* as much as for this later work on behalf of free-will, that Champneys's thinking is best seen as a flowering of the Lollard-rooted tradition of English radicalism which, by the mid-century, was becoming increasingly heterogeneous.

* * *

Cerberus, the Three-Headed Dog of Hell

In 1566, Robert Crowley, the longtime Protestant pamphleteer who was by now a clergyman in the emerging Puritan movement, published *An apologie, or defence, of those Englishe writers & preachers which Cerberus the three headed Dog of Hell, chargeth wyth false doctrine vnder the name of Predestination*. The work defended a writing he had penned eighteen years earlier, *The confutation of .xiii. Articles, wherunto Nicolas Shaxton, late byshop of Salisburye subscribed . . . M.D. xlvi. whē he recanted in Smithfielde*. However, Crowley's new antagonist appeared to be no defender of Shaxton's relapse into Catholicism; when quoting the title, he had truncated it so as to avoid mentioning the former bishop, and had attacked more than just Crowley himself.[61] The publication which stirred Crowley to take up the cudgels in 1566 appears to have survived in only one original printed copy, kept in the Codrington Library, at All Souls College, Oxford; *The Copie of an answere* would otherside have depended for its preservation upon the fact that Crowley, like John Knox is answering the "aduersarie of Gods eternal Predestination," chose to reprint his opponent's work, interspersed with his own refutation of it, passage by passage. Crowley's reproduction, fortunately, has been entirely faithful to the original. That original, though giving neither date nor place of publication, is believed, by the compilers of the *Short Title Catalogue*, to have been printed in the Netherlands in about 1563, three years before Crowley's response.[62] The anonymous author claimed that he had been charged with Pelagianism by a "certayne letter," and Crowley, conjecturing that there was no such letter in the first place, suggested that he "hath fayned this, as a grounde . . . to write and set abrode in print. . . ."[63] If charges of Pelagianism really had been made, Crowley argued, the aggrieved party would have done better

> to haue set downe in writing the copie of the letter that he sayth he Aunswereth, and the name of him that wrote it: so might those that he nameth in hys aunswere, haue had some waye to haue founde out the Auctour of the Aunswere. . . .[64]

Crowley was clearly vexed that his antagonist had sought anonymity to the point of vagueness about who had charged him with Pelagianism. Unable to address him by name, Crowley disdainfully referred to him as "Cerberus, the three headed Dog of Hell;" nevertheless, he suspected that "Cerberus" was one of his own acquaintances who ought, rather than attacking him in this public way, to "haue had conference w^t Crowley (for belike he knoweth him well ynough)."[65] Instead, "this aunswere . . . was first cast about in the streates of Londō," attacking Crowley, Knox, and the writings of others whom it did not name.[66]

The burden of "Cerberus's" work was to refute charges that "I and other sholde holde the errours of Pelagius, . . . deny the predestination of God: and seeke a iustification by free wyl, & by deseruing of workes," but his writing nevertheless constitutes an attack upon reformed doctrines of predestination in the name of Augustine.[67] "Cerberus" claimed that the slanders against himself and others stemmed from a genuinely Pelagian statement in William Samuel's *Prayer to God for his Afflicted Church in Englande,* which had been printed "beyonde the seas in Quene Maryes time," but protested that Samuel "is a man vnto mee | of very smal aquaintāce."[68] This slight acquaintance with Samuel is almost the only personal detail which "Cerberus" gave about himself, though some of his statements seem to indicate that he could have been part of a group of others similarly inclined; he pointed out that "both I & many other mislike" doctrines currently being taught "vnder the name and colour of godes predestinatiō," "& haue diuerse tymes with some of them [the predestinarians] in priuate and frendlye talke perswaded to leaue" those teachings.[69] "Cerberus" also seems to have been well aware of the free-will men who had suffered under Mary; he complained that the reformed knew well enough that those, whome they now so specialye accuse, to be suche haters of Godes predestination, are in deede moste intyre louers of the same, & many of those whome they accuse to be popishe Pelagians . . . haue bestowed both their goodes & their liues against that filthy & detestable sect.[70]

If this is a reference to the free-will men associated with Henry Hart and John Trew—and it is hard to imagine to whom else it might refer—then "Cerberus's," description of them as "most intire louers" of the doctrine of predestination is disingenuous, to say the least.

Indeed, disingenuousness seems to be the keynote of the work as a whole; nearly a fifth of it is devoted to quoting Augustine against Pelagius, but on the issue of the damnation of unbaptized infants, on which the two ancients agreed, Calvin is cited against both of them "because Caluine is with so many of vs, which are gospelers, in auctorite fullie sufficient to encounter with Augu. [stine]."[71] Nevertheless, it is clearly Calvinist views of predestination which were the real object of attack, since the section of Crowley's *Confutation of .xiii. Articles* which deals with predestination, and Knox's *Answer to a Great Nomber of blasphemous cavillations written by an Anabaptist, and aduersarie of Gods eternal Predestination,* are denounced by name (though, rather coyly, the word *Anabaptist* is not included in the quoted title of the latter!).[72] Of Crowley, "Cerberus" told his readers

thou seest . . . who they are that so odiouslie are noted with the name of free wil men | Not only the Papiste, against whome he pretendeth there to write but namelie all those that saie, God hath not predestinate any man to commit murther, or suche like wicked abhomination.[73]

It seems, then, that "Cerberus" was coming from a radical perspective in attacking current predestinarian doctrines even if, in his denunciation of Knox's *First Blast of the Trumpet,* he likened that work to (among other things) "reuelations of blinde Anabaptistes," an expression which indicates the writer's concurrence in the use of the description "Anabaptist" as a general term of denunciation.[74] (His reference to Knox's book was irrelevant to his argument, but was presumably intended to embarrass the Puritan fraternity by reminding his readers of a notoriously impolitic work from the ranks of the Genevan exiles.) Not only did he attack *A briefe treatyse of election and reprobacion,* whose author he did not name (it was Anthony Gilby), but also countered several statements made in "an Englishe boke trãslated out of Frenche, lately set forth in printe, and entituled, a briefe declaration of the table of predestination."[75] This last writing was part of a work entitled *A briefe declaration of the chiefe poyntes of Christian religion, set foorth in a Table of Predestination* by Theodore Beza. The quotations are identifiable as coming from this work, though no copy of the original edition of William Whittingham's translation, published in Geneva in 1556, is extant; comparison must be made with the second edition, which Pollard and Redgrave's *Short-Title Catalogue* estimates to have been published in about 1575.[76] Beza, of course, was the chosen successor in Geneva of the very man whom "Cerberus" suggested was "in auctorite fullie sufficient to encounter with Augu.[stine]," which perhaps accounts for the reticence about naming him! Only just before the end of his work did "Cerberus" relax his guard sufficiently to attack the Geneva Bible's gloss on Rom. chapter 9.15, according to which "the onlye will and purpose of God is the cheafe cause of electione and reprobatione, so his free mercye in Christe is an inferior cause of saluation."[77]

Two thirds of a century later, when the radical connotations of "Cerberus's" writing would doubtless have become obscure to most readers, the work was reprinted. Interestingly, it appeared as the main section of a piece of Laudian propaganda entitled *An Historicall Narration of the Ivdgement of some most Learned and Godly English Bishops, Holy Martyrs, and Others; . . . Concerning Gods Election, and the Merit of Christ his Death, &c.*[78] A work of little more than a hundred pages, this advertised itself as including excerpts from the writings of Cranmer, Hooper, and Latimer, but only short extracts were given from the works of these men (only three pages from Cranmer); the bulk of it consisted of *The Copie of an answere*. Whether this publication of 1631 was based upon a surviving copy of the original or simply excerpted from Crowley's refutation is difficult to determine, but it purports to give information about the author not contained in Crowley's refutation.

Published about the Second or Third yeare of Q. ELIZABETH, by a Protestant Divine, who florished both in the time of K. EDVVARD and Q. ELIZABETH, and in the time of Q. MARY for his conscience endured voluntary exile."[79]

Admittedly, this information is fairly vague, which is perfectly understandable from the viewpoint of seventeenth-century propagandists for anti-Calvinism of the right, who would naturally have been most unwilling to acknowledge a debt to anti-Calvinism of the left.

Six years later, in 1637, William Prynne pointed out in his *Quench-Coale* that the "J.A. of Ailward" who had published *An Historicall Narration* was in fact "One *John Ailward* (not long before a Popish Priest)" whose book had been intended to affirm "the Errours of the Arminians, to be the Iudgement and Doctrine of the Church of England, and of the Martyrs and Reformers of it, both in King Edwards and Queen Elizabeths dayes."[80] Concerning its largest extract, Prynne claimed gleefully that this was "written by one *Champenies*" and had originally been printed

> without any Authours or Printers name thereto, or place where, or yeare when it was printed, or any intimation at all that it was ever licensed; All of which were plaine evidences that it was printed in a corner, without any license at all.[81]

This was a surprising criticism to make under the circumstances, since Prynne did not put his name to *A Quench-Coale*. Instead the author was given as "a well-wisher to the truth of God, and the Church of England!"[82] Leaving such inconsistency aside (it was, after all, in this very year that Prynne paid with his ears for his beliefs), the assignation to John Champneys is incorrect, although some historians (J. W. Martin e.g.) seem to have been inclined to take Prynne's word for it.[83] Prynne appears to have fastened upon Jean Veron's identification of Champneys, with whom the Frenchman had disputed in print on the same subject in 1561, and to have assumed that Veron's antagonist and Crowley's were one and the same.[84] In favor of Prynne's assumption are the undoubted facts that both had attacked reformed notions of predestination, both had been published without the names of either author or printer, and that both cited Augustine, the Book of Wisdom and 4 Esdras chapter 8 in support of their arguments.[85] There, however, the case for the identification of the two ends. *The Copie of an answere* nowhere mentions Veron or cites from him; the unnamed French author, as has been said, was Beza. But Veron had been responding to an opponent who had singled him out for attack and who, though like the author of *The Copie of an answere* he had declined to reveal his own identity, had been unmasked, but not caught, by the time of Veron's reply in 1561.[86] Since Crowley was writing five years later than Veron, any perplexity on Crowley's part as to the identity of his opponent would be completely unintelligible if he were responding to the same work as Veron had done. Furthermore, even after making all due allowance for the vituperative exaggerations which were the natural concomitant of sixteenth-century theological debate, Veron's observation concerning Champneys and his ilk, namely, that "ther be non so greate enemies vnto learninge, as they y^t be altogether vnlerned, & withoute godly knowledge, as this valyaunt champion of the free wyll men is," would seem singularly inappropriate if directed at the author of *The Copie of an answere,* and indicates that Champneys had not changed his views on this subject since his earlier publication, *The Harvest is at Hand,* of 1548.[87] Peter Heylyn, writing his anti-Calvinist *Ecclesia Restaurata* in 1661, seems to have been accepting Prynne's gloss on Ailward's information when he added to his account of Champney's recantation that the

Punishment so wrought upon him, that he relinquished all his former Errours, and entred into *Holy Orders,* flying the Kingdom . . . in the Time of Queen *Mary,* and coming back again with the other Exiles, after Her Decease. At what time he published a Discourse, in the way of a Letter, against the *Gospellers* above-mentioned [i.e., the pre-destinarians]. . . . His Discourse answered not long after by John Veron . . . and *Robert Crowley.* . . .[88]

For the reasons just discussed, however, Heylyn's reconstruction cannot be correct. His method of expressing himself, switching from details of the 1549 prosecution of a number of radicals to the supposed ongoing effects upon Champneys, indicates that Heylyn was dependent, not upon a single continuous account, but upon several documents with which he sought to reconstruct the whole. All of the "information" thus gleaned is contained in Ailward's brief account of the author of *The Copie of an answere* and Prynne's ascription of that work to Champneys, and it seems likely that these two were Heylyn's source.[89] It seems safe to conclude, therefore, that, Prynne, Heylyn, and J. W. Martin notwithstanding, Champneys's tract against Veron and *The Copie of an answere* are two separate works.

What, then, of the authorship of *The Copie of an answere?* Any conjecture as to whether Champneys might have been its author in addition to the unnamed, and apparently now lost, work to which Jean Veron replied in 1561, would seem to be out of order for stylistic reasons; if Champneys appears to have quoted Augustine, he nevertheless displayed to Veron a degree of the same kind of antiintellectualism that had been typical of Henry Hart and his group. Even assuming that it had been within his abilities, this would have made him an improbable candidate to have written within a few years in apparently admiring tones of the works of Melanchthon, Bullinger, Erasmus Sarcerius, "and manye other of the beste learned protestantes," and to have compared the views of Pelagius with those of Augustine and Calvin, while showing a familiarity with the writings of Eusebius, Beza, Gilby, Crowley, and Knox.[90] Champneys described himself as unlearned in 1548, and his name does not appear among the lists of matriculations or graduations at Oxford or Cambridge in any of the following years.[91] "Cerberus," on the other hand, showed himself familiar with the rules of formal logic (major, minor, etc.), and frequently quoted from his authorities in Latin, claiming that he "coulde easely proue" that God did not predestinate evil "by an infinite nōber of places out of the auncient writers (if shorteness wolde suffer)."[92] John Knox's "aduersarie to Gods eternal Predestination," whom most historians have conjectured, on inconclusive evidence, to have been Robert Cooche,[93] may have had the learning, though perhaps not the restrained style, to have been the author. But this is purely conjectural, and there may well have been other champions of free-will, radically inclined but without the aversion to learning displayed by the likes of Henry Hart and John Champneys, who succeeded in their aim of eluding detection by contemporaries and by posterity. *The Copie of an answere* remains anonymous still.

*   *   *

Robert Cooche: A Radical in High Places

It was the misfortune of Robert Cooche to have his writings published only by his enemies, in edited form, and for purposes of refutation. As has been mentioned,[94] he was a keeper of Queen Catherine Parr's wine cellar, and later a singer in Elizabeth I's chapel.[95] In this respect, he was probably the most highly placed socially of all the midcentury radicals. Neither the dates nor places of his birth or death are known, however, and his personal biography is more difficult to reconstruct than is an outline of his religious ideas.

Probably in the year 1550, he wrote to Peter Martyr, who had assumed duties as Regius Professor of Divinity at Oxford in 1548, concerning the issue of the lawfulness of pædobaptism. This letter is not extant, but Martyr replied from Oxford on 1 December, in tones that express a mixture of indulgence and irritation.[96] He apologized for the long delay between Cooche's letter and his own reply, mentioning the amount of business that he had had to attend to, but then adding some straight talking.

> Not to dissemble with you: this did somwhat hinder my desire to answere, that in the question which you mooue, I perceiue you sticke to those arguments wherewithall by speech you delt with me. . . . I answere therefore rather, least I should seeme to want curtesie than that I thinke you can be remooued from that conceit wherein so stifly you haue settled your minde.[97]

Whether the two men had met at the royal Court or in Oxford is not apparent, though the former seems the more likely, given Martyr's national importance. Despite his firmness, Martyr addressed Cooche as "deare friende in the Lorde" and "deere friend in Christ," so he apparently did not regard him as a heretic who had put himself beyond all brotherly regard.[98]

One of the most striking things about the letter is the knowledge that Cooche clearly had of patristics and of church history. Martyr did not take up the biblical arguments made in Cooche's letter, considering this "superfluous: partlie for that I discovered them vnto you at large when you talked with me."[99] Otherwise, he promised to answer Cooche's objections to pædobaptism "in such order as they are propounded of you," and proceeded to answer arguments based on regulations made by Higinus, the second-century bishop of Rome, and texts from Tertullian and Origen, as well as the opinions of recent writers such as Juan Luis Vives and Erasmus.[100] Martyr felt that Tertullian's viewpoint was of little weight in the controversy, "for as you know, he fell to Montanisme. . . ."[101] He also pointed out to Cooche that Origen was capable of being used for ammunition by both sides of the debate.

> Concerning Origen it is certaine, he saith, that ye baptisme of children is a tradition of the Apostles. . . . you alledge for your opinion testimonies, both out of these Commentaries vpon the Epistle to the Romans and out of his Homilies vpon Leuiticus. . . .[102]

It seems that Cooche had even felt sufficiently informed about his subject to question Origen's authorship of the commentary on Romans; at least, Martyr's letter implies as much. "But that Ruffinus rather than Origen should be the authour of those thinges that there bee read, howe shall we knowe?" Concerning the opinions of "Ludouicus Viues vpon the 26. Chapter of the first booke *De ciuitate Dei* what else should I answere," Martyr asked, "but that he is deceiued, when he saith that none but of ripe yeares were baptised of old?"[103] The Papacy was later to be equally shy of actually engaging with Vives's arguments; just to ensure that nobody else was "deceiued," the Spanish scholar's work was placed on the index. One thing really stands out in this debate: however ham-fisted, both now and later, he sometimes appears to have been, Cooche's apparent ability to argue at this level with the upholders of magisterial Protestantism has no parallel among English radicals of this period.

Sometime during the year that followed, Cooche wrote a book attacking doctrines that had been propounded by William Turner in a lecture at "Thistelworth" (Isleworth, near Richmond). Turner had been appointed Dean of Wells in March 1550/51, and the historian W.R.D. Jones conjectures that the lecture in question was given before his departure thence from his house in Kew, on the duke of Somerset's Sheen estate, between Isleworth and Brentford.[104] As in his dispute with Martyr, Cooche had previously met Turner in oral debate; the latter complained that Cooche argued unsoundly concerning the sacraments "as ye did ones in my chamber, reasonynge wyth me."[105] However, though he may have heard some of Turner's arguments beforehand, he had not actually been present at the lecture he was attempting to refute, and seems to have gotten the wrong end of the stick concerning one of Turner's illustrations. His description of the beginning of the sermon bears this out. "Master Turner . . . began fyrste, as I am enformed, to commend vnto hys audience. . . ."[106] Cooche's book drew a reply from Turner, entitled *A preseruatiue, or triacle, agaynst the poyson of Pelagius, lately reneued, & styrred vp agayn, by the furious secte of the Annabaptistes,* which was published in London on 30 January 1551/52 for Andrew Hester, by a printer who clearly had an even greater propensity than was normal for jumbling up the letters *n* and *u*. W.R.D. Jones observes that Turner, in this book, "sometimes proves a facile rather than an always consistent debater."[107] The epithet "Anabaptist" was, of course, a familiar enough term of abuse, applied more or less indiscriminately to religious radicals, but its use in Cooche's case, as is apparent in the letter from Peter Martyr, may well have been justified. If so, then Cooche must have been unique, or nearly so, since no other identifiable Englishmen (apart, presumably, from "S.B.," who attached himself to a group of Dutch Anabaptists in the 1570s) are known actually to have embraced believers' baptism. Cooche may or may not have gone so far. He had certainly advanced to antipædobaptism, which is not necessarily, of course, the same thing, and he spoke out for the baptism of believers only, though whether or not he practiced it is another matter.[108] Antipædobaptism was a view tenable either by spiritualists, who might maintain that all ceremonies were unimportant and that biblical texts referring to them were to be understood metaphorically, or by those who rejected the validity of sacraments performed by an insufficiently purified established church; this latter may have been the position adopted by Hart's free-willers. Cooche fell into neither of these categories; either he had himself received believers' baptism, and thereby become the exception to John Bale's observation about no native Englishmen having done so, or else he had failed, through lack of courage or of what he might have felt to be a proper opportunity, to act out his own beliefs.[109] What is quite clear is that he unequivocally supported the baptism only of those "as haue not only heard the good promises of God: but haue also thereby receyued a syngular consolation in their hartes through remission of synne whiche they by fayth haue receyued."[110] He added that "yf any receiue baptim without theis persuasion, it profiteth hym nothyng," for "sacramentes do not profit them whiche heare not the promys, and knowe not what it meaneth."[111]

Though Turner did not say in so many words that it was Cooche who had written against his lecture at Isleworth, there is internal evidence in *A preseruatiue* which shows that that book was directed against him: of several prefatory poems, one ends with five lines in which the initial capitals are spaced noticeably back from the lines which begin to spell his name.

C   ommune tryall techeth them, that be wyse,
O   ff thynges forepast to fynde, what will befall,
W   ee haue seen, herof what end dothe aryse:
C   Confounding of kyngdomes, decay of all,
H   eede taken to warning saueth from fall.[112]

Furthermore, Turner began one of his sentences with: "Couche, of thy conscyence (yf thou haste any at all) tell me. . . ."[113] In any case, John Parkhurst, bishop of Norwich, informed Rudolph Gualter, the Zürich reformer, more than twenty years later that "Contrà hunc [i.e., Cooche] scripsit libellum (dum in viuis esset Edouardus Rex) . . . D. Gulielmus Turnerus, in quo illius sententiam de peccato originali refutauit. Perperam item tamen de baptismo Infantum sentiebat."[114]

In the work, probably never published, to which Turner's book was a reply, Cooche had not only attacked the lawfulness of pædobaptism, but also the doctrine of original sin.[115] It is possible that it was his dispute with Martyr that had caused Cooche to reject original sin for the sake of consistency with his position on baptism. Martyr had pointed out that "if you admit Originall sinne to be in children, and yet will not permit them to be baptised, you are not of Origens iudgement. . . ."[116] Implicit in Martyr's observation is the idea that to accept the fact that infants are under the curse of original sin and then to deny them the remedy of baptism is to be somewhat heartless toward children. If Cooche had come to see, by the time of his clash with Turner, the close connection that Martyr saw between the practice of pædobaptism and belief in original sin as the malady it was designed to deal with, then the repudiation of the one logically implied the rejection of the other. Turner, a herbalist and physician, as well as dean of Wells, sought "to aunswer hym [Cooche], in the one of his opinions; and (God wyllyng) when I haue set out my Herbal, I shal aunswer hym to the other."[117] It does not appear, however, that he ever did answer Cooche on the subject of original sin beyond the few pages devoted to that topic at the end of the book. That end is sudden and inelegant, and the author again felt constrained to excuse himself with: "Meruell not good reader . . . I haue so muche ado wyth the settyng out of my Herball. . . ."[118] Even by sixteenth-century standards, this shows a lamentable lack of finesse!

One of Turner's more jocular arguments against Cooche, expressing the basic point that the absence of biblical precept (in this case for pædobaptism) does not amount to prohibition, supplies some interesting details about Cooche's life and character.

> Christe neuer commanded yow, to were a ryng on your finger, and be cause it shuld not be smothered vnder your gloue, to make a wyndow to let the ayre cum in to it, I dare not say that it myght be seene, nether cōmande he yow to syng in his church any pypyng Christe neuer commaunded prycksong or any besy discant: therfore ye offend to be a curions [sic] musician. God neuer in his worde expressedly commaũded his Apostelles to suffer suche tal men as you bee to lyue syngle: ther fore your curate doth wroug [sic] to suffer yow to lyue syngle.[119]

On this evidence, Cooche appears as vain and eccentric in respect to his behavior concerning the ring; perhaps he found himself in a significantly higher social position than that of his birth, and could not resist flaunting the fact.

More importantly, Turner's jest that "your curate doth wroug [sic] to suffer yow to lyue syngle," not only reveals Cooche's un-

married state, presumably (if the jest was to have point) at an age
when most men might be expected to have married, but also shows
that he was assumed still to have dealings with his local clergyman.
He appears already to have moved on from working in the royal
wine cellar to a position similar to that which he was to hold during
Elizabeth's reign. This is strange, since Turner accused Cooche
elsewhere of virtual separatism. "Ye . . . separate your selfe both
in the supper of our Lorde, and also in baptyme, and in the vnders-
tandyng of original sin, from vs. . . ."[120] That more than a meta-
phorical, merely intellectual "separation" was meant, is shown by
several references to Cooche as having disciples of his own: "ye
captaynes of catabaptistrye;" "ye haue with your importune bab-
lyng bewitched certayn vulnearned [sic! = unlearned] simple mē,
that thei beleue to be true what soeuer ye say. . . ."[121] "Let your
I sayes," Turner sneered, "haue autoritie amonge your bewitched
scholars, as much as ye wyll: but they shal haue none with me;"
they should be "ashamed of suche an vnlearned and dotynge sco-
lemaster."[122] If Cooche had a circle of followers of his own, then
the fact that he continued to see his curate and to sing "prycksong"
and descants in church calls for explanation. It may be that
Cooche's following was a Lollard-type group that met for conventicles without having any consistent ideology of separation from
"the world," and for whom antipædobaptism was simply one more
radical doctrine whose full implications for ecclesiology were, as
with Hart's free-will men, felt rather than clearly worked through
and articulated. Nonseparatist conventicles are. a recurrent theme
in mid-Tudor radicalism. The intellectually ramschackle nature of
much of that radicalism may be partly responsible for the failure to
draw the full ecclesiological conclusions from their own theological
ideas; the Lollard tradition of nonseparatism undoubtedly played
a part also. It is just possible that Cooche was beginning to appreciate that a complete cleavage existed between the aspirations of the
radicals, and those of the established Protestant churches such that
men like himself were as alienated from the latter as from the
Catholic church which they had replaced. He spoke of "a poke
that is now begynnyng to spryng vp, not of a romysh pok, but of
an other deuelysh pok, as euell as it."[123] Though he added that this
was "syn" which "is not healed but thorow faythe," it seems that
it was established Protestantism to which he was really referring,
and that "syn" was but his description of it; on any conceivable
view, "syn" sans phrase had not originated with the Reformation!

    It seems, then, that Cooche continued to participate in the estab-
lished church, not only as a citizen, but professionally as a singer,

yet at the same time dissented from that church's theology and organized a following of his own. While the author of the antipredestinarian tract, *The cōfutation of the error of the careles by necessitie* (whom many historians believe to have been Cooche) may well have belonged to a separatist or Anabaptist congregation in the late 1550s,[124] there is no suggestion in Parkhurst's letter to Gualter of 1574/75 that Cooche was anything more, during Elizabeth's reign, than an isolated individual of unorthodox opinions.

Peter Martyr had complained that Cooche, in his letter to him, had merely repeated the arguments of their earlier conversation; certainly, the arguments of Martyr's reply had still not dissuaded him from utilizing them against Turner the following year. Turner disputed Cooche's claim that it was "Iginius byshop of Rome" who first "ordered to baptyse an infante" in much the same way that Martyr had: he argued that that bishop had made regulations about a practice that had existed before, rather than actually instituting the practice itself.[125] Cooche had appealed once more to the writings of Erasmus, whom he had cited, as Turner said, "amonge a great sorte of heretikes, which wrote agaynst the baptim of infants," including "the antoritie [*sic*] of the Donatistes, Anabaptistes, and Pelagians. . . ."[126] Turner had compared the great distance in time at which Erasmus had lived from the events about which he made his assertions, with that of Cyprian, "which lyued and florysshed, within .cc.lvij, of Christes byrth: and Saynt Austen, which liued but .CCCC.xlij. after Christes natiuite," who had both affirmed "that the baptisyng of chylder came vnto vs from the apostels handes."[127] This would have been a stronger argument, perhaps, had he not inconsistently complained, a few pages later, that some of the usages cited by Cooche dated from "CC. yeres and more, after Christes byrth."[128] How early was the early church? It was perhaps fortunate for the magisterial Protestants that few of the radicals were equipped to answer them back on this subject, for if Augustine qualified, then the period in which Turner and Cooche were writing might fairly be described as the High Middle Ages.

Cooche insisted that it was the usage of the early church that "they that cam to be baptised" did so only "after dewe proofe of vnfayued [*sic*] repentance, & thereby were called competentes . . . and then were taught the principles of the christian faith and were fyrst called Catecumeni."[129] Only after this were they baptized, and then only on either "easter euen" or "wit sonday euen." Such an argument, much though it may have shown off Cooche's erudition, was a godsend for Turner, who was able to ridicule this procedure by repeatedly comparing it with the accounts of baptisms in the Book of Acts. He pointed out that an argument from church history could not compete against one based upon the Scripture.[130] This was a nice turning of the tables from the usual battle-lines between stubbornly biblicist radicals and deviously erudite champions of Protestant orthodoxy. Turner was not slow to point out as much. "Who wolde haue thought before this, that catabaptistry wolde haue leaned vpon any suche foundacions? Ye hadde wont to rattel, and crake nothing but scripture, scripture. . . ."[131]

If, as Turner conjectured, Cooche's clash with Peter Martyr had pushed him toward the rejection of the doctrine of original sin, then the encounter with Turner may have had a similar effect in respect to the doctrine of predestination. His views on the subject are not entirely clear, and such suggestions as the contents of *A preseruatiue, or triacle* provide are certainly capable of an interpretation that would not require Cooche to believe at this juncture in the preselection of individuals to salvation. That said, the hints in the text do point that way. Turner was a strong predestinarian himself ("the vertue of his passion [in the eucharist] shulde be delt to all them that are elect, and chosen to be saued"), and held to a limited atonement ("Christes body was broken for all them that shal be saued").[132] He did not raise any arguments with Cooche about the fact of predestination, but only about its implications. "Baptim, say ye, is onli dew to the elect churche, chosen in Christ Jesus, before al worldes," and went on to ask whether the murderous Münsterites had been elect or, if reprobate, why they were baptized.[133] Cooche claimed that it was "certaine . . . that God is able to saue hys chosen Churche wythout thes meanes [baptism and preaching]: But thys is hys ordinary waye, to saue and damne the whole worlde. . . ."[134] It presumably cannot be known whether Cooche used the expression "chosen in Christ Jesus" as merely a piece of empty rhetoric, or as the key to understanding the concept of election, but it may be, given Turner's response, that Cooche concurred with him in accepting some kind of predestinarian formula. That concurrence Turner was able to use to good effect.

The essential point in Turner's remark about the Münsterites was the unknowability of the identity of the elect. That being so, children may as well be baptized as faith-professing adults. Cooche rejected pædobaptism, Turner alleged, merely "because ye cannot perceyue, whether chylder entend vnfaynedly to aměd theyr lyues, or no: & know not by theyr lyuyng, whether they be chosen, or vnchosen."[135] But if Cooche would baptize only "suche as, ye know whether they be elected," then no adults could be baptized either, "for no man can know the harte."[136] The recurring issues of the inscrutability of the human heart and the need for the judgment of charity had once more raised their heads in radical-orthodox debate. Turner pressed home his advantage. "Take yow .iiij. men of .xl. yeares of age to baptise," he challenged Cooche, "& let me take .iiij. infantes of .iiij. dayes olde: tell me how that ye know that your iiij. men of .xl. yeares, ar more elect and chosen," and added the triumphant refrain that "noman [sic] can tel, what an other mau [sic] intēdeth or what is in hys harte."[137] That was the shared assumption of predestinarian and antipredestinarian alike: if God had chosen some persons, who could never fall away, before all worlds, the plain experience of mutable professors around them showed that one could never know who the elect really were. That being so, infants might as well receive the same blessings of baptism as adult believers. If Cooche did share a belief in predestination, then the logic of Turner's arguments must surely have given him cause to review that belief.

In some other ways, however, the encounter between the two men was not a true meeting of minds. Turner argued, as Luther had done before him, that infants did have faith, for "they please GOD:" (he cited Jacob, Jeremiah, John the Baptist in the womb, and Jesus blessing the children), "therefore thay at [sic = are] not without al fayth, for Paule sayeth: without fayth it is impossible tho [sic] please GOD."[138] He proceeded from this somewhat tendentious use of the Scripture to argue that, if Cooche really believed infants to be without faith, then he must hold that state to have derived "ether of their first creation, or by Adās fall."[139] The former, he contended, was impossible, since God made all things good, and unbelief was bad, and, if Cooche wished to plead the latter, "then haue we found agayne orygynall synne. . . ."[140] Turner seems to have failed to appreciate that, precisely because his opponent did reject original sin, infants' lack of faith in a Saviour would not, on Cooche's view, necessarily damn them. Similarly, when Turner argued that, since the Scripture teaches that "he that beleueth not, is condemned alredy," children must either be considered as believers or as under condemnation, he was presupposing what Cooche would obviously deny: that, since the text referred to all people tainted by original sin, its scope included infants.[141]

At one point, Turner showed his incomprehension of Cooche's Zwinglian view of baptism as a sign or pledge of allegiance by man to God, by casting around to find in what way Cooche thought it "effectual."[142] He could only see baptism passively as "the sygne, or sacrament of the promise, that GOD made to vs," and concluded that "therefore baptyme belongeth as wel vnto chylderen."[143] He was irritated by Cooche's description of the baptismal waters as "onli water, leuing out of baptim."[144] Cooche, on the other hand, gave Turner the choice of either conceding that pædobaptism was a "vayn & bare sygne, vnfruitfull and vnprofitable," or of assigning "vertue vnto the work wrought."[145] Turner's answer to the *ex opere operato* charge was both weak and vague; baptism did profit infants, he insisted, "not thorowe the wrought worcke it selfe, but thorow the promysse of GOD and hys worde."[146] He apparently did not consider that, if that was so, then the promise alone might have been deemed sufficient! A little later, observing that Cooche would withhold baptism from children until they were fourteen years old, he complained that by that time "they haue done many actuall synnes, whyche hadde nede to be wasshed awaye, wyth the bath of baptime"—an argument which sounds suspiciously close to *ex opere operato!*[147] When better expressed, Turner's sacramental theology was clearly good Calvinism, distinguishing between the sign and the thing signified, and teaching that the latter is received under the former. He wrote that children may "haue it [baptism] as surely, as they haue the thyng sygnyfyed by the sygne."[148]

The historians I. B. Horst and J. W. Martin have both felt that some of the allusions to a "wood spirit" in *A preseruatiue, or triacle* were actually references to Henry Hart, the leader of the freewill men.[149] Certainly the arrest of many of Hart's circle after a conventicle at Bocking in Essex would still have been very recent news at the time when Turner wrote his book. The reference in the title to "the poyson of Pelagius" could have been penned with Hart in mind, but is more likely an allusion to Cooche's denial of original sin; none of his other doctrines at this point would seem to have been vulnerable to charges of "Pelagianism." A poetaster , Thomas Norton, had penned some lines "to the reder" at the beginning of the book, warning that "pestilent plage a poysonons [*sic*] ill

> Hath sowen sores in certaigne now of late:
> A wood sprited hart: with a wayward wyll:
> A stubborne stomache, to nourishe debate:[150]

Whether this was a reference to the Pluckley Pelagian is hard to ascertain. Later in his book, Turner asked his adversary: "What wood spret taught you this folish philosophy? . . ." and spoke of "the wood sprete, who taught yow yowr diuinite," adding that Cooche would have been well advised not to have "made your self a cōpaniō wᵗ the murderīg scribes, & pharises, in vsing their churlish cheke agaĩst one of Christis mēbres."[151] He had chided that "ye haue be like authoritie of youre wood spirite to make new textes of scripture, and to bylde thereupon what ye lyst."[152] These references could suggest, whether legitimately or as an attempt to smear, that Cooche had been a companion, and even a pupil, of the leader of the free-will men, but only on the prior condition that "wood spirit" is code for "hart," and that this in turn means "Henry Hart." This is to be doubted. Referring to the contest between himself and Cooche, Turner told his opponent that "ye may se what it awayleth your wood sprete to fyght agaynst the scripture;"[153] this suggests that the term *wood sprete* was being used in an impersonal (or, rather, immaterial) sense as in "spirit of lawlessness," "spirit of anger," and so forth.

In any case, Cooche's doctrines do not appear to be the same as Hart's, albeit both men were drifting in a separatist direction. Cooche, as has been seen, was still making statements capable of a predestinarian interpretation at a time when Hart's group had made antipredestinarianism a central doctrinal plank in their platform. Neither do the free-will men appear to have opposed pædo-baptism. Thomas Cole, who recanted in a sermon before Cranmer in 1552/53, had been accused of denying original sin, while Hart appears to have been equivocal on the doctrine, endorsing it in 1548 when it offered a stick with which to beat "the flesh" and implicitly denouncing it in 1554 when debating predestination with Bradford.[154] Most importantly, however, Cooche shared none of Hart's reserve about solafidianism. When deriding any idea of inherent merit in the act of baptism, he had asked whether water could scour away the corruption resulting from the fact that "all the worlde hath synned, and is defyled in Adā," and then answered that it "is washed away, but wyth the only fayth in the bloude of Christ."[155] He spoke of believers' "remission of synne whiche they by fayth haue receyued," pointing out that "syn is not healed but thorow faythe," and even his antagonist noted that "ye graunt wyth open mouthe" the doctrine of justification by faith.[156]

The cõfutation, a work dated variously (since apparently no original copy survives) as 1557 and 1559,[157] has been claimed by several writers as the work of Cooche. On this question of authorship, A. G. Dickens takes his cue from G. H. Williams, who in turn got the idea from the *Transactions of the Baptist Historical Society,* which reported that Cooche had been "provisionally identified" as the author by "Mr. Laing" (the midnineteenth-century editor of Knox's works) in 1856![158] Doris Witard also seems to believe this story, but claims only that "a modern writer suggests" as much.[159]

Perhaps the writer in question was J. H. Shakespeare, who also believed it, and who, like his fellows, cited no evidence.[160] In fairness, *The Transactions of the Baptist Historical Society* added "the fact that R.C. was a prominent opponent of John Careless on this very question of Predestination," and "in the choice of a title the name of John Careless seems to have been too tempting to pass by," although the precise reference of this evidence was not given.[161] If Bradford's letter, arguing for predestination, to "N.S. and R.C." was being referred to, however, "R.C." is not Cooche but Robert Cole. This letter was printed by Foxe, and is another example of his care to protect the reputations of Robert Cole, who later defected from the free-willers anyway, and Nicholas Sheterden, whom Foxe depicted as a heroic Protestant martyr.[162] The conjecture that the title of *The cōfutation* was a play upon the name of John Careless is an intriguing one, however. If Cooche were the author, it may indicate that he was in contact with the free-will men, and if he were not the author, that one of the free-will party may have been, though it exceeds in literary skill any of their other works and, on that ground alone, it certainly cannot have come from Hart's pen. Alas, despite the lamentable tendency of historians to lean upon one another rather than upon the extant facts of this matter, Cooche's authorship of *The cōfutation* is far from impossible, but the only respectable statement on the matter seems to have come from Burrage who, noting Shakespeare's claim, frankly admitted that "I know of no evidence whatever that Cooche wrote it."[163]

Cooche's first book, against Turner, appears only to have circulated in manuscript form, and his second (accepting for the moment that he was responsible for *The cōfutation*) was to suffer a similar fate. Ironically the "publication" of both works, the former in quoted scraps and the latter in full, was due entirely to the efforts of his opponents, who printed them only in order to hold them up to ridicule. His third attempt does not appear even to have gotten this far. On 13 August 1573, "compelled by the force of conscience," he wrote a letter from the Queen's Palace to Gualter in Zürich, asking his opinions about the administration of communion and the timing of the Last Supper.[164] He had written, he informed Gualter, "some pages upon these subjects, which I intend to print," but "nothing can be printed here in England without the licence of the bishops."[165] Cooche implied that support from Gualter for his own views would help him to obtain such permission. This letter prompted Gualter to inquire of Parkhurst about Cooche; the bishop informed him in a letter of the following

June that he had already written enough about him in previous letters, but eight months later (i.e., in February 1574/75) he gave a terse account of Cooche's career in another letter to Gualter which is the source of most of the biographical information about him that survives.[166] This last letter also shows that Cooche, after long and fruitless discussions with Parkhurst, Coverdale, and Jewel had failed to convert him, nevertheless abandoned his Anabaptist opinions some years prior to 1574, though the cause of this renunciation is not mentioned.

The opinions about communion which Cooche expressed in his letter to Gualter range from the biblicist to the idiosyncratic. On the one hand, he argued that a supper should be exactly that, while "a most minute morsel of bread and three drops of wine" was "in mockery of a supper;" on this point, he claimed, the church had been in error "almost from the time of St. Paul."[167] This biblicist note might be taken to indicate the continuing literalist mind-set of one long committed to Anabaptism, even if he was referring his difficulties to a Reformed leader such as Gualter. His opinion that communion should be a real supper, however, was one that he had held for more than twenty years. William Turner had answered his jibe about why infants were not admitted to communion as well as to baptism with:

> A mā might answer you, yᵗ they wer lyke to be lurched at your gluttenous supper, yf that they were with you: for ye wolde haue at the supper of the gluttenous catabaptistes (whiche ye call the supper of our Lord) befe, mutton, vele, capons and such harde meates, as the pore sucking childer can not eat. . . .[168]

In the light of Cooche's letter to Gualter, it certainly seems that W.R.D. Jones is mistaken in thinking that this scenario of Cooche's ideal of a communion was "unfairly attributed" to him by Turner.[169] Cooche sounded self-important and nit-picking in explaining how he differed from

> Beza and others as to the day when Christ took supper with his disciples. For they assign the supper to the fourteenth day, I to the thirteenth, in which, according to the law, the old passover was not to be sacrificed. Christ therefore instituted a new passover. . . .[170]

Gualter's unfavorable reply and Cooche's failure to get into print were both equally predictable.

Robert Cooche appears to have spent the best part of a lifetime irritating people in high places without actually obtaining a platform for himself and his views. Parkhurst seems to have considered him more loquacious than effective. Though Cooche's extant letter to Gualter would seem to bear out that judgment, *The cõfutation*—on the assumption that it is his—throws a kindlier light on him. Cooche was atypical of English radicals, not only theologically (no other known Englishman of the time explicitly argued for believers' baptism), and intellectually (his knowledge of church history and of the fathers is unequaled by any other known English radical of the period) but also socially, since few were as well-connected. To posterity, however, Cooche is typical of his radical peers in that much vital information about his character and biography is lacking, and reconstructions by historians must at many points be both tentative and somewhat impressionistic.

*   *   *

John Knox and the Errors of the Careless

When Hart and Bradford clashed on the subject of predestination, the ecclesiological consequences of their theological differences came briefly to light but, due to the lack of any thoroughgoing theory of separatism (or of anything else!) in Hart's thinking, the point did not become the focus of the dispute.[171] More important to the radicals than any Anabaptist-type separation from the state, was the need to exclude from the church those whose lives were clearly ungodly, either by dint of moral defect, or by being tainted with Popery. This was to be a concern, of course, of later Puritanism, and, like those Puritans who later separated from the established church, these early radicals frequently separated themselves, though their practice probably outran their theory in this respect. If the Elizabethan separatists were sometimes less than consistent in their views of the relationship between church and state, however, the midcentury radicals had almost no articulated views on the matter at all; as has been argued in chapters 1 and 2, Hart and Trew had no more than a separatist "direction of thought." And, unlike the Elizabethan separatists, the earlier radicals emphasized their theological differences with the establishment. Predestinarian ideas, they claimed, allowed moral laxity to continue unchallenged, since they led to fatalism and presumption. Only quite rarely, as in the clash between Hart and Bradford, was the more ecclesiologically significant point touched upon that the identity of the elect, according to all traditional ideas on predestination, was unknowable, and thus, the radicals charged, a church espousing such beliefs could not exclude the apparently ungodly, since they might, after all, be elected to life. Bradford, effectively, pleaded guilty as charged, but since ecclesiology was of such slight conscious concern to Hart the admission was hardly damaging.

During Mary's reign, however, a radical tract appeared which took up the issue again. Its author is described by John Knox as an *Anabaptist,* which, given the looseness of contemporary usage of the term, may or may not mean what it says. The piece does not appear to have been printed, but rather to have been circulated in manuscript; this much seem to be implied by Knox's observation that

> the copie which came to my handes was in that place [the history of Gideon was being debated] imperfecte, for after the former wordes it had onely written ["]Confyr to the world["]. And because I will not take vpon me to alter any thing in your wordes I leaue them to be corrected by your selues.[172]

The writing owes its preservation to Knox's extensive citation as he refuted it, passage by passage, in his own work, entitled with typical immoderation, *An Answer to a Great Nomber of blasphemous cauillation written by an Anabaptist, and aduersarie to Gods eternal Predestination.* Knox's reply was printed by John Crespin at Geneva in 1560, and to it we owe even our knowledge of the title of the antipredestinarian tract, which he gives as "the cōfutation of the errors of the careles by necessitie."[173] "Necessitie" was a reference to the doctrine of predestination, while "careles" referred to the moral and spiritual indifference which the radical writer suggested such teaching would inevitably bring about in those who accepted it.

Knox had been concerned for some time about the effect that disseminators of radical ideas might have upon the prospects for the cause of reformed Protestantism. On 1 December 1557 he had written to his brethren in Scotland, warning them about sectaries.[174] Among their chief characteristics, he identified Christological heresy (he named Arianism), tendencies to perfectionism, and, above all, the denial of predestination.

> Finallie, the generall consent of all that sect is, that God, be [*sic*] his foirknawledge, consale, and wisdome, hath no assurit electioun, nether yit any certane reprobatioun, but that everie man may elect or reprobat himself be his awn frie will, whilk he hath (say thay) to do gud or evill.[175]

Even at this date, Knox clearly had it in mind to write against the radical opponents of predestination.

> But the fontane of thair dampnabill errour, whilk is, that in God thai can acknawledge na justice except that whilk thair fulische brane be abill to comprehend, at more opportunitie, God willing, we sall intreat.[176]

It may be, then, that Knox had already encountered a copy of *The cōfutation,* and that the *Answer* was his delayed response to it.

David Laing, Knox's nineteenth-century editor, thought it "probable" that Knox's work "may have been written at Dieppe in 1559, during the interval of his application for the permission which was denied him, to pass through England on his way to his native country."[177] Knox's more recent biographer, Jasper Ridley, on the other hand, believes that he "probably wrote it during the second half of 1558, and completed it before he left Geneva in January 1559, as he had very little time in which to do any writing during the next twelve months."[178] The archives of the town council of Geneva recorded on 9 November 1559, that the work had been composed at the request of Protestants in England after another Englishman had written against the doctrine of predestination.[179] Four days later, the ministers of Geneva having given their consent, the council permitted Knox's book to be printed on the conditions that the work would not state that it had been printed in Geneva and that John Baron and William Whittingham would guarantee its doctrinal trustworthiness.[180] Geneva in general, and Knox in particular, being as unpopular with England's new queen as they were, the council's caution was quite understandable.

Noting that "no attempt has hitherto [this was 1864] been made to identify the author of the Confutation," Laing believed that Robert Cooche, William Turner's antagonist of 1551/52, was responsible for writing *The cōfutation,* and most subsequent historians have followed him in this conviction, though Champlin Burrage noted the lack of evidence for it.[181] Laing, following Strype's account of the life of Cooche (whom both men referred to as "Cooke"), believed that the circumstances therein described constituted "nearly conclusive" evidence of Cooche's authorship.[182] Despite the exaggeration of this claim, however (the evidence is good, but all circumstantial), the candidature of Cooche has to remain the best "educated guess" at authorship. Cooche is known to have continued to hold Anabaptist views into Elizabeth's reign; at least, John Parkhurst, bishop of Norwich, writing to Rudolph

Gualter in Zürich on 6 February 1574/75, could describe Cooche's defection from opposition to pædobaptism and doctrines of original sin as still only "ante paucos annos."[183] There are few other Englishmen than Cooche to whom the epithet "Anabaptist" in the title of Knox's book could appropriately have been applied, though, as has been noted, contemporary usage was loose. Certainly the author of *The cōfutation* was acquainted with the fact of Michael Servetus' martyrdom in Geneva in 1553, and deplored it. He was also known personally to Knox, who expostulated that "thy manifest defection from God, and this thy open blasphemie" had "desolued all familiaritie, which hath bene betwext vs," and, screeching that he would seek retribution against him in "any comonwelth where iustice against blesphemers may be ministred," said he was giving him advance warning of the fact "lest that after thou shalt complein, that vnder the cloke of friendship, I have deceiued the."[184] Knox's adversary was one "whose corrupt maners, freindly ād secretly I haue rebuked, but whose malice I now know."[185] Such a degree of familiarity would certainly not exclude the possibility of Cooche's authorship; as Laing pointed out, "that Knox became acquainted with Cooke during his residence in London as one of King Edward's Chaplains, is at least highly probable."[186] If Cooche was the opponent in question, then the pattern set by his encounters with Peter Martyr and William Turner—of private discussion followed by written debate—had once more been repeated.

In a rare, and perhaps only token, conciliatory gesture, Knox begged any less determined opponents of predestination, whose error is only

> of ignorance and simplicite, not to be offended, as though I did stomack against them, if at any time I shall handle the impudent writer or collector of this booke (whose nature is bettet [*sic*] knowen vnto me then vnto many of them) according to his malicious frowardnes. . . .[187]

This confirms Knox's close personal acquaintance with his opponent, and also the fact that Knox believed him to have been associated with a wider circle of radicals. Indeed, the expression "collector" implies that the antipredestinarian tract may even have been the product of such a circle, and Knox's frequent use of the plural when referring to the opposition may reflect such a belief, as does his reference to "thee ād thy cōpagnions that collected these blasphemies."[188] In reference to the separatist character of radicalism, he complained that "most streitly ye inhibit all of your sect to frequent any cōgregatiō, but your own."[189] If Knox was correctly informed, then the author of *The cōfutation* was active in a radical congregation, or at least among a circle of like-minded friends.

These facts require the unnamed author to have been aware of events overseas (the death of Servetus) and well acquainted with Knox. Robert Cooche fulfills the criterion of having somewhat wider horizons than most English radicals, since he had worked in Queen Catherine Parr's court in the capacity of wine cellarer at the same time as Parkhurst was there.[190] His occupation as a singer in Elizabeth I's chapel must have made for a thorough-going Nicodemism on his part;[191] this is a fact which comports ill with Knox's statement, just cited, in which he assumes his opponent to be one of those who refuse "to frequent any cōgregatiō, but [their] own." Cooche was not formally educated, however, and William Turner commented in 1551/52 that

> al the learned men that haue disputed with you in your opinions, whit [*sic*] whom I haue spoken, iudge you to be so sklender a clerk: y^t ye neuer lerned nether sophistry, nor logike nether anye good scyence in all your life, sauing only musyke."[192]

This was a rather unfair judgment, however, in view of the theological awareness demonstrated by Cooche in the very work which Turner had set himself to refute. Knox made no similar charge against his opponent, though he did point out that he knew no Hebrew.[193]

The author of *The cōfutation* had at some time been considered an orthodox Protestant, either by Knox himself, or by those whose judgment he trusted. Only such an interpretation can account for Knox's use of an expression like "thy manifest defection from God," and his description of his adversary as an "open traitor to the veritie, which once thow professed."[194] It is not certain whether Cooche fulfills this criterion; certainly he was openly espousing radical opionions (denial of original sin, and the rejection of pædobaptism) in 1551/52, when William Turner responded to him in print, though Peter Martyr had addressed him a year before in a tone which, while fraternal, suggested that he was considered a "weaker brother."[195]

No other candidates besides Cooche strongly suggest themselves as possible authors of the piece which so angered Knox. There is nothing to indicate, for example, that John Champneys knew Knox. The anonymous author of *The Copie of an Answere* in the 1560s is a possibility. However, that work displays far more formal learning than is evinced by *The cōfutation,* whose author displayed no more evidence of a formal education than the knowledge that the "principale cause called Causa Causæ, is the cause of the secōd ād inferior cause called cause causate."[196] Cooche, of course, had a clear ability, demonstrated in his encounters with Martyr and Turner, to utilize patristic authority and church history when it suited his purposes. Given the sparse nature of the evidence about levels of erudition, therefore, it can be concluded that the character of *The cōfutation* does at least remain consistent with the possibility of Cooche's authorship.

W. T. Whitley, writing in 1914, suggested that the title was a play on the name of John Careless, the antagonist of Henry Hart and John Trew in the King's Bench debates.[197] This is an attractive idea, and would certainly have precedent; Hart had not hesitated to make this pun in the course of his arguments. "I feare ye eccepte a carles mane to be yor teacher and he hath tawght ye as carles a fayth."[198] If the title was indeed a pun upon John Careless's name, then a fairly close acquaintance of the author with the Marian Protestant underground can be taken for granted, though not enough is known of Cooche's biography during this period to ascertain whether this would be a pointer further toward, or away from him as the likely originator. John Knox, however, did not take up the allusion, though he may have been unaware of the predestinarian debates in and around the King's Bench during Mary's reign. He wrote a letter to Thomas Upchard after the latter's visit to Geneva, on his way to Basel, following his release from prison in England, but this letter indicates only the briefest of acquaintances between the two men, and gives no hint at all that Knox knew anything of his background as a former free-will man.[199] Knox's written works make no mention of Careless, and he seems to have been oblivious to any such reference when he wrote to his "anabaptist" antagonist, "Ye take your pleasure in resoning with vs, whom ye terme Careles by necessitie."[200]

Amusingly, he saw fit to add: "I will not recompence raling with raling;" of all the bitter invective poured out in the tracts examined by the present study, an aspect of the competition in which the Reformed, except for Bradford, consistently got the better of their radical opponents, Knox's work is the most venomous and distasteful of all! J. S. McEwen's judgment, that "the Treatise on predestination was something of a *tour de force,* and that Knox's heart was not really in it," seems well wide of the mark; so wide, indeed, that it is perhaps best understood as an attempt to excuse him.[201]

As with Hart's free-will men, the burden of the author of *The cōfutation* was the failure of the official Reformation and its adherents to exhibit any significantly greater degree of practical righteousness than the Catholicism they sought to supplant. "How many of thē [the predestinarians]," he asked, "cā we perceave by their conversatiō, that they have cast of the old mā ād put on the new mā, walking sincerely in their vocation ād the true feare of God?"[202] Mere participation in a Protestant congregation, he alleged, anticipating later Puritan complaints on this point, was adjudged sufficient to account professors "faithfull brethren," and "the surest tokē of their electiō they think to be that they be of your congregation."[203] During Mary's reign, of course, it probably was enough; persecution ensured that few but the sincerely convinced would expose themselves to the hazards of identification with the Protestant cause. Perhaps the writer was remembering the Edwardian phase of English Protestantism. As a kind of parallel with Hart's antiintellectualism, the author identified predestinarian Protestantism with a pandering to the rich; their preachers "haue respect of persons preferring the welthie . . . if they be liberal, thoghe they be drowned in many vices."[204] This was an easy charge to make, of course, and a hard one to disprove, but it is revealing of the accuser's social prejudices, and his perception of predestinarianism as being in some way aligned with the rich and the powerful representatives of officialdom.

Most revealing of all is the writer's equation of predestinarianism with inclusivism, and his entire agreement with Hart about the lax ecclesiological effects of teaching doctrines of predestination. He charged that

> you vse to help vp such sores with this saying: there is none during this life that cā be knowē to be in the election, be he neuer so vertuous, nor any owt of the electiō be he neuer so vnrighteous, after this maner ye do heall thē vp, so that they nede not to indeuor them selues to bring furth the frutes of liuelie faith[205]

This is not, of course, quite the same reasoning as Hart's. Hart had argued, and Bradford had concurred, that the unknowability (according to predestinarian teaching) of the saved and the damned made it impossible to exclude the latter from the church.[206] The author of *The cōfutation,* on the other hand, emphasized that all incentive for godly living was taken away by this unknowability, though, like Hart, he also noted as a subsidiary point, that ungodly livers (expecially if they were rich) were by the same token judged too charitably and were not excluded from the church.

Although not entirely consistent in his reply, Knox gave a very different explanation to that which Bradford had given to Hart. He began by denying that "to be ioyned with this, or that cōgregation" was considered to be a "certen signe of election," and noted that "many fals brethren" were joined "with the company of the best reformed churches."[207] He agreed that "somtymes the elect, as touching mannes iudgment, is lyke in estate with the reprobate. And againe that sometimes the reprobate do beautifully shyne in the eyes of men for a space, as exemples be euident."[208] But then, paradoxically, he added, "yet I am sure, that you be neuer able to proue that we affirme, that in this life, no difference may be knowen betwext the two."[209] He explained that both the elect and the reprobate made themselves evident by their fruits, despite the fact that he had just taught the contrary.

> from election cometh faith, from a liuelie faith do good workes spring, in wᶜ the elect continuing and going forward, not onely make they their own election, sure, as, S.Peter doeth teache, but also giue a testimonie of it to others, before whom their good workes do shyne. And so by yᵉ cōtrarie signes and effectes, we affirme that the reprobate do manifest and vtter themselues.[210]

He expressed amazement that his opponent should charge the Reformed with holding "that no man can be knowen ether to be in the election, or out of the election, during this life."[211] Knox was atypical of Calvinists of that generation in the rigor with which he supported the logic of predestinarian ideas. He made his own supralapsarian views clear: it was "before all beginning" that "God . . . hath reprobate others: whom . . . he shall adiuge to tormentes and fier inextinguible [*sic*]," and these will thus "in tormentes glorifie the most iust & most seuere iudgement of God. . . ."[212] With outspoken frankness, he claimed that the Anabaptists "make the loue of God common to all men and that do we constantly deny."[213] Those who sympathized with Beza's extension of "Calvinism" to include a limited atonement, would eventually join the search for personal assurance that they were among those whom God loved and for whom Christ had died in their own outward works, as R. T. Kendall has argued in *Calvin and English Calvinism to 1649*.[214] When such ideas were taken together with the Puritan emphasis on church discipline, and the Presbyterian conviction that ungodly livers should be excluded from the church, the way would become open for a subtle change of emphasis in which it could slowly become assumed that the elect were, in some meaningful sense, visible. In both respects, Knox, if unrepresentative of his own generation, was a pointer toward the future.

This is not to say that Knox was always consistent in his defense of predestinarian ideas. His opponent raised the familiar charge that predestination made God the ultimate author of sin, and attributed a dark, secret will to God which was in antithesis to his proclaimed will, whereas in fact he "hath but one will which is euer onely good . . . nether hath he any secret will contray [*sic*] to this . . . he tempteth no man to sinne. . . ."[215] Knox believed that it was the

fre consent of man to rebellio̅, whose will was neither inforced neither yet by any violence of Gods purpose compelled to consent. . . . Conuict vs now (if ye can) that we make gods absolute ordinance . . . to be the principall cause of sinne."[216]

This line of argument is not necessarily inconsistent with even a supralapsarian individual predestination if it is on the basis of an event—the Fall—which is only foreknown, rather than predetermined. But it does leave at least one event in universal history—and human history at that—in which God was not the prime mover. Such a view inevitably led Knox to argue that "ma̅ when he sinned, did . . . consent to the will of the deuill, which did manifestly ganesay gods reuelled will;" the explanation he provided was that his disobedience was part of god's secret will, which he presumably meant was permissive, rather than directive.[217] Later, however, Knox inverted this logic when arguing that the damned were foreordained to damnation, for "if he shall damne those unwillingly, who̅ willingly he wold haue saued, then is he not omnipotent."[218] Why the allowance of a "permissive will" in respect to the identities of the damned should be deemed to impugn God's omnipotence, while the allowance of such a respect to the origin of sin does not, Knox did not explain. In that sense, his charge that "you enraged Anabaptistes . . . can admitte in God no iustice, which is not subiect to the reach of your reason" might almost be taken as a tacit admission.[219] Writhing on the hook of Ezek. 18.23, which teaches that God "will not the death of a sinner, but rather that he conuert, and liue," Knox resorted to what Jasper Ridley has rightly called "verbal quibbling" over the indefinite article, and seems to have sought to imply that "a sinner" referred to some particular person; it could not be true, from Knox's perspective, that God willed the death of "no creature."[220] Much though he thundered, Knox found it hard at times, it would seem, to be entirely comfortable with his own defense.

Knox's antagonist identified predestinarianism as the creed of official Protestantism; at least, he seems to have perceived a close correlation between those beliefs and a penchant for persecuting dissenters. He moved naturally from observations about the lax living encouraged by a belief in ineluctable predestination, to charges of intolerance: "but, such lippes, such letuce, such disciples, such masters. of your chief Apollos be persecutors on whō the bloode of seruetus crieth a vēgeāce."[221] What better, he asked, could one expect? The predestinarians' disciples were bound to be unrighteous when their very teachers were tainted by support for persecution. Michael Servetus, notoriously, had been executed in Calvin's Geneva for his unorthodoxy on the subject of the Trinity. But if Servetus was a victim of the very citadel of predestinarianism and the civic power of the church, there were "others mo whom I could name. but . . . God hath partly alredie reuenged their bloode and serued som of their persecuters, with the same measure wherewith they measured to others."[222] Knox understood this to refer to Joan Bocher, some of whose persecutors had subsequently lost their own lives under Mary.

I think ye meane . . . your prophetesse Ione of kent . . . none other cause do you se of yᵉ shedding of yᵉ blood of those most cōstāt martyres of Christ Iesus, Thomas Crammer, Nicholas Redley, Hugh latimer, Iohn Hooper, Iohn Rogers, Iohn Bradfurth, and of others mo. But that God hathe partly reuenged their blood, yᵗ is of your great prophet and prophetesse, vpon their persecuters.[223]

This suggestion, plausible as it must have seemed in those days when retributive justice was widely taken for granted, does not seem to have dissuaded Knox from resolving thunderously there and then to seek the death of his antagonist and similarly tempting the wrath of Providence. "I wil not now somuch [sic] labor to confute by thy pen, as that my ful purpose is to lay the same to thy charge if I shal apprehend the in any comonwelth where iustice against blesphemers may be ministred."[224]

Despite his bluster, Knox was effectively pleading guilty, and proudly so, to the taunt that his predestinarian creed was inextricably associated with religious coercion. The author of *The cōfutation* had pointed out that the Reformed were not merely succumbing to weakness or "humane infirmitie" on this point, but persecuted on principle. "They have . . . sett furth bookes affirming it to be lawfull to persecute, and put to death such as dissent from them in controuersies of religiō, whome they cal blasphemers of God."[225] Knox agreed, and thereby added another book to the list of those that so taught. However, it is his response to the charge that in justifying persecution the reformers made themselves hypocrites that is most significant. Before "they came to autoritie," averred the radical, "they were of an other iudgement, and did both say and write, that no man oght to be persecuted for his conscience saik. but now they are . . . becom persecuters."[226] This argument, Knox insisted, was to "abuse . . . the name of conscience," since conscience "must haue a testimonie of gods plaine wil reueled. which ye shal not fynd to be your assurance."[227] Knox's opinions had such a testimony, while those of his opponent did not; only the former, therefore, could be accounted "conscience." Conscience was only a valid court of appeal if it was in alignment with the truth! Hence the Protestants could plead for respect for their own consciences under a Catholic regime without admitting any obligation to yield the like concession to others when they were the established religion. Erroneous conscience, such as that of an Anabaptist, was no conscience.

> We say the man is not persecuted, for his conscience, that declining from God, blaspheming his Maiestie, and cōtemning his religion obstinatly defendeth erroneous & fals doctrine. This mā I say lawfully conuicted, if he suffer the death, pronounced by a lawful Magistrate, is not persecuted . . . but he suffereth punishement according to gods cōmandement pronounced in Deutronomie, the XIII, chapiter.[228]

Knox was familiar enough with Anabaptist arguments to anticipate the distinction his opponent might make between "externall crimes" and "maters of religion." He knew that the radicals would plead that "yᵉ conscience of euerie man is not a like persuaded in yᵉ seruice and honoring of God, nether yet in such cōtrouersies as gods worde hath not plaiemly decided."[229] Knox asked: "if that be a iust excuse, why pernicious errors shall be obstinatly defended, ether yet that gods established religion shall be contempteously dispised?"[230] Most moderns, and Anabaptists even then, would doutless have shocked Knox by replying in the affirmative to what he clearly considered to be a rhetorical question. But it was his antagonist who had raised what was perhaps the most telling question of all on this subject: "be these I pray you the shepe whom Christ sent furth in the middest of wolues? can the shepe persecute the wolf?"[231] To this, Knox gave no reply at all.

What Knox did, however, was to insist that Anabaptist views, such as the antipredestinarian radicalism expressed in *The cōfutation,* led inevitably to violence and social anarchy. He gave an extensive account of Continental Anabaptism, mostly describing the events at Münster, and concluded that "what so euer ye speake of charitie and loue, . . . yet shall you in the end produce no other frute then these your fathers haue done before you."[232] In making parallels with the revolutionary apocalypticism of the 1530s, it may be that Knox was sincerely invoking a wider apologetic against Anabaptism that had been gleaned in the Reformed hothouse of Geneva, rather than merely repeating what was becoming a familiar smear against all radicals. His references to the separation of Anabaptists, just mentioned, and to "your great angel Castalio"[233] (the Genevan defector, Sebastian Castellio) may reflect an assumption that radicalism was all of a piece, and that this English manifestation was somehow inevitably connected with these Continental counterparts, rather than reflecting definite information that he may have possessed about his adversary. Certainly the example of that "most perfect school of Christ" was never far from his mind, and toward the end of his work he dragged in a defense of its polity. It is certainly not impossible that Knox was conducting his entire attack upon his Anabaptist opponent with one eye, as it were, upon the European, and particularly the Genevan, scene, and that he interpreted "Anabaptist" arguments in that light. Whether or not Knox was correct in perceiving an inevitable propensity toward social revolution in Anabaptism, his diagnosis of such a propensity emphasized, by way of implicit contrast, the perception of his own doctrine as conducive to social stability.

*   *   *

S.B.—An English Anabaptist in Prison

Genuine English Anabaptists in this period were, as has been seen, very rare birds. One other person who probably does deserve the title is a carpenter imprisoned in Newgate in 1575. He attached himself (whether in prison or before is not known) to the Dutch Anabaptists apprehended at Easter, in 1575, two of whom were subsequently burned at Smithfield. He is known only through one surviving document recording his debate in prison with William White, a radical Puritan of separatist sympathies, and in this document he is referred to simply as "S.B."[234] The document takes the form of alternating paragraphs by each of the protagonists, and was produced as a reply by White to the views of S.B., though the margin includes a few comments made afterward by the latter.

White met S.B. in Newgate and had already heard that he was "inclyning to the sect of the Ana[ba]ptistes," so it does not sound as if he had firmly joined the group at that stage.[235] Furthermore, he appears to have addressed and referred to the group as a third party in his discussions with White, in a manner that makes him sound peripheral to it, though this may have been due simply to language difficulties or "newcomer status."[236] For these reasons, it seems that S.B. may not have been baptized as a believer; hence the element of doubt as to whether he should be referred to as an Anabaptist. Because of his undoubted commitment to their cause, however, and because White described him as such in this very specific sense (as opposed to its vaguer, inaccurate usage denoting radicalism in general), it is perhaps wisest to give him the title.

S.B. told White, some time after their first meeting, about the business losses he had sustained from cheats and how, true to his Anabaptist principle of nonresistance, he "would neither contend in lawe, complaine to the meagistrate, nor warne them to the Courte of Conscience."[237] These affairs had presumably taken place before his imprisonment, so it does seem that his first acquaintance with Anabaptism was not made in prison. This in turn indicates that his arrest may have been in respect to that connection rather than, say, for debt as a result of his financial losses. Certainly an alternative scenario would require some surprising coincidences.

The substance of the debate between White and S.B. was concerned with the lawfullness or otherwise, of oaths and of bearing arms, and also the proper attitude toward civil authority. The document is entitled, rather unecumenically, "A conference between a christian and an English Anabaptist," a description which gives the key to understanding White's harsh attitude to his adversary.[238]

Despite the soft answers of S.B., which failed in any case to turn away the wrath of White, he showed a stubborn insistence in these debates on taking the New Testament injunctions literally. "Christe saith sweare not at all," he observed, and added that "true Christians . . . ought to belieue one another" without an oath. Oaths were pointless, since a liar would forswear himself as easily as any other lie; after Peter "had saide falsly, he swore as falslie"—presumably the reference was to the apostle during the night following the arrest of Jesus, recorded in Mark 14.66–71. White countered with arguments from Abraham, the Old Testament, and the political necessity of oaths as "an end of all strife."[239]

S.B. also took literally Christ's affirmation that "all y^t strike w^t ye sword shall perish w^t the sword," and insisted that Christians may not carry weapons; his opponent responded that "Christ speaketh of such as vse the sworde unlawfullie."[24] Against White's plea that it was only "a revenging mynde" in the bearer that made weapons unlawful, the Anabaptist answered, reasonably enough, that "none hath revenged himself by weapon, but he had a revenging mynde."[241] Appealing to the example of Christ, who "would onelie suffer for the gospell, & not fight for ye gospell," S.B. conjectured that, if all men were of his mind, "kinges shoulde liue w^{t}out feare in their kingdomes." His Puritan opponent responded that Christ's example does not "so binde vs to suffer for the gospell, but that in some case we may allso fight for the gospell."[242]

Again, the Anabaptist "thought it not lawfull . . . to revenge my wronges done vnto me by extremity of lawe," because "Christ saieth, be m^{er}cifull as yor heauenly father is m^{er}cifull." He asked whether, if he were to prosecute an evil man, who had cheated him of "100 m^{er}kes and . . . cast him [into] prison till he satisfie me to the vndoing of his wife & familie in this doing doth my light shine before men? or are thei occasioned by this evill facte, to glorifie the heavenly father?"[243] White answered sourly that, if this principle were to be followed, one would soon keep company with "whores baudes thieues, traitors, heretiques etc.;" if

> a godly brother and faithfull subiect should finde your crewe at yor next meeting, and cause the magistrate to apprehend you all, should not his light shine and god therby be glorified, when the reprobate heretickes should be punished, & the deceiued elect converted? I trow yea.[244]

The pattern is very evident: The Anabaptist stood by the letter of the dominical injunctions, while White sought to evade their full force in the name of good order in a godly commonwealth.

In great measure, this is a battle between the Old Testament and the New. White answered the quotations of Christ's commands with appeals to the Old Testament and the insistence that the two could and must be harmonized. According to him, "you may not vrge such man^{er} of speeches [the commands of Christ], further than is meant."[245] S.B. answered that Christ had instituted a more perfect law than the Old Testament, forbidding a number of things (he cited divorce, polygamy, and resisting injuries) which it had permitted; the same process applied to swearing.[246] This, according to White, was to set "Christe and the Apostle James against god and the prophet Jeremy."[247] His ideal, like that of the magisterial Protestants generally, was the old Testament Israel; for them the New Testament altered the means and availability of salvation, but not the social and political framework within which that salvation took place. For radicals, the discontinuity was more drastic. Bishop Reginald Pecock had written that some of the fifteenth-century Lollards had held the New Testament alone to be authoritative, while others allowed what was "in the Newe Testament or in the Oold, and is not bi the Newe Testament reuokid."[248] This last was almost exactly the line taken by S.B. "I thinke the old testam^t to belong to xx[christ]ians, so much as is not abolished by ye newe."[249] It was to no purpose for White to appeal to Nehemiah as an example of arms-bearing to defend the work of God unless he and his ilk were setting about to "build a new materiall temple" along the lines of the Old Testament.[250]

In the new covenant, as S.B. saw it, the godly were a minority within society, and so a godly commonwealth was impossible. White saw only that the Anabaptists, which he called a "sect in a corn,^{er}" thought themselves "to be wiser and to vnderstand more then the whole wo^{r}ld besides."[251] The true church, White thought, might be called a little flock, "yet is it vniuersall and 10000 times greater, than a poore deceiued secte."[252] S.B. commented that, though his opponent thought the number of the deceived was bound to be smaller than those adhering to the truth, "I say vntruth is greater in multitude than the truth."[253] No remark, perhaps, sums up more aptly the different conceptions of the church presupposed by the defenders of magisterial Protestantism on the one hand, and the sixteenth-century radicals on the other.

The insistence that the Old Testament was subjected to the New did not detract from the Anabaptists' biblicism. S.B. testified as to how the Scriptures had transformed his life, and called them the "piller & ground of truth, on wch truth, god graunt me to builde and no other;" one of his Dutch sisters rejected White's offer of a loan of a book by Calvin on the grounds that her group did not depend upon men.[254] "The foundation wch I alledged of ye sufficiency of holie scriptures," S.B. wrote,

> I am sure it is true, For men haue & do erre, but the scriptures haue one sweete harmony & consent: but Augustine, Ambrose, Jerome, Origen, Chry^{o}stome, Luther, Calvine, Zwinglius, Brentius, Hemingius, haue no such concorde, but are one against another.[255]

Of these famous writers, one, Calvin, stands as a spectre behind the entire debate. It was Calvin whose book White proffered to the Dutch woman, Calvin again whom he had quoted in his previous letter to S.B. and Calvin whose words he produced with obvious relish to clinch his argument for resorting to civil magistrates, the law, and to weapons.[256] "S.B." scribbled in the margin that "I meane to leane to a more sure pillar than is Mr Calvin."[257] Other radicals, before the imprisoned Anabaptist, had identified this reformer as having possession over the mind-sets of their state-church opponents. Knox's Anabaptist had scorned at Calvin as the god of the predestinarians and magisterial Protestants, and Knox had proved him to be not far wrong by responding to the insult with a lengthy quotation from the oracle of Geneva.[258] The author of *The Copie of an answere* had sought to disarm the problem by quoting Calvin with approval on an irrelevant point in order to remove the sting of undermining Calvinist views on predestination; even so, he recognized the need to tackle the reality of the dominance of Calvin's system over the minds of many of his countrymen.[259]

*   *   *

All of the writers surveyed here, except S.B., made an appreciable impact on public opinion; none of their voices was allowed to pass unchallenged, and all called forth refutations or, in the case of *The Harvest is at Hand,* prosecution. This opposition came from magisterial Protestants outraged at the threat the authors seemed to pose to an orderly reformation. Clearly the state-church reformers took the ideas of these radical writers very seriously, and recognized in them plausible alternatives to their own theology, alternatives which they were determined to beat down.

4

Shaking the Foundations: Arianism and English Familism

Arianism in England

THE reigns of Edward VI and Mary saw the rapid increase in the numbers of adherents of radical, sectarian, and heretical ideas in England, of which only that minority who left written records, either of their own or in the accounts of their adversaries, are accessible to the historian. Hart, Trew, Bocher, and their respective, sometimes overlapping, circles, Champneys, Cooche, "Cerberus," and whatever followings they may have had, are all known to posterity as a result of official records, their own literary efforts, or the efforts they inspired in others who were determined to refute them. But these were not the only active radicals. Frequent complaints were made by Edwardian clerics of swarms of "Anabaptists," Arians, Libertines, and others, and not all of these worries can be attributed to paranoia or exaggeration. Bishop Hooper came across not only Monophysites, perfectionists, and libertines, but also those who claimed that God himself "acts under some kind of necessity," who denied the existence of the soul, and those who called Christ "a mischievous fellow and deceiver of the world."[1] Five men burned at Smithfield in April 1557 agreed that "all mens wyves ought to be comon to all men," but exhibited a bewildering range of views on other subjects, from the opinion that Christ had not yet come to the belief "y^t he was not equall w^{t}h the father in godhead."[2] This last, antitrinitarianism, was met with increasingly from the mid-Tudor period onward. The month after the five burnings, William Prowtyng, a sawyer of Thornham in Kent, John Symes of Brenchley, and Robert Kynge of Peckham, all denied the deity both of Christ and of the Holy Ghost under questioning by Nicholas Harpsfield.[3] If they had been held for a long time before this interrogation, it is just possible that some of these were the Arians present in the King's Bench alongside the free-will men and the predestinarians in Mary's reign; John Philpot wrote an *Apology* for spitting upon one of them.[4] But most of these sectarians are not even identifiable, far less accessible to theological analysis by moderns; they peek out at historians through a reference here, an allusion there. The most that can be hoped for, is that those individuals and groups whose histories, in some measure, survive, are broadly representative of radicalism as a whole; it is to be feared, particularly in view of the paucity of detailed knowledge about English Arianism, that they are not.

One bare paragraph in Cranmer's Register records the abjuration of the priest John Assheton "person of Shiltelington," of anti-trinitarian heresies on 28 December 1548.[5] He had attributed the doctrine of the Trinity to "the confession of Athanasius," implying that it was not a teaching held by the New Testament church. Assheton had also explicitly denied the deity of the Holy Spirit and of Christ. The former he had asserted to be "only a certeyn power of the Father." While he had affirmed the virgin birth and that Christ was "a holy prophet and speciallie beloved of God the Father," he had denied his deity on the grounds that Christ "was seen and leved, hungred and thirsted." Finally, he had attributed to Christ's passion merely the merit of bringing to man a knowledge of God's testament and power. John Bland, the parson of Adisham, also seems to have made a passing remark about the doctrine of the Trinity not very different from Assheton's though he does not appear to have got into particularly serious trouble for it. He had reportedly told his parishioners on 18 March 1542, "that the image of the Trinity is not to be suffered and he cannot find *Trinitas* throughout Scripture, but that Athanasius put it in his *Symbolum*."[6] Unlike Assheton, however, it is not possible to say whether Bland went so far as actually to reject the doctrines concerning the person of Christ and of the Holy Spirit which the doctrinal construct of Trinity is an attempt to reflect.

It would seem likely (the claim can be put no more strongly than that) that it was the case of Assheton which prompted John Proctor to take up the cudgels for trinitarian orthodoxy in his *Fal of the Late Arrian*. This book was published in London on 9 December of the year following Assheton's abjuration by a printer, William Powell, who (as will appear) was clearly running short of lower case *w*'s. Proctor was a religious conservative who would conduct propaganda for the government in the following reign. Now he took the opportunity to insinuate that this manifestation of the ultimate heresy was a natural consequence of the abandonment of most restrictions on the exposition of Scripture. Given the "daungerous

surfeitynge of the people . . . as haue ben in these later times prac-
tised amongest them," he asked: "what els was there to be loked
for, but that some of them wolde at last eumoet and spue forthe
some suche monst[r]uous portent" as Arianism?[7] It was a fair
point. If the break with Rome in the 1530s had acted as a spur to
religious dissidents, Henrician ruthlessness appears to have kept
the lid on the situation. But with the death of Henry VIII in 1547,
and the relaxation of restrictions on religious inquiry under Somerset, there does seem to have been an upsurge of radical activity,
or at least of complaints about it. Proctor was right. The number
of significant heretical variations on Christian orthodoxy being
strictly finite, Arianism was bound to occur sooner or later.

Proctor sought in his book to confute "the opiniō of a serten
man who lately denyed Christ deuinitie," but to do so "not disclo-
synge his name . . . whom I wold be lothe to displease, if he hath
Recanted . . . as some saye that he hathe."[8] Though he wished to
protect the Arian's name, Proctor's vagueness about the other details of the case appears to have been due to a lack of information
on his part. He did not know who had procured the indictment or
whether the person had recanted, or whether the Arian had been
imprisoned or otherwise punished. Proctor's copy of the heretic's
"prouffes in writying," originally written at Cranmer's request,
presumably to aid the prosecution, had been "sent to me, from a
friend of myne,"[9] he wrote. Some time had clearly elapsed between
his first receiving this document and his writing the refutation. It
seems that Proctor knew little of the case but what he had read in
the Arian's own articles. Assheton had certainly appeared before
Cranmer at Lambeth, and had confessed to having "presumptu-
ously affirmed by subscription of my proper handy writing thes
errours," so there would appear to be at least some correspondence between the details given by Proctor and those known of
Assheton.[10] No other "Arians" are known to have been prosecuted
during the year between the cleric's abjuration and the publication
of Proctor's book. If Assheton were the man in question, Proctor's
ignorance would have been understandable, since the former was
no London-based radical likely to have met many of Proctor's
friends or contacts, but seems to have been brought to the capital
for the purpose of resolving his case of heresy. Against the possibility of Assheton as the heretic in question is the fact that the articles
quoted by Proctor refer to Christology alone, and have nothing to
say on the subject of the Holy Spirit, or of the Trinity as such.

The Arian refuted by Proctor, had committed his views to paper,
"beyng required to Write, for the reuerence which I oWe vnto your

Lordship [Cranmer]," and had "purposed briefly and compendiously to commit in Writyng what I think touching tharticles."[11] He confessed that he thought this to be an unnecessary exercise, since his views should have been plain enough from his previous communication with the archbishop. He had already been brought by Cranmer to a disputation "before many Wytnesses" (Proctor had mentioned a meeting with "serten of the Counsell & dyuers other Learned men"), and had then spoken privately with the primate.[12] He was more than merely literate, and was familiar with the writings of Erasmus Sarcerius and Conrad Pellican, though he considered them "garbages."[13] His main argument was that Christ, as a man, could not be God, since the attributes of the former were clean contrary to all the main doctrines concerning the nature of the latter. God's nature was "single, comunicable to no creature: cōprehensible of no creat vnderstāding: explicable with no speche."[14] The doctrine of incarnation seems to have ben repugnant to his conception of divine impassibility. He asked: "hoWe may it be thought true religion Whiche vnitethe in one subiecte [i.e., Christ] contraryes, as visibilitie, and inuisibilitie, mortalitie and immortalitie &c."[15] Making mischievous use of patristic authority, he argued that "if Iesus Christ . . . was God, so shal he be a visible God, comprehensible, and mortall, Which is not counted God With me, q[uoth] great Athanasius of Alexandrye. &c."[16] Noting Christ's hunger, thirst, weakness, and fear in the Gospel accounts, he denied "that this nature subiect to these infirmities and passiōs is God or any parte of the deuine essens," for this would make God "mighty and of poWer of thone parte, Weake and impotent of thother parte," which he considered to be "madnesse, & folly."[17] But more than a commonplace rationalism was present; the biblicist note is sounded by the protestation that right faith was to be identified with that "which the scriptures do testify not in a feW places, & the same depraued and detort in to Wrong sense, but as ye wyll saye, throughlye, with one and the same perpetuall tenor and concent."[18] Proctor's defense of orthodoxy was less than convincing, and is perhaps best summed up by his exhortation that "we must suspende reason, for it worketh treason to all Godds Misteries."[19] Protestants may have allowed themselves a wry smile at this display of polemical weakness by a conservative but, even so, the orthodox of all stripes must surely have expected more in defense of Trinitarianism.

In April 1551, some sixteen months after Proctor wrote, Cranmer found himself dealing with another case of Arian heresy, this time in the person of the "iniquitatis diabolicae alumnus et filius, Georgius van Parris."[20] Van Parris was a surgeon from "Flanders," and seems to have spoken little English; at least, the services of Coverdale were required to translate the proceedings for him. Coverdale revealed that the prisoner "beleveth, that God the Father is only God, and that Christ is not very God, is noon heresy."[21] Asked whether he would retract and abjure this opinion, "he saith, no." Miles Hogarde, a hostile commentator writing five years later on behalf of the Marian regime, and seeking to demonstrate that neither holiness of life nor steadfastness in death were sufficient in themselves to make a sufferer at the stake a true martyr, claimed that the surgeon lived a life of voluntary austerity, and "woulde fall prostrate vpon the grounde, & geue thankes to God the father" before his (infrequent) meals.[22] Condemned to be burned at Smithfield, Van Parris embraced martyrdom, according to Hogarde's account, gladly and without fear.[23] He was only the second person actually to be executed for his religious opinions under Edward VI. He was also the last.

George van Parris was not, however, the last person in England to be in trouble for Arianism during the midsixteenth century. John Strype recorded that two Arians were imprisoned in the King's Bench under Mary, and were duly shunned by the participants on both sides of the predestinarian quarrels.[24] John Philpot wrote an *Apology for Spitting on an Arian;* to read the work is to confirm that "Apology" was intended in the sense of "apologia" rather than as any acknowledgment of fault.[25] He asked his readers to

> bear with me, who, . . . being blasphemed by an . . . Arian, making himself equal with Christ, saying that God was none otherwise in Christ than God was with him; making him but a creature, as he was himself; vaunting to be without sin, as well as Christ,—did spit on him.[26]

If the Arians in the King's Bench believed as Philpot reported them to do, then their radicalism extended beyond simple denial of the deity of Christ. They also, apparently, denied the deity of the Holy Spirit as Assheton had done.[27] Furthermore, they rejected the need for such prayers as "Lord, have mercy upon us miserable sinners," and even "Forgive us our trespasses" on the grounds that true believers were without sin, and they denied "the benefit of repentance to any person that sinneth after baptism."[28] This last remark, of course, suggests that the "Arians" in the King's Bench took an Anabaptist view of baptism, and this, depending on whether Philpot was speaking literally or only metaphorically, would seem to be confirmed by his reference to "these new baptized Arians."[29] If the Arians were indeed Anabaptist, no new precedent would have been set thereby, except perhaps within England. Most Dutch Anabaptism was colored with Christological heterodoxy; the Melchiorites, in their anxiety to affirm the deity of Christ and to exalt spirit above flesh, had endorsed Monophysite views. In this their successors sometimes differed. The orthodox evangelical Mennonites followed the Melchiorite tradition in this respect, while Adam Pastor was expelled for leaning to the opposite view and for denying the deity of Christ. The Melchiorites' other successors, the Davidjorists and their fellow-travelers and, later, the followers of Hendrik Niclaes, endorsed an allegorizing, mystical view likely to be compatible with the more explicit denials made by the Arians.

On 28 May 1561 at Guildford in Surrey, Thomas Chaundeler and Robert Sterete signed a confession which reveals a congregation not very different in its beliefs from the "Arians" described by Philpot. The Surrey congregation denied Christ to be God, held perfectionism and mortalism, opposed pædobaptism, and apparently practiced believers' baptism.[30] These sectarians had connections with a number of similar congregations across the country, and later seem to have been subsumed into Familism; it is possible that Philpot's "Arians" were members of this, or of a related, group. The not dissimilar instances of Philpot's "Arians" in 1555, and the Guildford sectarians in 1561, casts a new light on comments made by Hooper in a letter to Bullinger back in June 1549. Then, Hooper had complained of the "Anabaptists" who disturbed his lectures that they

> deny altogether that Christ was born of the virgin Mary according to the flesh. They contend that a man who is reconciled to God is without sin, and free from all stain of concupiscence, and that nothing of the old Adam remains in his nature; and a man, they say, who is thus regenerate cannot sin. They add that all hope of pardon is taken away from those who, after having received the Holy Ghost, fall into sin. They maintain a fatal necessity, . . .[31]

Taken by itself, this sounds like the jaundiced account of an uncomprehending figure of authority confronted by religious diversity among the no-longer-docile attenders at his sermons; Hooper was listing heresies, each of which may have been found separately in some person or group, but not, surely, all together! Seen alongside Philpot's report of those whom he called "arians," and the confession of Chaundeler and Sterete, however, Hooper's complaint appears much more credible as an actual picture of given individuals. Perhaps, after all, this kind of eclectic ultraradicalism, generally spiritualist and perfectionist, and prone to Christological heterodoxy (either Monophysite on the one hand or Arian on the other) really was quite widespread. If so, then it is almost undocumented apart from the references discussed here, but would have accounted for most, perhaps even all, of contemporary allusions to "Arianism."

It certainly does seem that the men known to Philpot belonged to an active congregation. Philpot warned his readers that "if they will go about to pervert you from the true faith in corners and dens, as they do very diligently, as I hear say, . . . tell such that the truth seeketh no corners. . . ."[32] Perhaps a wider organization existed—the congregations listed by Chaundeler and Sterete may have been precisely that—but if it did, these ultraradicals were successful in eluding the attention of the authorities and left no records to posterity.

As a further isolated example of an organized attempt at the active propagation of Arian ideas in England, the case of Christopher Vitel deserves attention. Vitel is something of an exception in another respect also, namely, to the general scarcity of information about individual Arians. He was a joiner by trade,[33] and though he was later to become the chief propagator of the Family of Love in England, his activities and contacts prior to that allegiance are illuminative of doctrinal radicalism generally during the mid-Tudor period. William Wilkinson, writing against Familism in 1579, printed the account of Henry Orinel of Willingham, Cambridgeshire, concerning his encounter with Vitel "about the third yeare of Q. Maries raigne. An. 1555. at Michaelmas or not much after."[34] Wilkinson made it plain that it was the recent report of a witness still alive that he was publishing, rather than contemporary documentary evidence, and the slight vagueness over dates, even as to the exact year, bears this out.

According to Orinel's account, he had stayed at "a cōon Inne" at Colchester, along with "William Rauen of S. Iues," who had "likewise fled beyng in daunger for Religion" from the Marian authorities.[35] There they encountered Vitel, who taught many doctrines which Orinel had not previously heard of. The teachings imputed to Vitel were that children ought not to be baptized until they come to years of discretion; that the Edwardian Litany was not the service of God; that Christ was not God; that the godly do not sin; and that Antichrist was to be identified with all the ungodly, and not with the person of the Pope.[36] Orinel recounted that "one Iohn Barry seruant to M. Laurence of Barnehall in Essex came to the same Inne, to reason with the Joigner [Vitel] about the Diuinitie of Christ."[37] Vitel's debating skills, however, "put Barry to silence & blankt him so that he had not a word to say," which perturbed many, especially two "women Gospellers" who had come with Barry (John Barre) to hear the debate. Orinel was sufficiently worried as to resolve to go to Oxford to speak with the imprisoned Ridley and Latimer, but his doubts were assuaged by someone else in the meantime. Sometime later, presumably after Queen Mary's death, Vitel visited Orinel's home town of Willingham, and sought to meet Orinel at an alehouse, "but I sent hym word that I would not come to hym nor haue to doe with him."[38]

Despite the vagueness as to dates, there seems no reason to doubt Orinel's accuracy or Wilkinson's truthfulness, and every cause for trusting them. The scene described is convincingly vivid and, since it portrays the worsting of Trinitarianism in a tavern debate, and since Barre, the champion of that Trinitarianism, was—apparently unknown to Wilkinson—in the circle of the very free-will men whom that writer had just denounced on the previous page, it can safely be assumed that neither Orinel nor Wilkinson had any reason to have invented or significantly embellished the incident.

Orinel had been in more radical company at Colchester than he—or Wilkinson—knew. With delicious, if unconscious, irony, the fondly remembered contender for the deity of Christ was one of the free-will men associated with Henry Hart, whom Wilkinson had just a page before blamed as being in some vague way responsible for the receptivity of some in England toward Familism.[39] John Barre had helped William Laurence to write an antipredestinarian tract addressed to Augustine Bernhere, Latimer's servant, and was very probably a believer in conditional immortality.[40] It is rather surprising, therefore, to see Laurence and Barre characterized as "orthodox Protestants" by the historian J. W. Martin.[41] By 1579, Orinel did not know "if he [Barre] be aliue," so it may safely be assumed that he had not had a continuing radical career of any marked notoriety.[42]

Vitel remained an Arian throughout Mary's reign, according to Robert Crowley, who had cause to dispute with him, though to no avail, on several occasions.[43] The joiner told his cousin, Joan Agar, that "Christ was not God: but onely a good man, and a Prophet: and that there were men shee did know liuing, that were as good, and as holy men, as he was."[44] Vitel's career as an Arian came to an end with his recantation at Paul's Cross during the first year of Elizabeth's reign.[45] Thenceforward, he became completely involved with the work of extending Hendrik Niclaes's Family of Love in England. As A. Hamilton, the modern historian of the Family of Love, sagaciously observes, Vitel's former Arianism "could easily be suited to the essentially allegorical interpretation which Niclaes always gave of the incarnation."[46] Vitel was not alone in turning to Niclaes; other ultraradical groups appear to have done so as well, and with them went any prospect of forming an identifiable Arian presence in England beyond the appearance of the occasional individualist. Instead, Arianism proved to be the seedbed for the growth of the Family of Love.

*   *   *

The Origins of English Familism

In the alehouse at Colchester, where Henry Orinel and William Raven met him in 1555, Vitel sang the praises of the life and doctrine of a man "who liued as he sayd beyond the seas . . . whom afterwardes I vnderstode to be one Henry Nicholas a Mercer of Delph in Holland."[47] Hendrik Niclaes was the founder and prophet of the Family of Love, but only the last of the five doctrines supposedly taught by Vitel at this time ("that the Pope was not Antichrist, but he which doth not that which God's law commaundeth, . . . & so there are many Antichrists") is distinctive of Familism.[48]

The story of the Family of Love has been ably recounted both by J. D. Moss and by A. Hamilton, and it is not proposed to duplicate their efforts here more than is strictly necessary.[49] The former noted that "when and how Familism first began to take root in England, like much of its history on the continent, remains a mystery to historians."[50] The enigma existed for contemporaries as well; William Wilkinson sought a solution by alleging connections between midcentury radicalism and Elizabethan Familism, though he was unable to pinpoint any precise link beyond that of temporal contiguity: "from this presēt yeare, in the which this [the predestinarian prison debates] happened the doctrine of HN. began to pepe out."[51] However, Wilkinson sought to add weight to his allegation by charging that "neither cā this Louely Family abide the most blessed and comfortable doctrine of Predestination," and cited a statement from a Familist letter to John Rogers of late 1578 or early 1579.[52] But Familist views on predestination were somewhat ambivalent, and will need to be considered separately. Shortly before Wilkinson wrote, Rogers, another antagonist of Familism, had made a similar conjecture about the group's growth in England.

> For as much as their beginning was in Englang [sic!] about the latter end of Queene Maries rainge [sic] when many of our brethren were entred into that gulfe of freewill . . . and likewise certeine Arrians, with Pellagians ioyning together, found an author for their purpose, vnder a newe deuised name of Familie of Loue.[53]

Rogers confessed, however, that this reconstruction of events was but "my simple coniecture," and offered no supporting factual basis for his theory.

If the evidence for any direct connection between the freewill men and English Familism seems slight, that for I. B. Horst's conjecture, that under Edward VI "Hart . . . was a consistent separatist and later under Mary accepted or turned in the more spiritualistic direction of the Family of Love," is nonexistent.[54] Horst believes that Hart's ability to escape the flames of martyrdom may have been due to a willingness to conform outwardly to established religion while inwardly dissenting from it, which was a Familist trait, and that this willingness developed during Mary's reign, accounting for a supposed imprisonment early in the reign while avoiding martyrdom. Horst cites the testimony of Thomas Chaundeler of Wonersh and Robert Sterete of Dunsfold given at Guildford in 1561 on this point; their group initially refused to attend parish churches during Mary's reign, but later resorted to a policy of Nicodemism.[55] That Chaundeler and Sterete's group is representative of Familism as a whole may be doubted; Vitel implied that even in 1561 the Surrey group was not solidly Familist.[56] Of course, Horst's argument does not require Hart or anyone else to have been solidly Familist, but merely to have been moving in that general direction. Even so, his case takes in two misapprehensions and an unproven conjecture. He believes that Hart was imprisoned "during the early years of Mary's reign," and finds it "remarkable that Cuthbert Sympson was sent to the stake, while Hart who was associated with him and seemingly a more notorious heretic escaped the fire."[57] The misplaced beliefs in Hart's imprisonment and that the Sympson of his circle was Cuthbert have been dealt with elsewhere in the present work; several of Hart's group did, of course, embrace martyrdom for their beliefs, and a warrant was out for Hart's arrest at the time of his death in 1557.[58] Horst also believes that the English "Henry" who was reported to be "of like mind" with David Joris (a forerunner of Niclaes and model for many of his teachings) and financed a conference of Anabaptist leaders at Bocholt in 1536 may have been Hart; he offers no evidence beyond the coincidence of the rather common first name.[59] In any case, a tendency toward Davidjorism in 1536 would be unlikely to have lain dormant (none of Hart's extant writings betray such) until "later under Mary." Furthermore, there is no evidence whatsoever that Hart or any of his circle had connections with the Surrey group or inclinations toward spiritualism. Hart's strong aversion to speculative ideas and abstract theological constructs has been noted in chapter 2; the fact that Familism frequently borrowed antiintellectualist rhetoric would have been unlikely to be sufficient to reconcile him to its esoteric nature.

If Horst's case seems purely speculative and "dare-say," this has not prevented other writers from building upon his speculations. T. Wilson Hayes, in his 1986 article, "The Peaceful Apocalypse: Familism and Literacy in Sixteenth-Century England," takes the statements of Horst, whom he surprisingly describes as "the best authority on Hart" (J. W. Martin's essays were already in print), as indicating a belief that Hart definitely "became a Familist during Queen Mary's reign."[60] To be fair, Horst does not quite say this, though his guesses in that general direction (which is all they are) seem wild enough. Hayes feels constrained to point out that the free-willers' rejection of predestination, their antiintellectualism, and their denial "that children were . . . born in sin" or that anyone "was irrevocably saved or damned" were all ideas "espoused by the Radical Reformation group that originated in the Netherlands and was known in England as the Family of Love."[61] He might more aptly have pointed out that these ideas were all radical commonplaces; in any case, as will be seen, it is by no means certain that the Family of Love did entirely reject predestination.

Even so, John Rogers presumably had some grounds for his conjecture that "certeine Arrians" of the Marian period, "with Pellagians ioyning together, found an author for their purpose" in Hendrik Niclaes.[62] The career of Christopher Vitel himself, clearly atypical of English Familists in general in its scope, may not have been so different in its spiritual dimensions, that is, in coming to the movement from a different type of religious radicalism. The beliefs of individual English Familists show a degree of lack of uniformity that might be thought surprising in a movement so clearly marked by loyalty to the actual person, as well as to the teachings, of a strong leader such as Niclaes, to whom revelatory gifts were ascribed. Stephen Batman, in a preface to John Rogers's *Answere*

vnto a wicked & infamous Libel made by Christopher Vitel, one
of the chiefe English Elders of the pretended Family of Love, alleged that Vitel "hath in corners drawen companyes togethers *[sic]*,
of the which some haue refrained, and others yet too many abiding."[63] If he was correct in this report, it would seem that the
gathering together of a conventicle was comparatively easy; it was
the holding of it in conformity to a given sectarian organization
structure or pattern of belief that was difficult. The explanation
for the relative diversity within English Familism, as for the clear
existence of a prehistory of the Surrey group that was exposed to
the glare of the authorities in 1561, is perhaps that Familism took
root among groups and individuals previously inclined to radicalism, and open to changes of direction where Familism seemed to
offer a better hope.

Certainly this was Vitel's own experience. He was a man who,
as Rogers reported,

> all the dayes of Queene Marie was a teacher of these famous heretiques
> the Arrians, and at Paules Crosse did solemnly in the first yeare of our
> soueraine Ladie Queene Elizabeth, recant the same errours, as by the
> register of y[e] bishop of Londō doth manifestly apeare.[64]

In a tantalizing reference to this earlier period, Vitel explained that
"although I had red certayne bookes of sundry wryters; yet was
I moued to search whether they were grounded vpon the Lords
promyses or no. . . ."[65] Unfortunately, it is unclear whether he was
speaking of books which acted as a point of departure for his first,
radical-Arian inquiry, or whether this remark concerns his later
movement from Arianism toward Familism. What is certain, however, is that Vitel had been a habitual religious searcher before
becoming, to his own satisfaction, a finder. Rogers wondered, not
only why Vitel had become an Arian in the first place, "and many
yeares became a leader of many pore soules into that gulfe of
mischiefe," but why, having done so, he then chose to "forsake
that opinion, and imbrace this absurde impietye of HN [Hendrik
Niclaes]."[66] Stephen Batman made it plain that, as he saw it, the
Family of Love was itself Arian in any case, and that Vitel had
thus recanted at Paul's Cross "as I thinke the same error which
he now stiffely defendeth."[67] This was a jaundiced view, however;
Rogers himself conceded with a frankness generally foreign to debates of this kind that "whereas they haue been charged with diuers
articles before the highe commissioners, yet by no argument that
I can learne, doe I finde that they holde all the errours conteined

in the same."[68] Even so, explicit Arians were not unknown on the periphery of the movement; one such, who had signed a confession of Arianism as recently as 24 March 1574/75, was identified warily by Wilkinson as "*W. H.* of *B.*" in Cambridgeshire.[69] He was "perhaps vnto the Family . . . not vnknowen" even in the late 1570s, "for that *Vitels* had sometymes lodged in his house, and hee vseth to conferre with them concernying their opinions."[70]

Vitel provided no clear explanation of his metamorphosis from Arian to Familist—the phenomenon that had given Rogers such cause for wonderment—though he did give a general account of his conversion to Familism.

> The̅ saw I, that all people vpon earth which were without the house of Loue, were all wrapped in vnbeliefe; and that there was nothing among them but variaunce, . . . and euery one would haue right, and be the comminaltye of Christ, and condemned all others for heretickes, and false Christians.[71]

Vitel felt that his previous way of life had been a mistake: "so haue I humbled my selfe before the Lord and his Minister HN. as the greatest sinner among sinners, desiring the Lord that he . . . woulde . . . forgeue me al my offences. . . ."[72] He did not date this conversion but, the tone of his own account notwithstanding, it may have been a gradual process rather than a crisis experience. If he had been speaking highly of Niclaes to Orinel in the autumn of 1555, he retained his Arian views—which were not characteristic of Familism—not only then but presumably until the early part of Elizabeth's reign (his recantation at Paul's Cross is unlikely to have been in respect to offenses committed long before). Looking back on this time from the vantage point of two decades, he seems to have been tacitly admitting that his Arian and Familist periods had overlapped to some extent, and to have been seeking to exonerate the idol of the latter from the taint of the former, when he wrote that

> all these [sects, errors, etc.] come hereout, because the man will iudge the workes of the Lord with his naturall wisdome, or lernedenes. And hereout, namely, out of the wisedome of the flesh, sprang all Christopher Vitelles [i.e. my] errors, but not out of any other ma̅s councell or bookes.[73]

If Vitel had erred during that time, he seems to have been implying, it was not as a result of reading Niclaes's books, but due to the follies of his own "naturall wisdome" superimposed on the teach-

ings of Niclaes. Though, as in most things, his manner of expressing the point is vague, the point itself would appear to be valid.

Another Familist, "E. R.," the author of one of several letters
sent to Rogers responding to the first edition of his *Displaying of
an horrible sect of grosse and wicked Heretiques, naming themselves the Family of Love, with the lives of their Authours, and
what doctrine they teach in corners,* and printed in the second
edition of March 1578/79 related an account of his life that also
suggests a seeking attitude, comparing the rival claims of different
groups and writers. "I haue read many authours bookes within
this 35, or 36, yeares. . . ."[74] He was "not ignoraunt of the Lande
of strife and contention that ye walke in"—presumably a reference
to the mutual anathematizing that had pushed Vitel into the arms
of Niclaes—and had "wandered vppe and downe there ouerlong,
and consumed much time there about, to my great greefe and sor-
rowe. . . ."[75] The writer, whoever he was, seems to have had a
background in religious activism of a radical type prior to joining
the Family of Love.

Alastair Hamilton, the recent historian of Familism, has commented on "the marked dichotomy between the confession made
by individuals before justices of the peace and ecclesiastical authorities, and the printed apologies and replies to Puritan attacks."[76] This dichotomy he attributes to the difference between
the "unsophisticated interpretations" of ordinary Familists interrogated in the late 1570s, and the skillfully constructed defenses of
the "Familist elite." There is undoubtedly something in this distinction. However, the fact that the former sometimes differed mark-
edly, not only from the latter, but from the teachings of Niclaes
himself (insofar as Niclaes's teachings are susceptible of reduction
to uncluttered propositions at all!), suggests that English Familism
was less monolithic than its apparent fixation on the person of
Niclaes would suggest, and perhaps that it took at least some of its
support from undercurrents of English radicalism which antedated
Familism and continued to survive within it.

The confession of Leonard Romsey is a case in point. Although,
as Hamilton points out, "it is hard to resist the feeling either that
he was speaking with deliberate malice or . . . that his statements
were prompted" by his interrogators, some of his statements do
not bear such obvious hallmarks.[77] Romsey, an apprentice glover
of Wisbech, appears to have had no long prehistory of radicalism,
but to have gleaned his beliefs from the Familist group which recruited him in the 1570s, and principally from his master, John
Bourne, whom he seems to have been determined to damage as

much as possible. These beliefs included the doctrine that "Christ did not receive flesh of the virgin Mary," "that there is no resurrection of the body after the natural death thereof," and that hell is "no other thing but the grief of conscience in this life."[78] Niclaes did not explicitly teach these doctrines; though the flat mortalism of Romsey and his fellows has no documented English parallel outside the circles of Familism, Monophysite Christology had a long history in English radicalism, and the (implicit) denial of hell had a precedent in the writings of William Laurence and John Barre.[79]

The confession of Thomas Chaundeler and Robert Sterete on 28 May 1561 at Guildford also indicates a less than simple origin for Familism in England.[80] These two men belonged to a group of radicals in Surrey; Chaundeler was a clothier of Wonersh and Sterete a clerk of Dunsfold. Their congregation was already in existence "in the beginning of Queen Mary's reign," and the group initially considered it "damnable" to attend the parish churches, "and did excommunicate such of their sect as they knew faltered therein."[81] In this they were in line with some of the underground Protestant churches, and with groups such as the free-willers. However,

one year after [i.e. in 1554?] they were changed from that opinion openly declaring to their brethren that they were all bound to come to the church and to do outwardly all such things as the law required . . . although inwardly they did profess the contrary.[82]

A similar shift toward Nicodemism is evidenced by the abandonment of the group's original opposition to the bearing of weapons: "at the length, perceiving themselves to be noted and marked for the same, they have allowed the bearing of staves."[83] This Nicodemism may have several sources: it may be a strain of Lollard nonseparatism reasserting itself, or have its origin in contacts with one of the forms of Continental Anabaptism, or be evidence of Niclaes's early influence upon the group. It might also be a purely local response to the practical pressures created by strict separatism, with the appeal to "submit yourselves to the ordinance of the higher powers" as a rationalization of the change in policy. One practice, the refusal to "say 'God speed,' 'God morrow,' or 'God even,' but to those that be of their sect and to others they say 'speed,' 'morrow,' or 'den,'" is strongly reminiscent of Lollard and free-willer refusal to greet "a Synner or a man whome they knowe not."[84] The comprehensive radicalism of these beliefs defies any attempt to locate a single likely source, and suggests an eclectic use of Continental Anabaptist and radical connections. Rogers admitted that "they haue reformed some of these grosse matters since that time," and these reforms were presumably a turning away from their own idiosyncrasies in favor of closer conformity to Niclaes's own teachings.[85] Though Hamilton asserts that "there is little in the doctrine described by Sterete and Chaundeler which corresponds to Niclaesism," the Nicodemism, antipædobaptism, and perfectionism may certainly be laid at the door of Hendrik Niclaes.[86] The other beliefs, however, cannot; Niclaes never taught believers' baptism, while his sin committed against orthodox conceptions of heaven and hell or against Trinitarianism were implicit rather than explicit, and resulted from his spiritualizing, allegorizing language rather than any flat denials. As Hamilton notes regarding the Surrey sectarians, "there are numerous features . . . far more similar to the Anabaptists than to the Familists. . . . The most we can say, therefore, is that the sectarians of 1561 were ready to receive the Familist doctrine."[87] John Rogers insisted in 1578/79 that the depositions of 1561 were "of one or two of the Familye," but Vitel responded cageily that "what they were, that is that, but of *HN*. his doctrine at that time they knew not," while the Familist letter writer "E. R." insisted more forthrightly that they "are, nor neuer were of the Familie of Loue."[88] "E. R.'s" claim was less than truthful, but Vitel may or may not have been lying; Chaundeler and Sterete had reported their knowledge of "Henrike, a Dutchman, the head of all the congregation," who was "permanent in no place, but still wandereth to visit his flock."[89] This may well have been a reference to Niclaes; if so, it could imply that he was actually in England at that time, rather than in the Netherlands. Even if a different "Henrike" was being referred to, however (Dutch influence in radicalism of this type was not insignificant), thereby vindicating Vitel's disclaimer with strict reference to 1561, nevertheless, as Rogers retorted, "this is certain, one of them [Chaundeler and Sterete] is liuing, & knoweth you but to well, and is a welwiller to your Family, and scoller of Allin."[90] Several months previously, in his second edition of *The Displaying of an horrible secte of . . . the Familie of Love,* Rogers had claimed that both informants were still alive, and his modification probably reflects information received in the interim; Allin, on the other hand, was an elder of the group in 1561, was known to Rogers as an activist and propagator of Familism in the 1570s, and, as a "neare neighbour" of the Surrey men (he was from Wonersh), "did more instructe them, and lead them forward into your error," before dying "soudenly by the high way, going to Farnam to be examined before ye bishop of Winchester."[91] Chaundeler and Sterete, or at least the survivor of the two, clearly reverted to heresy after 1561; it would appear unlikely that the congregation of which they were a part was destroyed by their revelations to the authorities. In sum, it seems certain that this ultraradical group, whose ideas included rationalistic, Anabaptist, and spiritualist elements, was drawn inevitably into the Familist ambit, and that this process was moderately advanced as early as 1561.

That there were in England during the 1550s and early 1560s groups whose eclectic doctrinal radicalism might well make them prone to such a development is illustrated by the Arians encountered by John Philpot in the King's Bench prison in 1555. According to Philpot, the two men in question not only denied the deity of Christ and of the Holy Spirit, but espoused perfectionism and believers' baptism.[92] They apparently practiced Nicodemism to some extent; at least Philpot complained that they evangelized "in corners and dens," and compared this habit unfavorably with the apostles, who preached openly despite persecution.[93] They seem to have anticipated Familist emphases on the need for a secret and esoteric knowledge given only to the illumined.

When the scriptures be so clearly alleged against them that they have not what to say, these be their foolish answers, . . . —if ye were of us, ye should perceive more than ye do. Thus under the pretence of a hidden secret, which they say is revealed unto them above all other, they would, through curiosity, have men to call their faith in doubt, and so to deny the same.[94]

Like their second-century Gnostic predecessors, they allegedly denied the Old Testament to be of any authority, thus taking the common radical emphasis on the New Testament to an extreme conclusion.[95] The doctrines imputed to these men by Philpot, though startling in their radicalism, are so similar to many of those confessed by Chaundeler and Sterete six years later that Philpot's veracity might well be considered vindicated by that fact alone. If the martyr's unwelcome prison fellows were not members of the congregation to which Chaundeler and Sterete belonged six years later, they certainly seem to have been a part of a similar group, which would, for the same reasons as the Surrey congregation, have been disposed to receive Niclaes's doctrine as it was disseminated.

The Licentious Doctrine: Predestination and the Familists

A certain ambivalence discernible among the Elizabethan English Familists concerning the doctrine of predestination may also indicate that, for some of them at least, their proneness to radicalism lay in an unease with exactly those facets of magisterial Protestantism that had brought many of the mid-Tudor radicals to prominence. One might, perhaps, expect from a movement such as Niclaes's a definite, even if not necessarily prominent, doctrine of predestination; mystical movements without strong doctrines of ecclesiastical separation from the world had traditionally tended to teach that the elect were chosen rather than choosing. The *Cloud of Unknowing* had assumed this, as had other medieval mystical works.[96] G. H. Williams, observing that not all of the European radicals rejected predestination, explains that the predestinarian sector consisted chiefly of "spiritualist Rationalists," such as Camillo Renato, Johannes Baptista Italus, and the followers of Faustus Socinus.[97] Concerning this type of predestinarian view found "here and there" among "radical Italian Evangelicals," he points out that

> back in Italy, rebaptism could never have become ecclesiologically constitutive in a loose Catholic context. . . . "Classical" (Germanic) Anabaptism . . . presupposed either a predestinarian, solafideist state church or the old Catholic Church fiercely defended by Hapsburg princes and Catholic leagues.[98]

The "loose Catholic context" that existed in pre-Tridentine (and early post-Tridentine) Italy prevailed also, of course, in the Erasmian-influenced Netherlands.

In point of fact, a mildly expressed predestinarianism is found in Niclaes's writings. The claim that it was for "his Chosens-sake" that God had "shortened the Dayes," and the frequent references to "vs Littleons and God-his Elect" certainly suggest predestinarian assumptions.[99] According to Niclaes, not all those who heard the Familist message were true disciples, but only "those which . . . are touched; by yᵉ Lordes Grace; in their Inwardnes: and to whom it is likewise graunted to see-into or to knowe their

Sinnes."[100] God would manifest himself by "his Elect Saints, . . . his chosen."[101] These disciples, added Tobias, Niclaes's fellow-elder, could be assured that "the Lord . . . forsaketh not [his] Elect."[102] These allusions, of course, are more suggestive than definite in respect to predestinarianism, but then the same could be said of almost all Familist teachings.

Whence, then, the supposedly general opposition among English Familists to the doctrine of predestination? William Wilkinson based his claim for free-willer paternity of English Familism partly on the charge that "neither cā this Louely Family abide the most blessed and comfortable doctrine of Predestination."[103] By way of evidence, he cited the single extant remark to which such an accusation could have been attributable. This was an aside made in a letter to John Rogers from his Familist critics, which lamented that "at this present your [i.e., Rogers's] brethren in Christ (for their good faithes cause they haue in your licentious doctrine of predestination and free election) fill all the prisons almost in England."[104] The implication was that a belief in ineluctable predestination inevitably encouraged crimes both moral and civil, since the elect were saved, do what they would, and the reprobate were damned, do what they might. The same letter spoke of Rogers and his ilk as "you free ones or Lybertines."[105] A further letter from the Familists took a step back from these accusations, and was more conciliatory in tone. This pleaded

> for our minde concerning Gods predestination, take vs not therein so short, for we allowe of it simplie and reuerently, in his kinde; and yet further also, euen as the holie Scriptures allowe the same; but wee like not to contende therin, nor desperatly to seeke libertie of life thereby, neither foolishly to serch therein for things aboue our capacities.[106]

This is a vague statement, of course, and as it preceded a passage purporting to describe Familist views of justification in terms that were suspiciously orthodox, it may simply have been intended as an answer to turn away wrath. As Rogers complained,

> in your letters you shewe your dislyking of such doctrine [predestination], terming it licentious[.] Is not this deep dissembling, and yet call it plaine dealing? I would not haue you . . . set downe pointes of doctrine agreeable with vs, and say it is your confession of faith, where you conceale the cheefe matters in variance between vs.[107]

Even so, the same letter from the Familists had, in a less obviously diplomatic passage, included sentiments which, if not exactly predestinarian, at least expressed the Reformed idea of the convert as one "wrought upon" by divine grace.

> Wee will not go about to conuince you by the testimonies of holy Scriptures, for that lyeth not in our power, neither were wee so dealt withall. It is the Lord (by his grace) that hath conuinced vs, if he also conuince you, then are ye rightly conuinced, and so the praise thereof appertayneth onely vnto him.[108]

Probably the first letter was from but one individual Familist acting on his own account, for he signed himself, "Your vnknowen friend," while the later one seems to have come from a (presumably more authoritative) group; "we" and "our" are frequently used and the letter is concluded with "Your louers and friends. F. L."[109] However, even the diplomatic "allowing" of the doctrine of predestination is sufficiently muted to betray a degree of unhappiness with the full rigor of Puritan expressions of it. The attack on its "licentious" nature, whatever the status within Familism of the attacker, shows that, for some Familists at least, some of the old sources of radical discontent with magisterial Protestantism remained; such dissidents would certainly, two decades earlier, have been sympathetic to the free-willer cause. In sum, Niclaes himself and the Family of Love in general appear to have had no hard-and-fast line on the issue of predestination, though their mystical approach inclined them slightly in its favor. However, the English adherents they collected were to some degree those who had been attracted by the participatory aspects of Protestantism while repelled by parts of its formal theology, such as predestination. If there is no evidence of real continuity between midcentury free-will radicalism and Elizabethan Familism, the movements were at least tapping some of the same kind of impulses among the religiously active and inquiring. In this, strictly limited, sense, the insinuations of Wilkinson and the "coniecture" of Rogers concerning English Familist origins may not have been too far wide of the mark.

The Dutch Connection

A further qualification needs to be mentioned in regard to any continuity between earlier indigenous radicalism and Elizabethan Familism, however: the Dutch influences upon, and presence within, the latter were very considerable. Alastair Hamilton has detected possible Familist connections among a number of Dutch and other Continental merchants and scholars in London during Elizabeth's reign. He admits that his evidence is inconclusive, warning that "if the Flemish merchant scholars residing in London ever did believe in Familism it was . . . humanist Familism," in contrast to the "Familism of the English communities," which "may have owed a debt to Lollardy" and to other earlier "nonconformity."[110] But, even if there were two types of Familism, they can hardly have been entirely unconnected. In respect to the leadership and the prophetic, even messianic, role accorded to Niclaes himself, the leading figures in England seem to have been either Dutch or with strong Dutch connections. Chaundeler and Sterete, who laid bare the dealings of the Surrey group in 1561, mentioned not only "Henrike, a Dutchman, the head of all the congregation," who, as has been already noted, may well have been Niclaes, but also another Dutchman, "a shoemaker that followeth the court, . . . he is an elder."[111] Vitel himself seems to have been either Dutch or of Dutch extraction. Rogers, addressing him, stated that "I am informed, you are of the Dutch race your selfe," and sneered that his activities in bringing heresy "to our countrye, and translating the bookes, . . . was not done lyke . . . a true English harted man."[112] Even so, he claimed to have "heard you at Paules Crosse recant the blasphemies of Arrius doctrine" nearly two decades before, and if he required information from a third party as to Vitel's Dutch origins, then Vitel's English must have been sufficiently fluent and free of a telltale accent, even at that date, for Rogers not to have noticed anything unusual in that regard.[113] If Vitel was a first-generation immigrant, he was no recent arrival. Finally, the Dutch-ness of Niclaes's writings (not to say the double-Dutch-ness!) was consciously retained in Vitel's translations. Vitel admitted that "I haue geuen forth certayne bookes, which are translated word for word as neare as we could, out of the bookes of HN."[114] That Vitel's translations of Niclaes were intended to be word for word can hardly be in doubt; the English works are extremely cumbersome to read, abounding in hyphenated words ("raised-vpp," "bring-in," "of-one-minde," "for-that-cause," "wonderful-woorkes," and "chosens-sake"), which reflect single words in the Dutch. Rogers reported that Familist leaders attempted to justify to him the "darke speeche" of the writings and the frequent absence of "matter in the Authour, that may bee drawen into argument," by arguing "that the Authour hath written in the Dutch tongue, which wanteth his grace and eloquence beeing turned into our rude Englishe."[115] On this evidence, it rather sounds as if the Familists with whom Rogers had discussed the matter might have been Dutch themselves. The advantages (according to the Familists) and the barbarousness (according to Rogers) of the Dutch language, and of things Dutch, frequently became an issue of contention in the debate between the two sides.[116]

In summary, then, it must be said that the origins of English Familism seem to have sprung from more than one source. The influence of Hendrik Niclaes himself was clearly preeminent, particularly once his books had been translated and published in the mid-1570s. Prior to this, his ideas seem to have been spread by Dutch disciples, and particularly by Christopher Vitel. But the indigenous recruiting ground seems to have included people who might previously have been prone to involvement in, or even actually committed to, one or other of the earlier radical groups in England, certainly including those who, like Vitel himself, had formerly leaned toward rationalism or Arianism, and perhaps not excluding separating free-willers.

*　　*　　*

Familism and the Problem of Religious Authority

If the message of the Family of Love found answering chords in some who had had previous contacts with religious radicalism in England, what of the generality of its recruits? It does seem that many of them were converted from Protestantism, a point not entirely unworthy of remark when it is remembered that the population of Elizabeth's England was Protestant more in name than in fact, and that traditional beliefs and practices remained strong, particularly in the first half of the reign. "The greatest greefe that I can conceiue against ye nouices of the Family," John Rogers lamented, lapsing as he did so into a somewhat cloudy style reminiscent of Niclaes himself, "is that some of them haue beene professours of Christ Jesus Gospel according to the brightness thereof, which . . . he hath reuealed in this latter age most plenteously."[117] The recruits to Familism had left "the certainty of doctrine which once they so earnestly imbraced."[118] It is possible, of course, that this last remark of Rogers is unduly euphemistic concerning popular devotion to the teachings of the official church, but his personal contacts with individual Familists appear to have been so extensive that it more likely reflects his actual knowledge of the histories of those individuals, and that these had been convinced Protestants.

The religious conflicts in England certainly appear to have exacted a toll in the dispositions of some who were later to join the Family of Love. The "certainty of doctrine" so apparent to Rogers may have given way to doubts in many minds as the frequent changes in the religious complexion of the established church during the mid-Tudor period were followed by the Elizabethan disputes within that establishment over church polity. The long-term effect of authority speaking with several conflicting voices is not only the creation of confusion, but also the fatal undermining of that authority. The proliferation and conflicts of competing orthodoxies were apt to make many turn in disillusionment in a spiritualistic direction, as had occurred on the Continent with those who accepted the ideas of men such as Caspar Schwenckfeld and Sebastian Franck, as the Münster débâcle had affected Obbe Philips, and as renewed religious conflict and uncertainty in seventeenth-century England were to facilitate the rise of Seekers and Quakers. John Rogers noted of the English Familists that "nothing is heard more common in their mouthes, then these tearmes, ye are at variaunce amongst yourselues: no vnitie of doctrine is obserued: ye are of diuers opinions and sectes."[119] Rogers's Familist correspondent, "E. R.," remarked in the same vein, "I am not ignorant of the Lande of strife and contention that ye walke in . . . I haue wandered vppe and downe there ouerlong."[120] Vitel, too, purported to be appalled at the way in which "euery one would haue right, and be the comminaltye of Christ, and condemned all others."[121] There are at least two kinds of response that the devout might make to such a realization. The former is the repudiation of all kinds of dogmatism, and a refusal to give unqualified acceptance to any professing "true church"; this, in general, was the response of the groups and individuals mentioned, and amounts to a kind of "devout agnosticism" in the face of competing claims. By the nature of the case, these have been organizationally so loose that only the Quakers have flourished as an ongoing group. The second response is that more usually associated with the modern cult; the implicit assertion that, in a world of competing truth claims, almost anything might be true, and the rise of a new organization claiming to be the entirely authoritative vehicle for proclaiming an esoteric truth of its own. The paradoxical nature of the Family of Love is that it amounted to a manifestation of both these impulses. Vitel's account of his conversion sums up the contradiction perfectly: although he professed to be saddened at the way in which every church "condemned all others for heretickes, and false Christians," yet "thē saw I, that all people vpon earth which were without the house of Loue, were all wrapped in vnbeliefe."[122] This contradiction, on the one hand the spiritualizing enterprise that evacuated dogma of much of its content, and on the other the authoritarian, messianic role accorded to Niclaes and the exclusive claims made for the group, are a distinctive, perhaps even a unique, feature of the Family of Love.

Dark Speeches: The Spiritual Meaning of Scripture

To deal with the spiritualizing first: Rogers noted that "there is no matter in the Authour [i.e., in Niclaes], that may bee drawen into argument, but . . . it seemeth to be as a riddle, or darke speeche."[123] The accusation of "no matter" was hyperbole, of course; Rogers had set himself to tackle, not harmless rambling, but what he saw as a serious outbreak of actual heresy requiring refutation. But it was heresy hidden in an outer pulp of "darke speeches" of Niclaes "that we simple ones can not vnderstand; and no mauell [sic], for surely I doubte he vnderstandeth not him selfe."[124] Niclaes did not actually say that doctrinal content was unimportant; he expressed, in his usual misty fashion, the idea that the literal reading of the Scripture was inferior to the spiritual. "No man," he wrote,

> how wyse or vnderstanding soeuer hee be, in the Knowledge of the Scriptures; can by any-meanes comprehend or vnderstand the Wisdom of God • nor-yet see, knowe, finde, nor receaue, the Guiftes of God . . . but onlie they, that stand goodwillinglie and obedientlie sub-mitted, vnder the Woorde of Life. . . .[125]

Those who trust in a literal understanding of the Scripture "haue not out of their litterall Knowledge, vnderstoode the secreat minde of God."[126] John Knewstub, adding his own contribution to the flurry of anti-Familist literature pouring from Puritan pens in the late 1570s, pointed out that Niclaes substituted "is" for the Creed's "was" when saying that Christ "is conceiued of the holie Ghost."[127] This he attributed to a belief in Niclaes that every time someone becomes a Familist Christ is conceived. While such an explanation is certainly possible, the tendency to use the present tense is more probably due to the mystical impulse to dehistoricize the Christian verities, removing the facts of the redemption story from their spatial and temporal locations in order to heighten the awareness of them as present realities. Rogers noted with concern that "the history of Christ his birth: hys miracles, passion, death resurrection &c. They regard not, but allegoris vppon euery part thereof most daungerously and vngodly, . . . making no accompt of the history."[128] Niclaes declared that "the holy Spirit of Loue . . . teacheth and declareth" to the elect

> all what was spoken vnto them in time-past; concerning the Trueth; as Parables or Similitude. For in times-past (thewhiles [sic] . . . was yet . . . the Vaile; which is the Flesh of *Christ;* still before the Cleernes of the Face of God and *Christ*) they coulde not endure Thatt which is the Cleernes of the holy Gost it self.[129]

This is spiritualism, in which past revelation is parabolic and the historical Christ of flesh and blood is but a veil which we are called to see beyond. The step from such a mystic position to actual denial of the historicity of the details of the redemptive drama is, perhaps, a short one, and the Familists' Puritan critics were ever on the lookout for signs that it had been made.

The cloudiness of Niclaes's style of writing made him less vulnerable to accusations of actually denying orthodox doctrines than the more plain-speaking, less wary, ordinary Familist whom Rogers, Wilkinson, and Knewstub encountered. This did not deter attempts to pin such charges on him, but it did make them less plausible when they were made. Knewstub, for example, felt that he had proved, at different points in his own work, that Niclaes held Christ to be "no man, but an estate of men"; not God; the second birth; "the oldest Father in the familie of loue"; and the doctrine of perfection.[130] In all cases, Knewstub was applying criteria more suitable to the Ramist logic that was becoming popular in Reformed circles than to what he admitted was the "bastardly broode of Allegories" that constituted Niclaes's language.[131] Citing the account of the incarnation in Niclaes's *Evangelivm Regni. A Joyfull Message of the kingdom,* Knewstub professed certainty that "Christ with H.N. is the head of Abrahams faith, but not of Abrahams, [sic] flesh, which opinion oeuethroweth [sic] his humanitie."[132] It is far from clear that this proves anything of the sort, but both here and elsewhere in his work Knewstub appears to have been determined, on feeble evidence, to find Monophysitism.[133] Similarly, he insisted with weak logic that Niclaes's teaching that all true believers partake of Christ's divine nature amounted to Pelagianism.[134] Even he conceded that, though "ye see this horrible heresie of Pelagius to be reuiued agayne by H.N. and his family," the heresy was propounded "somewhat subtilly for feare of beyng espied."[135] Too subtly, one suspects, for most. If other aspects of Niclaes's writings lay open to the charge of Pelagianism, this appearance of it was such that few readers but Knewstub could espy it.

Other passages in Niclaes appear remarkably orthodox: near the beginning of his *Dicta HN. Documentall Sentences* he used an unmistakably Trinitarian formula in speaking of God, while in the *Evangelivm Regni* he gave an account of the atonement which, though inevitably confusing, seems to be within a stone's throw of orthodoxy.

> Through Christ, and through his Service in the Beleef, God hath . . . manifested and accomplished the true Offering; to the Forgeeuenes of Sinnes | and to an euerlasting Attonement of ye Generation of Mankinde; in the Holie.[136]

The marginal references here are to Isa. 53, Heb. 9 and 10, and the passion narratives in the Gospels of Matt. and Mark. Whether these encouraging passages of Niclaes really signified the orthodoxy they implied is, as with so much that he and his followers said and wrote, open to question. Rogers confessed himself confused, for example, as to what actual content the Familists gave to the word *Loue*, since sometimes they used it in a way that appeared to mean God, sometimes Christ, at other times "your wholl doctrin and profession," and on yet other occasions it seemed to signify a "property or vertue proceeding frō God."[137] Rogers was right to be confused. Much of Niclaes's writing seems almost to have been designed to elude reduction to concrete propositions. This is true even down to details; "why they vse this pronoune [']the['], so much," Rogers complained, "I cānot well vnderstand."[138] To glance even cursorily at the literature with which he had to deal is to sympathize with him.

If Niclaes was hard to convict of heretical denials (though he made heretical affirmations), some of his English followers were more garrulous. "Confidently to beleue the truth of the history" recorded in the Scripture, reported an appalled John Rogers "(they say) is to abide in the letter which killeth."[139] Some of the heresies mentioned by Knewstub at the beginning of his book are recorded in a way that suggests they were gleaned from conversation rather than from Niclaes's books.[140] Two of the Familists examined by the bishop of Ely in 1580 confessed to having held heretical views on the resurrection of the body: the illiterate Margaret Colevill, described as "widow and gentlewoman," "confessed . . . that the body did arise again in this life, and that the wicked should not rise again in their bodies unto condemnation," while John Bourne, the Wisbech glover, "confessed that he had erred about the resurrection of the flesh."[141] The orthodox articles that they and their fellows were required to subscribe to, after their examinations, laid great stress on the corporeal, historical nature of the details of the story of Redemption, suggesting that the denial of these things had been prominent in their interrogations.[142] Knewstub, warning his readers against the exegetical practices of the Familists, denied that any place in the Scripture could be "vrged, in an Allegoricall sence, vnlesse the same taken litterally, and in the Grammaticall sence, shall establish some thing repugnant, eyther to faith, or Charitie."[143] The irony in the fact that such an argument should be employed by this upholder of the established church against sectaries is delicious; he might have disallowed Knewstub's qualifying phrases, but the sentiment expressed would otherwise have gladdened the heart of John Champneys.

The Lord His Elected Minister:
The Authority of Hendrik Niclaes

Wilkinson reported that some Familists with whom he had conferred "affirmed, that the scripture is hard for a simple mā, and therefore the bookes of HN. do make an easie passage, and geue a readyer [= readier?] way to the vnderstanding thereof."[144] Niclaes supplied that which leaders of cults have continued to provide their followers: a resolution of the problems of interpreting the Scripture in the form of an authoritative interpretation. As the Familists themselves stated in a letter which Wilkinson published, Niclaes was being used as an instrument of God "(accordyng to his promises written in the Scriptures) all controuersies growne among men about their misunderstanding of the scriptures to bryng ye same to an end."[145] Proceeding from this belief with flawless logic, they asked: "What iniurie were it (seing that it procedeth by the same spirite) to valew it [i.e., Niclaes's work] equall with those same sacred scriptures."[146] Niclaes implied that his own work was to be regarded as on a level with the Scriptures, he himself being a mouthpiece for the "liuing Voyce" of Christ.[147] The Scriptures testified to Niclaes and his message; more ordinary methods of exegesis were to be rejected, for it was "meere Lies or vntrue, what such Scripture-learned; through the knowledge which they get out of the Scripture; bring-in, institute, preach, and teach."[148] Despite his repudiation of the "Scripture-learned" (an expression which recalls the pejorative "Schriftgelehrten" so beloved by Thomas Müntzer),

Niclaes employed an average of about ten marginal Scripture references per page in his *Evangelivm Regni*. The Scripture was not so much to be rejected as to be subordinated to the authority of its truly authoritative interpreter. The real value of the use of the Scripture seems to have lain, for Familists, in the spiritual authority of the exegete. True Christianity was to be expounded only "by Them that are chosen or raysed-vp thervnto by God."[149] Who such a chosen one might be hardly needed to be said; to anyone with any initiation at all into the sect, the answer was obvious.

These are classic cult tactics, of course. In our own day, one of the cults has refrained from informing new converts that its leader is the Messiah, preferring to present the "evidence," and to leave the initiates to draw the irresistible conclusion for themselves. Perhaps, as with some modern selling techniques, such conclusions are held to the more tenaciously if one feels that in attaining them the last step, at least, has been made alone. Similarly John Bourne, the Wisbech glover, confessed in 1580 that the "obscureness of the doctrine must not be declared unto them by any conference with men, but revealed unto them from God, and to be found and understood among themselves."[150] Even so, the open claims made for Niclaes and his personal authority were certainly very great. Tobias, one of his fellow-elders in the Family, warned that no one should presume to oppose Niclaes "because God the Father with his Son *Jesus Christ,* dwelleth and liveth perfectly in *H.N.* in the heavenly being . . . and that no man without the fellowship of *H.N.* or without the obedience of the requiring of his doctrine" could come to God.[151]

Wilkinson claimed to have been told by some of the Family that new recruits had their Bibles taken away from them for a time by the elders, and were given Niclaes's works to read.[152] Presumably the idea was to ensure that Niclaes's spectacles were, so to speak, firmly placed over the proselyte's eyes before his access to the Scripture was resumed. The teachings of the prophet were to dispel doubt, and to provide certainty and inner quiet. Rogers noted that any inquiry of Familists as to why they allowed themselves to be recruited brought forth a tale of "marueilous conflicts, much trouble and vexation of minde, and could neuer attaine any quietnes, vntill by the doctrine of H.H. [*sic!*] they found rest vnto their soules."[153] This may have been a stock answer (Vitel had testified similarly concerning himself),[154] but it does seem that the Family of Love was meeting a spiritual need that the Puritans were missing, and that this need concerned the area of religious authority. As has just been noted, Wilkinson was told "that the Scripture is hard for a simple mā," and that Niclaes's works provided "a read-yer way to the vnderstanding therof" in order to "bring controuer-sies . . . to an end."[155] Niclaes himself declared that argumentative souls with a good knowledge of the Scriptures "did daylie increase; to a more Intangling; with much Contending and Disputation of Christ and his Services and Ceremonies."[156] The observation seems tailor-made in view of the vestiarian and presbyterian dis-putes in England, and would certainly have rung true to many people. Niclaes continued: "many goodwilling heartes . . . searched the Scripture . . . and sighed and prayed vnto God" in confusion, but now—and what was most to the point—God had "heard the Sighing and Prayer of the Poore | and for his Chosens-sake" had "raised-vpp Mee HN" to proclaim the truth.[157] To de-scribe the prophet's works as an actual explanation of the Scrip-ture, however, might be to invite ridicule; the most amusing statement in the writings of Niclaes, who does not appear to have been given overmuch to humor, is perhaps the summary at the end of his *Evangelivm Regni*. "I suppose that this groundlie Instruction and inconfutable declaration, is sufficient | for to satisfie throughlie all Vnderstndinges, which loue the Trueth!"[158] Whatever it was in his readers that derived satisfaction from studying Niclaes's works, their understanding must have been the least of it. That which has, in Rogers's words, "no matter . . . that may bee drawen into argument" is inconfutable by definition. Niclaes's followers, of course, saw the murkiness of their hero's literary output in a differ-ent light.

> Whereas ye finde fault at the obscuritie and darcknes of the Authors writyng, I might aunswere that it might seem so much the more to be the same, that it geueth forth it selfe for (*videl,* a worke proceedyng from the spirite of the Lord). . . .[159]

The obscure nature of the books was itself testimony to their divine inspiration; the wisdom of the wise was, after all, to be destroyed.

The existence of a personality cult around Niclaes is unmistak-able, and it extended beyond mere reverence for his writings. Rogers was horrified that the Familists with whom he came into contact appeared to believe that Niclaes "hath onely the truth: and all the world else seduced and deceiued."[160] Some believed their leader to know all languages, as well as having the biblical gift of the word of knowledge, telling an arriving messenger what his message was before he could open his mouth to deliver it.[161] John Bourne gave his name on a piece of paper to an elder by the name of Jones, who promised to pass it on to Niclaes. The latter would "register him in the book of life" (a—for the Family—unusually literalist conception!), and this Bourne believed to have been done.[162] The problem was not the uniqueness of such messianic claims; they had been made before. Rogers cited a man by the name of More from Sussex and one Ellis Hall of Manchester who had pretended to a similar role in recent decades.[163] These two, however, had been shut up as lunatics; the trouble with Niclaes was that he was believed. The constant use of the initials "H.N." to refer to him was not without significance; according to Rogers, some Familists intimated that the letters stood for "Homo Novus."[164] Others wrote to him in February or early March 1578/79 in more mysterious vein, stating that just as Christ's name "is shadowed by two carecters A.O." so "there is some meaning, more then you or wee can well tell, in these two carecters H.N."[165] Rogers declined to be unnerved by this revelation, and his comment, that "you must deuise some hidden secretes, whereby to cary a shew of profound matter" is almost certainly a correct analysis of the real impulse behind the making of such claims.[166] The same letter denied that "wee slyly meane H.N. by [sic] the white stone spoken of in the Apocalips," but contended that the reference was to "all such as ouercome in that battaile, and not by any one particularly."[167] Was it the stone they took as referring to all overcomers, or the initials? The meaning is, probably deliberately, unclear. The Familists were masters at the game of appearing to agree with those who opposed them while in fact continuing to dissent. To debate with them was frequently to chase the wind. The separatist leader Henry Ainsworth, writing in 1608, grumpily, but perhaps not unreasonably, concluded concerning "H.N." that the "mystical letters may rightly be read Ha Nachash, that is | The Serpent" of Genesis 3.1.[168]

Some of the cultlike traits of English Familism have already been referred to in passing. The Familists practiced, both through the kind of debating ploys just mentioned, and in their Nicodemism, what one modern cult has euphemistically called "heavenly deception." Some of their other practices bring modern analogies to mind. Elidad, one of the chief elders, forbade members to debate with outsiders in general and with former, or lapsed, Familists in particular.[169] John Bourne confessed that "whosoever cometh to the Family of Love must forget all that he had learned before."[170] Like the restriction on reading the Scripture until a convert had been familiarized with Niclaes's works, the idea seems to have been to isolate members ideologically to some extent from their environment. Understandably in an organization which laid such stress on the spiritual authority mediated through its leader, it was perhaps felt that, to make converts steadfast in their adherence, more was needed than simple reliance on the inner assurance that an individual's relationship with God might bring. Niclaes warned against those who, having obtained and read some of the Familist writings, refused to be incorporated into the organization, but set themselves up as independent teachers; these were "false Brethren" with "vncleane vngodlie Heartes."[171] Clearly, it was affiliation to God's organization, not the correct belief, that made one godly by Familist criteria. As some Familists put it to Rogers, "there is no Catholick church nor comminaltye of Saintes but the Familye of Loue."[172]

The tension between these exclusivist claims and the spiritualizing, dogma-evacuating tendencies discussed earlier, cannot be better illustrated than by placing the former alongside some of the opening remarks of Niclaes's *Evangelivm Regni*.

> Vnto the Louers of the Trueth, . . . of what Nation and Religion soeuer they be | Christians | Jewes | Mahomites or Turkes | and Heathen. . . . Let euery Nation then haue among them, so many-maner of Groundes | Beleefes | Religions | Ceremonies | and Seruices, as they will | wherin they loue God-his Trueth | and the Righteousnes.[173]

It is not the call for religious toleration that stands in tension with Familist exclusivism. The adherence to the former tenet (which will be considered in a moment) was repeatedly affirmed, and is in any case consistent with the Familists' willingness to attend the services of whatever religion might be established by law. But the admission that in these men might "loue God-his Trueth | and the Righteousnes" comports ill with the claim toward the end of the same work that "who assembleth him not vnto us . . . he shall . . . beare the Burden of his Damnation," or that "they shall . . . all perrish, which remaine . . . with-out the Communialitie of his Loue."[174] In all likelihood, the winsomeness at the beginning of the book and the authoritarian claims at the end, were paradigmatic of many adherents' journey into the Family. Perhaps the elders would have had an (unintelligible) explanation of the paradox; consistency was not the Family's strong point.

The Membership

How many people joined the Family of Love? Rogers was told "by some of the same fellowship" that there were "at the least

1000" in England, an estimate he appeared to accept.[175] If this was the Familists' own estimate, however, conventional wisdom would disregard the "at least" and take the thousand as an absolute maximum. But the volume and range of Familist literature available in English from the mid-1570s needs to be borne in mind, and could suggest a larger number; the Familists, being the devious creatures they were, may have been anxious to play down, rather than play up, their true strength. Thomas Chaundeler and Robert Sterete, the Surrey men interrogated in 1561, indicated that their proto-Familist organization existed in the Isle of Ely, Essex, Berkshire, Sussex, Surrey, Hampshire, Devonshire, and London.[176] The first of these areas was certainly a cause for concern to the authorities at the end of the 1570s. Richard Cox, bishop of Ely, was told in September 1579 that in the isle of Ely and elsewhere in the diocese, "common fame reporteth, that dayly those swarmes [of Familists] increase," and that such developments would finally cause great religious disturbance, "as it hath already begonne in diuers places."[177]

The reports of the Family's antagonists are not always consistent concerning the social standing of the generality of recruits. On the one hand the elders are described as being generally weavers, basket-makers, musicians, bottle-makers, and others who made their living by traveling around, while their converts were "certayne vnlearned country people," most likely "some simple husbandman whose wealth is greater then his wit, and his wit greater then a care to keepe him selfe vp right in God his truth and sincere Religion." On the other hand, Knewstub lamented that no consolation could be drawn from supposing "that they are of the rascall sort," since "it is not generally true: these shamelesse dogges thrusting themselues (for a fatter soppe) into houses of great wealth."[178] It seems to have been agreed that the Family of Love was predominantly rural. This was a feature Familism shared with the Lollards, the free-willers and (in the next century) the Quakers, unlike early Protestantism and the various types of pre-Civil War separatism, which were predominantly urban. Whatever else it may have been, English Familism does not appear to have been a movement supported to any significant degree by clergy. Robert Sharpe, the parson of Strethall, Essex, who was examined in December 1574 and recanted at Paul's Cross six months later, seems to have been a lone exception.[179] Despite its rural strength, Familism appears to have recruited largely from those strata of society most prone to religious radicalism and sectarianism, the artificers and tradesmen, many of whom were of moderately independent means. Thomas Chaundeler of Wonersh, interrogated at Guildford in Surrey in 1561, was a clothier, while his fellow, Robert Sterete, was a clerk, "bishop" David Oram was a joiner, and Thomas Allen of Wonersh and John Gryffyne of Lockwood, Essex, were mercers like Niclaes himself.[180] Of the suspected Familists questioned at Wisbech in 1580, two were yeomen (one of whom was described as the wealthiest of the group), while the others whose occupations were given were a barber, a shoemaker, a glover, an oatmeal maker, and a widow who, though illiterate, was described as a "gentlewoman."[181] Vitel had been a joiner.[182]

Probably few, if any, of these were formally educated, and Knewstub commented on "the want of learning in the patrons of these heresies" but the fact that Niclaes's books were so widely and eagerly distributed indicates that most Familists could read.[183] Rogers asserted that Vitel's converts were "sundrie simple men," but when the Familists agreed with him and pleaded for those who had recanted and then relapsed that they were indeed "simple men, who can scarcely reade Englishe," Rogers reversed his position and pointed out that "Sharpe and his companie which recanted at the crosse" (presumably the parson of Strethall) were certainly not simple.[184] In justifying the fact that he himself, the "simplest of many thousandes," had ventured to become involved in the attack upon Familism, an enterprise "more fitter for men of learning, and knowledge," Rogers urged that the Familists' doctrine was "so vayne, and childish, that simple soules, and meanely exersized in holy scripture, are sufficiently instructed by the Lord, to manifest all their abhominations."[185] Clearly, he intended "manifest" to be understood as "make manifest" and the supreme irony of the alternative reading of his sentence was presumably lost on him; most of the English Familists, in all likelihood, were men like Rogers himself, literate, religiously aware, "meanely exersized in holy scripture," but without the formal learning imparted by the universities. In the Familists, Rogers was doing combat with his peers.

Intellect and Gnosis

According to John Knewstub, the Familists substituted a general inspirationism for the learning which they lacked. He sneered that

when simple men such as be artificers, thrust forth themselues . . . to be guides for others vnto God; forthwith that is fathered by the multitude vpon the miraculous and extraordinarie worke of God; and there-

fore they will haue all of them, who haue atteined vnto knowledge by
ordinarie meanes, of necessitie yeelde and giue place to their better
and superiour.[186]

Full weight was given, of course, to Niclaes's "miraculous and
extraordinarie" knowledge, but it does appear that somewhat
lesser, if not entirely dissimilar claims were made for the teaching
of other Familist leaders. Vitel agreed that "none should take in
hād to teach or preach, but the illuminate elders, which are Godded
with God, or incorporated to God, and with whom also, God
in one being and power of his spirite, is hominified, or become
man."[187] Here a typical allegorization of traditional Christian doctrine, in this case of the incarnation, was wedded to the idea of
illuminism. The apostle Paul had received his ministry straight
from Christ and, in any case, "what ministration (that euer was
true) came frō other then Gods owne mouth?"[188] It was a fair
question.

The Familists claimed that it was their elders who were illuminate. Stephen Batman observed three "degrees" within Familism,
with the "cōminalty of the holy ones" at the base, ascending to
the "vpright vnderstandinge ones," and finally to the "illuminate
Elders." Such a hierarchy is consistent with a generally pervasive
gnosticism in the Family. It was through the Family that "the secret
Treasures of God" were revealed; Niclaes's Terra Pacis was "a
secret Lande" that was "knowen of noman [sic], but of his Inhabitants, and of those which com into thesame [sic] and that be assembled with them."[189] The entire style of Familist writing, with its
elusiveness and "dark speeches" was expressive of the notion of
a secret knowledge accessible only to the elect, and even to them
only by degrees. The notion itself was propounded; defending the
proposition that "the truth hath not bene taught in the world since
the Apostles time, but nowe by the Familie," a group corresponding
with Rogers urged ingeniously that, since Christ's kingdom was not
of this world, "how can the trueth be taught, where the kingdom is
not?"[190] Just in case it should occur to their opponents, after they
had regained their breath from this awesome line of argument, that
such reasoning would exclude the Familists too, they hurriedly
tilted the usage of the word *world* to show that the Family of Love
was not actually in it: the truth "hath bene euer hid from the worlde
and her wise, but yet alwayes manifested amongst the outseuered
ones from this world."[191] Moses had shown his ministry only to
the Israelites, Abraham and Lot to their families, the prophets to
"Gods peculier children," and the apostles in private houses; the

argument was used to defend the policy of Nicodemism, but also illustrates the conception of a secret knowledge to which only a chosen few had access.[192]

The illuminism and gnosticism of the Family of Love raises once again in this study, of course, the issue of antiintellectualism. In its attack upon the supremacy of a learned elite, there was an element of continuity with the earlier, midcentury radicalism. But the form which that attack took has no continuity with it whatever. On the contrary, it stands in marked contrast to it. The earlier radicalism had been biblicist to a high degree. There had been little or no suggestion of inspirationism, except perhaps implicitly in the apocalyptic expectations of John Champneys's *Harvest is at Hand*. But he, perhaps more than any of the others, had been anxious to insist that it was "the true literall sence of the holy scriptures" that was to be paramount in determining the shape of Christian faith.[193] The Familists' belief that the truth "hath bene euer hid from the world and her wise" and manifested among the "outseuered ones" picks up, of course, on a theme of the first two chapters of the First Letter to the Corinthians; among the Familists, however, this theme is a pervasive presence. Niclaes rejected, not merely the learned, but also the "Scripture-learned" as being "contentious . . . disordable . . . diuided."[194] The "Masters of the Scripture" were "craftie, subtill, & peruerse of heart . . . darkened in their Vnderstanding."[195] Rogers noted that Niclaes "doth despise such as bring forth any doctrine out of the learnednesse of the Scripture."[196] Niclaes explained that "the scripture lyeth not, but al those which ar not instructed through the spirit of Christ, they lie & . . . expoūd the scripture . . . vpon an earthy or elementish foundation."[197] Instead, he exalted the authority of those who, like him, "God hath graunted . . . to speake wiselie," bringing the truth "to light through H.N. his elected Minister."[198]

During the course of the official Reformation in England, the authority of the Pope had been replaced, ostensibly by that of the Bible but in fact by that of the state. The processes entailed in this change, or rather, in this series of changes from the early 1530s to the end of the 1550s, had involved conflict and debate. These had not disappeared with the Elizabethan settlement, but had continued, and the basis for the existing established church was seen to be as transitory as the political balance of power within the country itself. The undergirding authority of that establishment was seen as flawed. Familism represented one possible response (and with perhaps more, perhaps less, than a mere thousand adherents it was certainly not a particularly weighty response) to that crisis of authority. But it was an option nonetheless. Paradoxically, as has been noted, it held together a "devout agnosticism" in respect to many traditional doctrines with an exclusivist counterauthority of its own. The attack upon the letter of the Bible was an attack upon the chaos of private interpretation in favor of a single authoritative interpretation. This, of course, was every bit as authoritarian as the established churches with which it competed, but with the advantage that the source of the authority was a man illuminated by God, and uncontaminated by the vagaries of political power which so obviously tainted the Protestant state churches.

*   *   *

The Religious Concerns of English Familism

There is some purpose in reiterating that it is "English Familism" which is being discussed here since, although the writings of Hendrik Niclaes must, by the nature of the case, play a central role in any consideration of "what Familists thought," it is the concerns of the Englishmen and women who responded to his teachings that is important in our consideration of the course of English religious radicalism in the sixteenth century. English Familists did not enjoy direct access to Niclaes's writings in their own tongue until the 1570s, and it was shortly after this that the force of the machinery of official suppression was turned against them. Both through the comments of their detractors, particularly John Rogers and William Wilkinson, and through the letters and statements of the English Familists which Rogers published interspersed with his own writings against them, it is possible to glimpse something of their central religious concerns. Many of these concerns are, unsurprisingly, not unrelated to those of other radicals of the mid-Tudor period.

The foremost of these was the fostering and living out of practical, experiential righteousness well beyond that which the official Reformation had succeeded in bringing about. Wilkinson conceded that "this accusatiō in some part be true, that many which professe themselues to be Gospellers . . . haue little list to lyue thereafter: abusing the pretence of the Gospell as a stalking horse to leuell at others by."[199] The allegation of one Familist, that "your licentious doctrine of predestination and free election" has wrought such fatalism and moral complacency among the general population as to "fill all the prisons almost in England," may not have been fully representative of the sect's views on predestination, but furnishes an excellent example of the way in which radicals were dissatisfied with the effect of Reformation teachings upon moral standards.[200] John Rogers's reply to the charge, while not conceding that there was any direct link between official doctrines and moral laxity, is nevertheless illuminating.

> Before the doctrine was set foorth, prisons haue beene full of leude persons, & such as regarde no religion. . . . And although some stumble at the same yet the faulte is not in the doctrin but in the persons, who take it by that part which it is not to be holden by.[201]

A statement coming closer to an admission that the new teachings had had strictly limited effect in promoting practical righteousness would be difficult to find.

William Wilkinson was conceding that the Familists themselves were generally of "godly conversation" when he stated that they "would fayne in lyfe seeme innocent and vnblameable . . . they walkyng very closely do iustifie themselues, because so fewe haue to finde faulte with them."[202] The misbelief of the Familists did not bring inevitable moral collapse in its train. "I know that some honest men of them in lyfe haue confessed vnto me diuers heresies in Religion."[203] Rogers admitted that the "simpler sort" of the Familists were "such as haue a desire to serue the Lord."[204] Wilkinson explained that the lives of many Familists appeared godly enough only because they had learned so to live from "the preachyng of the Gospell, before euer they were infected with HN. his heresie."[205]

The Familists, of course, did not believe this last remark. Niclaes himself seems to have viewed the Protestant doctrine of solafidianism as a veritable license to sin; such, at least, would appear to be the conviction behind his rejection of those who "bost them: they are free, it is all payde."[206] It may have been this or a similar remark that Wilkinson had in mind when he accused Niclaes of charging "the ministry of the Gospel . . . that it engendreth a false freedome or libertie."[207] Vitel responded to the complaint that Familists were "enemies to ye grace of God manifest to vs by Christ Jesus" (meaning, apparently, solafidianism) with a typically deft piece of verbal juggling which left Familist ideas intact while appearing to agree substantially with his opponents. "We confesse that there is no man righteousnes [*sic!*] vntill the Lord deliuer hym from his vnrighteousnesse, and through hys Christ make hym righteous: and then may he say that the Lord is hys righteousnes."[208] What is apparent, even from this obvious subterfuge, is that Vitel favored an experiential realization of righteousness over against the forensic justification of Protestantism. As John Knewstub complained, "to be gilty by the sinne of an other, or to be iustified by the righteousnes of an other, is a doctrine not onely not receiued of them, but throughout all their [the Familists'] bookes impugned."[209]

Niclaes and many who were recruited to the ranks of his Family had a deep respect for the certainties and ceremonial of the old Catholicism. Niclaes thought that "the catholick Church of Rome, hath obedientlie grounded itself on . . . Seruices and Ceremonies," though he insisted, of course, that these were but "figures or the Prefiguration of the true Christianitie."[210] Wilkinson was appalled that Niclaes "sheweth him selfe a frend to Rome."[211] Such friendship was shown by more than mere approval; in his distaste for Protestantism, the arguments of Edwardian conservative critics like John Proctor were being echoed by Niclaes, who wrote that it was "through contention and discorde" that the Protestants had "cast of the Church of Rome, and dyd blaspheme her with her ministries, and of their own braynes pretendyng the Scriptures, haue brought in other ministeries and Religion."[212] John Bourne, the Wisbech glover apprehended for being a Familist in 1580, was required, in the course of his recantation, to affirm that Niclaes "blasphemeth when he defendeth the Church of Rome as the true Catholic Church and accurseth those which have forsaken the same, as revolters from the true church."[213] When Rogers lamented the fact that Niclaes commended Pope and cardinals, the mass and other ceremonies, Vitel responded weakly that "there is none commended, but in their right order, if you marke the matter well," which sounds as close to an admission as to make no difference.[214]

Familist denials that the Pope was Antichrist employed arguments which, while attractive to historians by dint of their modernity, nevertheless pursued the moralistic approach which was such a central concern of the group. Niclaes, in a rare moment of plain speaking, flatly denounced the identification of the Antichrist with the Pope. "Oh, oh, no: the Antichrist is nearer vnto vs, were it wel known. The wisdome of the flesh . . . I say, the wicked nature of the Divil, (wherwith the man is one mind. . . .) is verily that same right Antichrist."[215] Antichrist was no particular man, but was to be identified with what or whoever was against Christ. Wilkinson's Familist friends told him the same. "The man of sinne and childe or broode of the Deuill and cōdemnation (beyng a right aduersarie or an expresse contrary vnto Christ. . . .)" was "raigning in all states of men generally."[216] Their Puritan antagonists did not need to look to Rome to find Antichrist; a glance within would suffice.

If, like most other sectarians, and in common with the Catholics, the Familists were concerned with practical righteousness, they pursued the moralistic direction decisively further than the latter, and also than most of the former, by teaching perfectionism. This was a crucial Familist doctrine constituting, as far as Rogers was concerned, "a principall difference betweene you and vs."[217] As with so many other of their controversial teachings, it was denied, of course. Niclaes assured two Protestant maidens of Warwick on that point.

> Herevpon mought some men say, ye would have the man perfect, No, my beloved, no; I speak not of the perfection of the man, but I speak of the perfectnes which Christ ought to have with the man, before he can be confessed and acknowledged.[218]

In case those overinclined to charity should doubt that this really amounts to a subtle affirmation of precisely the doctrine he was purporting to disown, it should be pointed out that Niclaes immediately explained that "man in his vnregenerated spirit is vnperfect" . . . implying, of course, that the regenerate man *was* perfect! Rogers was certain that the Familists held "that after regeneration we sinn not," and observed that they appealed in support of such a contention to 1 John 5.18, and to John 8.34 and 9.31, which texts teach that those born of God do not sin, that those who do are servants of sin, and that God does not hear sinners.[219] He countered that these and similar Scriptures meant only that sins were not imputed to the regenerate. The regenerate man's battle against sin, Rogers maintained, was "continuall, and shal neuer haue end vntill our earthly tabernacle shalbe turned to dust."[220] He denied that perfection could be "in this life attayned vnto, and that the law is possible to be kept."[221] His Familist corespondent "E.R.," on the other hand, made on this subject a rare—perhaps unique— appeal to the church fathers; he referred to Jerome's dictum, "Accursed be he which saith, God cōmaunded vnpossible thinges."[222] Rogers's pessimistic (or realistic!) view made its supporters, as far as the Familists were concerned, "aduocates for sinne," an expression which anticipates George Fox's charge, three quarters of a century later, that his opponents were "pleading for sin."[223] The letter which some Familists sent to Rogers sometime in February or early March, 1578/79 contains a suspiciously orthodox statement of faith denying, in apparently (the cautionary epithet is always necessary with this group) unequivocal terms, that the Familists held perfectionism. But even the author of this writing could not resist making the observation that "you take part ouermuch with the sinne (as we thinke) and we ouermuch with the righteousnesse (as you thinke)."[224] It may have been so, particularly since perfidy in debate does not seem to have come into the Familists' definition of "sinne."

Secret to God Only: Nicodemism and Toleration

Of all the practices and beliefs of the Familists, that which most enraged and frustrated their opponents, and made virtually impossible the task of eradicating the sect, was Nicodemism, the belief in the justifiability of denying their true beliefs to interrogators, either simply or by endlessly devious equivocation, or of recanting and then reverting to their heresies once they were released. These practices were by no means unique to the Family of Love, but the group's attempts to provide a theoretical apology for them were notorious, and heightened the alarm of pious minds among the orthodox, who saw these practices as an intensification of the threat posed by heresy. The royal proclamation of 1580 against the Family concluded that "they are more dangerous in any Christian realm" precisely because, "though many of them are well known to be teachers and spreaders abroad of these dangerous and damnable sects, yet by their own confession they cannot be condemned."[225] Archbishop Edwin Sandys denounced those who

> in open shew profess any religion, inwardly keeping their false hearts to themselves, Which practice the Family of Love hath lately drawn to a precept, and . . . say and unsay to any, saving such as be of the same family, with whom they must only use all plainness.[226]

It was, as Sandys said, the Familists' drawing of the practice to an actual precept that was so shocking. Heretics, it was generally held, might be persecuted with the full confidence that the persecutors could not find themselves destroying the truth by mistake; as John Knewstub reasoned, "true Religion spreadeth and increaseth vnder the crosse, so punishment and affliction is the baine of heresie and false religion."[227] The only danger was from the possibility that the upholders of heresy might evade "punishment and affliction," either by lying, or by recantation followed by immediate relapse. Henry Ainsworth, the English separatist leader, was expressing an assumption common to most Protestants when he maintained that "the outward meanes of mans salvation and of the righteous Christian life | is to be stood for vnto the death."[228] This conviction had not dissuaded him from fleeing to the safety of Amsterdam, whence he made this pronouncement, any more than it had prevented many Protestants from going into exile during Mary's reign, but he and they would doubtless have made a distinction between prudence and attempts to elude capture on the one hand, and actual dishonesty or denial of the faith once apprehended on the other. Doubtless the distinction was never cast-iron; John Careless had denied to his captors knowing Henry Hart, but had admitted to his diary that "I lied falsely" to prevent the Catholics from exploiting Protestant divisions.[229] Even so, Protestants in the hands of Catholics, and separatists apprehended by Protestant authorities, were expected by their fellows not to yield in their beliefs, and to die for them if necessary, though Vitel argued that Protestants in Italy and Spain "holde it good pollicie to defend them selues & their consciences" by Nicodemism.[230] Against the tradition of not yielding under persecution, Niclaes argued that

> if they take or lay-holde on vs with Force and Violence | and that then; although wee crye; ther cometh not any Power nor helpe vnto vs . . . and that they euen so rauish vs against our Will | so are we giltles of the Transgressing: For wee haue cryed, for to be released from the Tirannie of the Euell | and ther is no Helpe com vnto vs.[231]

Niclaes likened this to the situation described in Deut. 22.25–27, in which a woman who cries out for help when raped is considered guiltless if no help comes.[232] Wilkinson retorted that, if God did not "enable vs to resist and preuayle agaynst sinne," then that fact did not make God an accessory to the sin, as Niclaes's line of argument, in effect, made him.[233]

Vitel had held Nicodemist views during his Arian days; his cousin, Joan Agar, had told "M. Fulkes the Elder [William Fulke?], and others," that Vitel had accounted Latimer, Ridley, and the other Marian martyrs "starke fooles, and did not well in suffering death."[234] At that time he had persuaded waverers to go to mass (Wilkinson thought that Vitel had already come under Niclaes's influence on that point), and this was an issue of conscience which John Bradford had found it necessary to address in his tract, *The Hurt of Hearing Mass*.[235] By the late 1570s, Vitel had a ready line of defense for such secrecy. Without quite admitting that the Familists did, in fact, deny their allegiance "with their mouth, & keepe it still in their harts," he argued that his critics were worse, because "you confesse the Lord, with your mouth, and your hart is full of bitternes, and euen so you deny him with your hart, and mouth."[236] It is hard to see how the "and mouth" was justifiable, but presumably his central point was that a heart obedience was more important than an outward confession. Niclaes explained that the confessing of Christ "must stand in greater force or effect, then to be confessed with the mouth"; the general Protestant belief that "we for Christs cause should forsake our lives" was acceptable only if the injunction was understood as a forsaking of the self-life to "be the disciples of Christ."[237] Forsaking one's own life meant forsaking "the man of syn" that was in each of us. As with the denial that the Pope was Antichrist, so Nicodemism was turned in a moralistic direction. It was the self-life that needed to be surrendered; God was not "appeased with an elementish body," and so none should "boast yourselves in such an vncertayn confessing" as martyrdom.[238]

Whether or not the two Protestant ladies of Marian England to whom Niclaes wrote took his advice, the Familists did so. Which ever of Chaundeler or Sterete was still alive in 1579, the survivor was a Familist despite his recantation of 1561.[239] Allen, a Familist leader and weaver of Wonersh, Surrey, fled bail and, encountering on his travels a local justice of the peace, denied possessing Niclaes's books, but was searched and found to be lying.[240] Both he and Robert Sharpe, parson of Strethall in Essex, recanted Familist views at Paul's Cross on 12 June 1575, though Sharpe had been interrogated with half a dozen others only six months earlier and had made an orthodox confession of faith, adding with nice humor that "we think it unlawful and ungodly to speak one thing with the mouth, and think the contrary with the heart, as the Libertines do."[241] Allin relapsed into heresy again, and died on his way to Farnham to be examined by the bishop of Winchester, while the implication of Rogers's dire warnings about the "terrible example" of Sharpe's equally sudden death is that he, too, reverted yet again to Familism.[242] The Familists who wrote to Rogers in the early spring of 1578/79 admitted that some of the Family had recanted and then returned to the sect, but claimed that these were simple men; would Rogers allow that "euery simple man that heareth a doctor preache, should be compelled to deliuer forth all his diuinitie, or els to be committed to straight prison?"[243] The argument was spurious (most Familists were more deeply involved than the comparison implies), and the same letter conceded more frankly that it was "feare of your rigorous dealings" that had "made some of vs to flye & lurke in corners."[244] It was precisely this attitude, however, which the Familists' antagonists held in such contempt, for "if the doctrine of *H.N.* be a truth, why is it taught in corners?

why dare none step foorth to maintaine the doctrine?"[245] Secrecy
and truth were, it seems, mutually exclusive. Rogers pointed out
that, by the Familists' own admission, it was "feare of death doth
cause tham to be silent," and asked scornfully: "Did Christ or his
Apostles so?"[246] Familists in Flanders attended mass, while their
coreligionists in England attended the parish churches, and the
Familists who corresponded with Rogers did so anonymously.[247]

This last was an all but pointless precaution, since Rogers knew
many of them in any case, and could easily have exposed them
had he wished to do so. As he himself pointed out, "your persons
I haue not hated: For whome in their trouble I haue sought deli-
uerie, and haue knowne of your meetings if I had been enuiously
minded."[248] For all his taunts, he was clearly anxious to protect
the identities of those Familists whose activities had not already
made them notorious. He accounted it "not expedient" to identify
the authors of the letters that had been sent to him, "for as much
as I doe but guesse at the matter."[249] His guesses, one suspects,
would have been highly accurate and informed, for at least one
"friend of mine . . . is entred into that errour" of Familism, and
had drawn the attention of Rogers's pen to the sect in the first
place.[250] He did not say whether it was Sterete or Chaundeler who
had survived and remained "a welwiller to your Family," any more
than Wilkinson was willing to identify the Arian with whom he was
acquainted beyond calling him (presumably to show that the person
was not fictitious) "W.H. of *B*."[251] For moderns, of course, this is
welcome evidence that both men, who appear to have been likable,
were better, by non-Augustinian, twentieth-century lights, than
their persecuting principles. In this they were perhaps not unusual;
the willingness of nonsectarians to tolerate or seek to protect the
actual heretics known to them personally, even as they espoused
the principle of prosecuting heresy in general, will be discussed in
the concluding chapter.

But the Familists' unwillingness to suffer for their faith was
linked to a conviction that religious coercion was something which
no one had any right or duty to inflict. "Oh! What a lamentable
Thing," cried Niclaes, "is the Slaying or Shedding-of-bloud, for the
Consciences cause."[252] He seems to have been thinking primarily
of his own group ("of those that are zelous towardes the Righteousnes"), but declared that there was nothing "more lamentable
before God and his holyons | then the shedding of innocent
Bloud!"[253] He inveighed against those who "force Others to confesse and saye; Another kynde of Fayeth, then their Hearts alow
or Testifye."[254] But the strongest pleas for toleration came from the

English Familists themselves and, citing William Tyndale, these were couched in terms that made it plain that it was something approaching a universal toleration that was aimed at. "E.R." wrote to Rogers that

> it is not Christian like, that one man should enuie, belie, and persecute an other, for any cause touching conscience. William Tindale compareth them to Antichrists disciples, that do breake vp into the consciences of men, & compel them either to forsweare themselues by the Almightie God, . . . or to testifie against them selues. Againe, he saith, secrete sinnes pertaine to GOD to punish, and open sinnes, to the king. . . . If any man do willingly erre, he shall haue euerlasting damnation for his rewarde at Gods hand, vnlesse he do earnestly repent. Is not that punishmēt sufficient which God hath ordeined, but that one Christian must vexe, belye, and persecute an other?[255]

Another letter from a group of Familists also quoted Tyndale against prying into men's consciences, and added, "Let that which is secrete to God onely, whereof no proofe can be made, nor lawfull witnesse brought, abide to the coming of the Lord, which shall open all the secretes &c."[256] If "that which is secrete to God onely" refers to the condition of a given man's heart, then it must at once be said that this is a very predestinarian argument indeed. The heart is unsearchable, the saved and damned cannot be known in this life; why punish heretics on the assumption that they are reprobate? This would be a very weak argument, and Tyndale had been most unusual in making it. On the other hand, "that which is secrete to God onely," may refer to theological verity, so that toleration is based upon a kind of operational agnosticism on the part of government. Government has no right to impose any religion because it is no fit judge of what is, or is not, the truth of God. This would be closer to the Anabaptist view.

Either way, Rogers was in no doubt about the consequences: if it was not lawful "to chastice heresies, and to punish gainsayers of publick doctrine," then "so you would haue it, that euery man might be left to the libertye of hys owne will, and so should the world swarme with infinite dissentiōs and heresies."[257] Nothing could be more calculated to repel the sixteenth-century mind than such a prospect of religious anarchy. Orthodoxy must be maintained precisely because it was what Rogers said it was: "publick doctrine." It was the possession of all, assent to which guaranteed the social order. Indeed, assent was even more important than the actual content of what was assented to, which was perhaps why some of those in the Elizabethan hierarchy who were less piously inclined than the Puritans were apt to view the Family of Love with a more lenient eye than, say, the separatists. The former would, after all, assent; what they did among themselves was, perhaps, their own affair.

Rogers answered the Familists' appeal to Tyndale in a fairly muted way and, without actually defending the principle of persecution, insisted that the main point was the Familists' contemptible and cowardly secrecy.[258] As a general principle, however, few would have dissented from Wilkinson's opinion that "a Christian magistrate both may and ought to punnish by death and otherwise, those that are heretiques agaynst the fayth, and blasphemers against religion."[259] The fact that only some had been predestined to salvation did not mean that the reprobate should not be coerced in matters of religion because, thankfully from the magisterial Protestant point of view, neither group could be identified with any certainty. In any case, public order had to be preserved, and even the reprobate could glorify God. The Familist elder Theophilus, on the other hand, "will not haue any man compelled to religion, & therefore much lesse to be put death [sic] for the same."[260] Wilkinson called for legislation against the Family of Love, and in the following year, 1580, his wish was granted in the form of a royal proclamation.[261]

Knewstub made the usual magisterial Protestant appeal to the Old Testament in support of a policy of forcible eradication of heresy.[262] The typical radical counterappeal to the New Testament was deflected by Wilkinson; he argued that Gamaliel's counsel to the Sanhedrin (Acts 5.35–39), to let the disciples alone lest the Jewish leaders find themselves fighting God, was a "one-off" peculiar to that circumstance, and not a general principle.[263] Otherwise, he argued, with perfect circular reasoning, "many heretickes would stirre coles in the Church." The needs and circumstances of sixteenth-century established religion were the presupposition of this type of scriptural exegesis, and made the Old Testament commonwealth a court of appeal of continuing validity, while incidents in the New were for a dispensation only.

The Sheep and the Goats: A Time for Separation

The practice of Nicodemism, and a willingness to mingle with the congregation of the state church, was not necessarily inconsistent with belief in a gathered, or pure, assembly. Some of the Lollard "known men" had, after all, been ministers in the established church. The exclusion of the godless from the pure church did not oblige the godly to exclude themselves from the impure. This was not the way that either the Anabaptists on the one hand, or the English separatists on the other, perceived the matter, but certainly the Familists seem to have reasoned this way. To this extent, the claim of the physician John Jones that the Familists were "seuering themselues from the Christian cōgregation" was incorrect.[264] Niclaes announced that the time had now come for "ye Good; with all Repentantons" to "becom knowen and made-manifest from the Wicked," and that "they shall seperate them the-one from the-other."[265] The marginal Scripture reference given was to the separation of the sheep and the goats in Matt. 25. Whoever "assembleth him not vnto vs" would be condemned "with the Deuell and all wicked Spirites; with the Cheynes or Bandes of Darknes; in the Fire of Hell."[266] Knewstub picked Niclaes up on this passage, pointing out that as a reference to the last things, it was misapplied. As will be seen in a moment, however, tenses, always mutable in Niclaes's way of thinking, could easily be changed by an insistence that the last times had already arrived, that the scriptural "shall" had become an "is," and that the Familist message was itself a sort of last trump.[267] In his *Terra Pacis. A True Testification of the spirituall Lande of Peace . . . or the heavenly Jerusalem,* Niclaes encouraged anyone who might have "a Desyre; with all his Heart; to assemble him with vs."[268] Joining with the Family, assembling with them, was to make manifest that one was a sheep. The Wisbech Familists, however, were required by their interrogators to affirm the orthodox view that no such division was possible in this life.

> Although in the visible church the evil be ever mingled with the good and sometime the evil have chief authority in the ministry of the word and sacraments, yet for as much as they do not the same in their own name but in Christ's . . . we may use the ministry both in hearing the word of God and in the receiving of the sacraments. Neither is the effect of Christ's ordinance taken away by their wickedness.

Nor were the sacraments to be rendered invalid, "although they be ministered by evil men."[269] This confession reeks of Puritan embarrassment with the actual state of the established church, which was so very far from their ideal, but from which their theology forbade them to separate. Wilkinson went so far as to claim that it was the church which had been likened by Christ, in Matt. 13, to a field "wherein good seede is sowne by the paynefull husbandman, & corrupt seede scattered by the hād of the enemyes."[270] According to the actual text of Matt., the field was, of course, the world, but one can appreciate Wilkinson's difficulty.

The Angel in Midheaven:
Familism and the Internal Apocalypse

The coming of the Kingdom of God has been characterized by one modern evangelical theologian as "the presence of the future," a tension between future event and already existent reality.[271] If the generality of Christendom has tended to emphasize the former aspect, the Familists went in for a drastic redressing of the balance. Their tendencies to replace the "was" and "will" of the Creed with a potentially mystical "is," and to internalize the events of redemption history, making the Fall, the Crucifixion, and Resurrection more important as personal experiences than as historical events, have already been noted. Here, as with other aspects of their thought, the moralistic concern was to the fore. Assent to the history was as nothing; indeed, reliance upon it alone was to "rest grounded more on yᵉ litterall knowledge of the Christiā veritie then on the beyng of the same."[272] The "beyng of the same," the internal realization of the realities which the history described, was everything. Similarly, Niclaes's emphasis upon the imminence of the coming Kingdom was less "apocalyptic" in the traditional sense than some of his rhetoric ("euen-now in the last tyme," "the Ende shall come," "Therefore also is this Daye . . . the Last-daye") implied.[273] Again, the question is one of emphasis. A literal apocalypse was not denied, any more than Niclaes's claim to be "raysed-vpp by the highest God, from yᵉ Death" denied the historical Resurrection of Christ, but the use of language frequently implies that "now" is not only the penultimate phase before the end, but in a sense actually *is* the end. Not only is it the case that "after this Daye, ther shall no Daye of Grace more, com vpon the Earth," but in the judgment of God, "an euerlasting Death and Damnation of all Vngodlie" and "an eternall Life and Saluation of all the Holyons and Elect of God; becometh also executed therin." N. T. Burns notes of early modern mystical religion that

> anxious to persuade their fellows of the importance of having Christ formed within, some enthusiasts found it but a short step from saying that this regenerate state was the beginning of the salvation spoken of in the Gospel to saying that it was the *only* salvation.[274]

Niclaes's use of the present-tense "becometh" is significant. The judgment is now; it is executed through the acts of the Familists themselves. Commenting on Niclaes's *Evangelivm Regni,* Knew-stub complained that "the separation which shalbe at the last day, betweene the sheepe and the goates . . . is (as he [Niclaes] saith) fulfilled nowe, while some ioyne with his doctrine & that his family, & other seperate themselues from it."[275] Heaven, likewise, is within. "The whole outward World, is very-great and vnmeasurable . . . yet is notwithstãding the inward World; without comparison; much greater, inwardlie in vs"; similarly "the outward heauen . . . incompasseth the whole outward World," but "the inward Heauen; wherin God with his Christ and Holy-gost | and with all his Holy-ons, dwelleth and liueth essentiallie; is far-away much greater and gloriouser."[276]

Niclaes, in his *Evangelivm Regni,* constantly likened himself to the angel of Rev. 14.6, which is depicted as flying in midheaven, with an eternal Gospel to proclaim to those who dwell on earth. "Apo. 14. a." is given as a marginal reference eight times in the book, generally in conjunction with "Math. 24. b." which teaches that the Gospel of the Kingdom will be preached across the world before the end comes.[277]

The English Familists, however, do not seem to have picked up on this apocalypticism, even in its internalized form, to any great extent. Even so, Bishop Richard Cox of Ely, William Fulke, Richard Greenham, and the others examining the Wisbech Familists in 1580, thought it worth securing a subscription from their prisoners that "the last trump is not yet blown to any. . . . And therefore the doctrine of H.N. is not the last trump."[278] Leonard Romsey, one of their number, told his captors that "they hold their opinion that their kingdom which they call David's Kingdom is to be erected here upon earth," and that a prophecy current among them predicted a time not far off when "there should be no magistrate, prince, nor palace upon the earth, but all should be governed by the spirit of love."[279] Romsey, however, seems to have been trying to get his master, John Bourne, into as much trouble as possible by his confession. None of the other prisoners gave any corroborative hint of such beliefs, though their statements agreed on most other things, and the fact that no account was taken of this information in the recantations or orthodox articles which the Familists were required to sign is eloquent of the fact that the interrogators did not take Romsey too seriously. Nevertheless, Niclaes's writing on the subject of the last things worried Rogers sufficiently to ask:

> Why delite you your selues with such speaches? For in this world these thinges according to the letter, shall not happen, but they are spoken to assure vs of the resurrection, and to shadow the ioyes of the kingdome of heauen, whereby our harts should be lifted vp with expectation of his promise.[280]

It would be tempting to dismiss this as simply an instance of state-church amillennialism confronted with the unnerving spectacle of sectarian apocalypticism. The possible anachronism of a term like *amillennialism* apart, William Lamont has taught us some twenty years ago to be mindful of the sense of final struggle with Antichrist transmitted to English Protestantism generally by Foxe's *Acts and Monuments*.[281] Even so, the assumptions of Rogers's exposition are certainly reminiscent of what would now be called "amillennialism": the events described in the biblical prophecies concerning a coming Kingdom of God are not to be looked for in this world, but in the next; we are told of them that they might encourage us, not that we might, as it were, encourage them. This is the eschatology of Augustine and, like so much of Reformed theology, manifestly conducive to good social order. It is not clear if Rogers had much reason to be anxious. Apart from the reference to the "white stone" in Rev. mentioned earlier in this chapter,[282] there is little evidence that English Familists paid much attention to the idea of an imminent end of all things, whatever Niclaes wrote, and the Familist safety valve that tended to internalize all realities meant that significant social disruption would have been unlikely even if they had.

*   *   *

The ultraradicalism of the Arians and their effective successors, the English Familists, certainly worried the government and stirred several conscientious Protestants to raise their pens. Familism, however, seems to have been a little too esoteric to generate a mass following. Such appeal as it had was inevitably linked to some extent, though not as much as in Holland, with the life of its prophet. Despite the greater independence of English Familism, the death of Niclaes in around 1580, helped usher in decline toward the end of the century, though some Familist ideas may have lived on among the Grindletonians and, later, the Quakers.

5

Established Protestantism, Predestination, and Ecclesiology

DURING the course of the present work, notice has frequently been taken of the attitudes of the various radical groups and their magisterial Protestant opponents toward doctrines of predestination and free-will. So frequently, indeed, that it would seem necessary to turn aside from the radicals themselves for a moment to examine this concern of the upholders of the Protestant establishment. Why was the doctrine of predestination so important to them and, more pertinently to the present discussion, what were its ecclesiological effects? For it is those effects which, as will be seen, created for them a concept of the church which was irreconcilable with the programs (or at any rate, the implicit programs) of the various radicals. This theology was neither abstractly philosophical nor simply devotional; it had practical, even political, effects.

A number of historians of recent years, from C. D. Cremeans and O. T. Hargrave, to D. B. Knox and D. D. Wallace, have sought to analyze the varying shades of opinion among the early English Protestants and reformers, and later among the Puritans, concerning predestination.[1] Questions considered include whether given individuals held to sub- or supralapsarianism; whether or not they spelled out the doctrine of foreordination to damnation as a logical corollary to the elect's predestination to salvation; whether they clearly articulated the notion of a limited atonement or shrank back from voicing such a conclusion; whether they were influenced by Luther's (supposedly more moderate) predestinarianism as expressed, for example, in his *Bondage of the Will,* or by Calvin or Bucer. For the purposes of the present work, few of these distinctions, valid and important as they may be in other contexts, matter very much. Presumably some kind of predestination, at a minimum that which accepts that God has predetermined to judge the world at the return of his Son, must be accepted by virtually all groups claiming the title "Christian." But the word has generally been taken as having a meaning which, while not as specific as the distinctions considered by the historians just mentioned, is yet more specific than this generalized definition. "Predestination" simply defined, is taken here to mean the essential conviction that God chooses those who will choose him, and that the making of the latter choice is in that sense somewhat illusory, the choosers having been foreordained to that end from before the foundations of the earth. To most of the radicals discussed in this work, with the likely exception of the Familists (though Joan Bocher's views on the subject are not known), such a conviction was anathema; to the magisterial Protestants, it was fundamental.

The Henrician Protestant writers had all stressed the importance of the doctrine. William Tyndale, who was the author of the notes to "Thomas Matthews's" Bible published in 1537, as well as its real translator, included the topic of "Eleccyon," "Predestinacion," and "Prouidence" in "A Table of the pryncypall matters conteyned in the Byble." The first of these taught that "few are electe or chosen."[2] The section on predestination emphasized that

> God had predestynat before the makyng of ye world . . . for to saue & make vs his chyldren. . . . Then the carnall and sensuall people cãnot cõprehende the eleccyõ & predestinacyõ of God; because they stryue for to saue thẽ selves. . . .[3]

Tyndale considered Paul's Letter to the Romans "the principall & moost excellent part of the newe Testament | & moost pure Evangelion," probably because it was that part of the Scripture most supportive of those emphases which he and those of like mind wished to make. His notes on the book stressed that the ninth, tenth, and eleventh chapter concerned

> Goddis predestinaciõ | whence it springeth all to gether | whether we shall beleue or not beleue | be lowsed frõ synne or not be lowsed. By which predestinaciõ oure iustifyinge & saluaciõ are clene takẽ oute of oure handes . . . nether can eny man withstand or let him[4]

John Frith was even more forthright: "whom so euer he choseth them he saueth of his mercy: & whom he repelleth | them of his secrete & vnsearchable iudgemẽt he condempneth."[5] For Frith, election was not consequent upon faith, "but fayth foloweth the election," for the elect "are no doubte chosen before they had fayeth."[6] Robert Barnes was likewise certain, not only that "god saueth so fewe men | and dammeth so meny," but that "there be serten open places of Scriptur | that geue wonly the cause | to god alonly of eleccion and also of reprobacion."[7] Simon Fish also taught that eternal salvation was entirely "in the hondes & will of god to gyve it to whome he will by his mercy."[8] George Joye laid down the order of salvation as being "Firste" that "we are chosen of God in christe before the foundacion of the worlde was layed," and that the second birth is consequent upon this, "which gifte of faith" merely "certifyeth vs of our election."[9] Faith simply reassures the believer of what has been preordained in eternity concerning him; Joye reflected this scheme of things elsewhere in his writings.[10] Indeed, his *Refutation of the byshop of Winchesters derke declaratiō of his false articles, once before confuted by George Joye* exhibits some of the most rigid predestinarianism to be found in the writings of the Henrician Protestants. "Whom god hath predestined and chosen they shalbe saued, for god repenteth him not of his eleccion, but it must necessarelye and immutably come so to passe"; "God wil haue mercye of whom he lyst, and harden whom it lyketh him."[11] Lancelot Ridley, brother of the future bishop of London, wrote in 1540 that God "electeth and choseth whome he wyl" by predestination, and that the rejection of the Gospel by any was a "token that they be nat the children of saluacion" rather than the actual cause of their damnation.[12] Miles Coverdale does not fit into this overall pattern; even his strongest statement on the subject, that we are "chosen of god to shew now his wonderful workes," need not be understood in a predestinarian sense.[13] Even so, Henry VIII seems to have taken it for granted that a strong doctrine of predestination was central to Protestantism in general. His book, *A Necessary Doctrine and Ervdition for any Christen man,* published in 1543 and generally known as "The King's Book," contained an "article of Justification," which betrayed the semi-Pelagian monarch's fears of solafidianism, but added a cautionary word about what he must have considered its general concomitant.

> All phantasticall imagination, curious reasonyng, and vain trust of predestination, is to be laid apart. And . . . we ought . . . not to assure our selfes, that we be elected any otherwise, than by . . . the tokens of good and vertuous liuyng . . . and perseueryng in the same to the ende[14]

A similar article on free-will claimed that in preaching a balance should be struck between free-will and the grace of God, though the language makes it plain that it was the former which he was most anxious to conserve.[15]

In view of the foregoing, the conclusions of O. T. Hargrave on the subject might well be greeted with the utmost surprise. He believes that the Henrician reformers had "relatively little . . . to say about the doctrine," and that their comments were generally made incidentally to the discussion of some other, related subject.[16] But while it might be difficult to argue that predestination was central to the thought of all of them, the subject certainly was frequently mentioned and was by no means glossed over. The fact that the doctrine was often referred to, as it were, tangentially, in connection with other topics is good evidence that it was a controlling assumption in the theology of the reformers. In the case of George Joye, Hargrave's judgment is most definitely wide of the mark; predestination seems to have been the linchpin of his system. D. D. Wallace thinks, probably correctly, that Hargrave has attempted to "separate out earlier, more moderate strands in this [predestinarian] tradition from later, more "rigid" Calvinistic ones," though it is "doubtful that Calvin introduced anything distinctly harsher into the tradition than already existed."[17] Hargrave makes play of the fact that the Henrician Protestants left some possible ramifications of the doctrine undiscussed, and then concludes, most astoundingly of all, that "the basic fact is that they were not really interested in dealing with the problem; they seem to have been, in fact, quite anxious to avoid it whenever possible"![18] The most astonishing fact about this judgment, is that Hargrave refers to virtually all of the material, or at least to the same publications, that have been cited here. D. D. Wallace's judgment is sharp but not unjust.

> One suspects in such efforts to separate earlier Reformed theology from later Calvinistic theology that there is an underlying motive of clearing some favored movement or thinker from any imputation of "Calvinism."[19]

Hargrave, by his own confession, is searching for "the sources and origins of the liberal theology" of the seventeenth century.[20] Whether or not modern liberal theologians wish to become heirs to the Reformation legacy, the "sources and origins" of liberalism are not to be located, it would seem, where Hargrave has been looking for them.

Even the Edwardian picture might be thought to provide more sustenance for the view of early English Protestantism which Hargrave seeks to portray, though it is meager enough. At least John Hooper baulked at the idea of an immutable predestination to salvation or damnation. Writing in 1548, he expressed the belief that it was "oure office" to ensure that we do not exclude ourselves from the "generall grace | promisyd to all men"; though he denied that salvation was due to free-will, he felt that it was also wrong to claim that "God hathe wrotē fatall Lawes . . . and withe necessite of desteny | uiolently pullithe one by the here in to heauen | and thrustithe thother hedling into hell."[21] In fairness, it should be pointed out that D. D. Wallace is almost guilty of the opposite error to that of Hargrave here; referring to, but not actually quoting, this passage in its Parker Society edition, he comments that "John Hooper affirmed predestination . . . straightforwardly," a claim which, in the light of Hooper's actual words, looks like less than the full truth.[12] Admittedly, two years later Hooper wrote tersely, in *A briefe and clear confession,* "I believe that the Father in Jesus Christ his Son through the Holy Ghost hath elected and chosen those that are his own . . . before the foundations of the world were laid."[23] However, given the style of this statement, and seen against the background of the earlier obvious discomfort with the doctrine, this seems like a perfunctory acknowledgement of what was the dominant belief among his fellow-reformers. The earlier discussion had been fuller, clearer in its negation, synergistic, making sin the cause of reprobation and faith of election.[24] Even Henry Hart, one suspects, might have been happy with such an exposition. Perhaps this was why those whom he called "anabaptists," flocked to hear him and debate with him at his lectures in London.[25]

With the further exception of Hugh Latimer, Hargrave's comfort is almost at an end. The Edwardian bishop of Worcester seems consistently to have sought to disarm the doctrine of predestination, to make it palatable to his hearers, though he did not deny its truth. (Augustine Bernhere, his Swiss manservant, who was to dispute with William Lawrence and John Barre in the following reign, was, of course, solidly predestinarian.) Latimer's counsel from a sermon of 14 February 1552 is typical, in that it shifted the focus of attention from the inscrutable judgments of God to the faith of man.

If thou art desirous to know whether thou art chosen to everlasting life, thou mayest not begin with God; for God is too high. . . . The judgments of God are unknown to man; . . . but . . . learn to know Christ . . . that he came to save sinners. . . . Consider, I say, Christ and his coming; and then begin to try thyself, whether thou art in the book of life or not.[26]

His constant concern appears to have been the disconcerting effect that the teaching of predestination was bound to have upon the mass of simple hearers, and to mitigate that effect by assuring them that if they believed then they were chosen, so that "we need not go about to trouble ourselves with curious questions of the predestination of God."[27]

Most of the Edwardian reformers, however, were as unswerving in their support of Reformed notions of predestination as the Henricians had been. Many of the Protestant leaders, of course, were active in both reigns, and need not be cataloged again. John Bale could fairly be accused of paying little attention to the doctrine, but he affirmed readily enough that "they onlie shal posesse that [the city of God], which are wrytten in the lambes boke of lyfe or that were predestinate ther vnto in Christ before the worldes constitutyon."[28] These chosen ones are held by God in a "perpetual remembraunce," and by him they are "ordayned of goodnesse, chosē of mercy, called by the Gospell, iustyfyed throughe faythe, and glorifyed."[29] John Poynet, bishop of Winchester, wrote in a catechism of 1553, published under royal authority and intended for the use of all schoolmasters, that the principal cause of salvation is the love of God, "whereby he chose vs for his, before he made the worlde"; those who are in the faith were from all eternity "forechosen, predestinate, & apoynted out to euerlastīg lyfe."[30] The predestinarianism of William Turner has been noticed in chapter 3, while John Philpot, John Bradford, and others, were to take part in the King's Bench prison debates in Mary's reign, though they did not leave it until then to give voice to their predestinarianism. Philpot translated *Curio's Defence of Christ's Church* into English. This Italian Protestant work taught "all things to be done necessarily, if we regard the purpose or providence of God," though we appear to work "freely and of our own accord."[31] Asked by his Marian captors about Calvin, Philpot told them that "in the matter of predestination he is in none other opinion than all the doctors of the church be, agreeing to the scriptures."[32] John Bradford's predestinarianism has been referred to at length in the present work's chapter on the free-will men, and needs no further exposition here. In reference to the source of this theology in Bradford's case, the historian E. G. Rupp has described him as "perhaps the first Calvinist among the English Reformers."[33] Nicholas Ridley, Bradford's patron and the master of his college at Cambridge, as well as Edwardian bishop of London from 1550, wrote a treatise on predestination while in prison during the next reign and probably sent it to Bradford sometime after mid-April 1555.[34]

Bartholomew Traheron, the keeper of the young king's library, was a consciously committed Calvinist, who crossed swords with Hooper on the issue, and wrote to, and quarreled with, the latter's mentor Heinrich Bullinger, the Zürich reformer.[35] He told Bullinger that we should "ascribe actions to God, but leave to man whatever sin there is in them; . . . in some wonderful and ineffable manner that does not take place without his will, which is done even against his will."[36] A theology that was willing to embrace a paralogism like this as the price of a strong doctrine of predestination clearly held that teaching very dear indeed. Traheron agreed with Calvin that God "not only foresaw the fall of the first man, and in him the ruin of his posterity, but that he also . . . arranged it."[37]

The foreign influences in England that were encouraged by the government were those of reformed theology. Protector Somerset himself was in correspondence with Calvin.[38] Martin Bucer, Regius Professor of Divinity at Cambridge from 1549; Peter Martyr, Regius Professor at Oxford from 1548; and his convert Bernadino Ochino, prebendary of Canterbury, were all convinced exponents of the reformed doctrine of predestination. Bucer taught the doctrine,[39] and asked: "Quis ergo casus poßit obtingere tam grauis, qui reprobos faceret, quos Deus mutari nescius, ad æterno prædestinauit, uitæ & hæreditati salutis?"[40] Martyr denied that it was "any let to preaching, that the number of the elect (as it is in verie deed) is certeine and unmooueable" on the grounds that, by preaching, "we go not about to translate men from the number of the reprobate, into the number of the elect: but that they which perteine to the elect, might by the ministerie of the word be brought vnto their appointed end."[41] Reprobation he defined as "the most wise purpose of God, whereby he hath before all eternitie, constantly decreed without any iniustice, not to haue mercie on those whome he hath not loued."[42] Given the immense influence of Bucer and Martyr in England, the significance of these beliefs speaks for itself. Ochino went so far as to assert that "Christ can not sane [sic] a reprobate, not dam an elect," and concluded that "much lesse is it in oure power, if we be elect, to dāpne our selues, or if we be reprobate to saue our selues."[43] Ochino's views extended, not only to a limited atonement, but also to an active decree of reprobation. God "chaseth away yᵉ sinner, whē he doth not call hym. . . . Yet for all this god sinneth not, for he is not holdē nor boūd to geue vs this grace, he may hardē and mollify after his owne pleasure."[44]

Examples and quotations could be multiplied indefinitely. What should be clear, is that predestinarianism of one sort or another was central to the English Reformation, and was virtually synonymous with Protestantism itself. Hargrave, however, sees the Edwardian reformers as constituting a "shift even further in the direction of moderation," and insists that Hooper and Latimer were typical.[45] As has been shown, the two men were atypical; both the fact that Latimer deferred to the doctrine even as he tried to remove some of its sting, and that Hooper formally affirmed predestination to salvation in 1550, following his apparent denials in 1548, show that they recognized the vast majority of Protestant opinion to be against them to a degree that obliged them to acquiesce.

John Ailward attempted Hargrave's task before him. He wrote in 1631 to prove that the attacks of the Calvinists on the Laudian party were mistaken because the latter were not "Broachers of NEW Doctrine," whose ideas were taken from Arminius, but teachers of old doctrine, which "these *Holy Fathers and* Martyrs *did hold,* and Teach *touching the Matters of Gods* Election."[46] Although his work included writings from Hooper, Latimer, Cranmer, and Jewel, most of the book consisted of a reprinting of *The Copie of an answere.* The only substantial extract was of Hooper, from the work cited here. The extracts from Latimer are tangential to the issue, and the strongest statement in the minuscule excerpts from Cranmer and Jewel relate to their belief that Christ had died "for the sins of the whole world."[47]

The belief in a limited atonement, Christ dying only for the sins of the elect, as R. T. Kendall has shown, did not become a great issue until Beza popularized the idea after Calvin's death in 1564.[48] Cranmer said little on the subject of predestination, though his statement that Christ had come "to preach and give pardon, and full remission of sin to all his elected" sounds predestinarian, and his support was taken for granted by Bradford and Ridley in the disputes with the free-will men, the former sending him the copy of his "Defence of Election."[49]

The Book of Private Prayer, authorized by Edward VI and published in 1553, includes the petition to "make me, O Lord, of that number, whom thou from everlasting hast predestinate to be saved."[50] And, without entering into all the details of the doctrine, the official Articles of the Edwardian Church promulgated in 1553, nonetheless endorsed the overwhelmingly predestinarian emphasis of the leading reformers. The seventeenth article declared that

predestination to life, is the everlasting purpose of God, whereby (before the foundacions of the worlde were laied) he hath constantlie decreed by his owne judgemente secrete to vs, to deliuer from curse, and damnation those whom he hath chosen out of mankinde, and to bring them to everlasting saluation by Christ."[51]

The same article freely acknowledged that such a doctrine was likely to drive "curious, and carnall persones" to "desperation."[52] So there it was. Not, perhaps, sufficient to satisfy those who might have wished to spell out every possible ramification of the doctrine from limited atonement to decrees of reprobation, but still sufficiently explicit to make plain the official endorsement of the essential belief that God chose those who would choose him.

Hargrave would doubtless see the failure to force the fine print of predestinarian theology into the articles as evidence for his verdict that "the influence of these earliest [Henrician and Edwardian] traditions . . . laid the foundations for the broad tendency of caution and moderation which became so typical of the English attitude toward the doctrine."[53] A more probable explanation for the article's simplicity is the unpopularity of predestination, and a desire not to provoke the unprotestantized majority of the English population. In any case, the essential point of the doctrine was spelled out, and was repeated in the articles of 1561 and 1571.[54] Hargrave admits that "under Elizabeth the [Calvinist] tradition continued to gain ground." But as C. D. Cremeans, whose entire book was dedicated to demonstrating this hypothesis (though he meant the entire Calvinist system, and not just predestination), pointed out, "the doctrine of predestination was not the exclusive property of Calvin"; the present chapter demonstrates that other reformers were as rigorous as he, while almost all taught the doctrine in its essence.[55] Hargrave is intent upon showing that "the anti-Calvinist tradition" was "also a significant factor in Reformation England."[56] But the examples he can find prior to de Corro, Baro, Harsnet, and Hooker, the late Elizabethan precursors of Arminianism, of whom only the last two were English, are few indeed. He mentions Thomas Talbot, the 1562 petitioner against the enforcement of reformed doctrines of predestination, whose protestations appear to have passed without an echo, and his comment that "there must have been many others like Talbot" illustrates that he has been unable to locate them.[57] Apart from Talbot and whatever following he may have had, Hargrave is thrown back onto the free-willers, who as radicals to the left of the reformers cannot be described as proto-Arminians, and so can form no part of the case which Hargrave appears to be trying to make. Citing Owen Chadwick's wise judgment that, in "the formative period of reformed theology," there was no distinctive English school of thought but only English theologians falling under one or other of the Continental streams, Hargrave suggests a "possible (and probable) exception."[58] This, he asserts, is "of course, . . . the anti-Calvinist tradition, the closest approximation to a native school within this context." Whatever the patriotic appeal of such an analysis might be, if predestinarianism is dismissed as a nasty foreign influence, Protestantism cannot escape the same imputation, for the two are virtually inextricable. Hargrave concludes that

> the Arminian movement in England may have been rather more indigenous in origin than has heretofore been allowed. . . . the origins of the movement may well lie, at least in part, in the work of those English anti-Calvinist thinkers whose ideas anticipated, in some cases by as much as half a century, the work of Arminius himself.[59]

D. D. Wallace is right; this is wishful thinking. Antipredestinarianism in England there certainly was, but it was the property of either conservatives and crypto-Catholics on the one hand, or of sectarian radicals on the other. The magisterial Protestant reformers were predestinarian almost to a man.

Predestination and the Invisible Church

The question arises as to why this was so. D. D. Wallace has pointed out that it was used as a buttress to "the basic Reformation insight—that redemption was God's gracious gift apart from any human deserving," and was to be apprehended by faith, not works.[60] "How better," he asks, "to make that point than to insist upon God's eternal predestination?" Election thus understood took salvation entirely out of human hands and, at a stroke, completely undercut the Pelagianism and sacramentalism of the Middle Ages. As D. B. Knox has said, "This doctrine is the sheet anchor of justification by faith only."[61] Certainly there seems to be some substance in this explanation; Jean Veron doubted whether solafidianism could be defended without it, for otherwise "the whole doctrine of iustification by faith, as builded up on a sandy grounde, is moste easy to be blowne downe" while, as Peter Martyr pointed out, "the Pelagians . . . taught, that the election of God commeth by our merits. Free iustification also should perish, except we be rightlie taught of predestination."[62] It could not be true that God's grace was offered to all without distinction, for if it were then the difference between the saved and the damned must be some response in man. The Protestants' concern was to emphasize the totality of the difference between their Gospel and the teaching of the Roman Catholic church, and so even man's faith was likely to be seen as a "work" if it was not accounted a gift of God, given to whom he chose, and denied to the rest.

It is not intended either to elucidate or to argue with this explanation here, though it should be said that it seems an eminently reasonable one. For the purposes of the present discussion, however, it is the secrecy of God's predestination that was the key aspect. Via the secrecy of the identity of the elect, the distinction between visible and invisible church was maintained. Since the latter was insusceptible of visibility, the established church could continue to be all-embracing. Without such a doctrine, solafidianism was a teaching which seemed sure to destroy the institution of established religion, since only those who knew themselves to be converted were the true church. But such a destruction would have been utterly subversive of the sixteenth-century social order, since religion was the primary method of social control. Secret predestination rescued the situation, because it made it impossible for any person to judge, beyond a general conjecture, the state of his neighbor. In this sense also, the doctrine must be seen as supportive of justification by faith, since without it the latter could not have been tolerated within a territorial, coercive church.

There is no doubt that the leading reformers stressed the secrecy of God's judgments, and the impossibility of being sure of the election or reprobation of anyone, except oneself. The tendency of late medieval mystics to endorse predestination has been noted already;[63] Jan van Ruysbroeck provides an example of the teaching about its secrecy: "we bien nat knowyng whice bien ordeyned of god Þat shul be in Þe booke of lijf and whiche nat," although we must "truste sikirli Þat he haÞ ordeyned us to be of the nombre of his chosyn children."[64] Ruysbroeck distinguished several categories of relationship with God, rising from the "faithful servants" through the "secret friends of God" up to the highest group, the "hidden sons of God."[65]

John Frith, in a work published in 1533, stressed the secrecy of God's election: since "they that are chosen from the begynnyng are no doubte chosen before they had fayeth, we ought not therfore to geue suche vnaduised iudgements . . . seinge Goddes election is hidde from our eyes."[66] Even apparent pagans may be elect, and "there are many I doubte not whiche are thus spiritually baptised al though theyr bodyes toutche no water"; exactly who belonged to the true "electe sanctifyed and inuisible congregacion" was, by definition, "onelye knowen vnto God."[67] He argued that the biblical saints—John, Paul, "Mathew, zacheus, & the thefe and marye magdalen"—could not have been identified, even by themselves, as elect until their conversions, and concluded that "nether knoweth anye man of an others election but euerye man may knowe his owne thorowe his fayth and wil that he hath to fulfil the law of god."[68] "Goddes election," he affirmed, "is vnknowne to mā."[69] Lancelot Ridley denied that "outwarde workes" allowed us to distinguish between the elect and the reprobate; one could not make more than a mere "coniecture who be ordeyned of God to be saued and who to be damned," and that on the basis of response to the preaching of the Gospel more than of works.[70] William Turner had challenged the Anabaptist Robert Cooche to explain how one could be any more certain that men of forty years of age were elect than newborn babies, and took his presumption of Cooche's reduction to silence as an argument for pædobaptism.[71] John Bradford told Henry Hart that "as for who be the elect and who be not, because it is God's privilege to know who be his, God's people are not curious in others" and content themselves with tentative surmising on the basis of a neighbor's outward life.[72]

Bernadino Ochino believed likewise.

> But it is not now conuenient, that we may or can deserne distinctlye, the elect from the reprobate, to the ende we may be more fervent in exercisinge charite, with all men, as if they were brethern [sic] with vs in Christ, the which we would not do towarde the reprobate if we knewe thē distinctly: But in the ende, the tares shalbe seperate frō the good wheat; none then being in this present lyfe knoweth certainly of his neighbour, if he be of the elect or not, nor also whether he be in the fauour of God; we may only haue therof an obscure, confused, uncertain, and faylying knowledge by cōiecture of yᵉ outward lyfe and workes, of whom Christ speaking, sayd, Ye shall knowe them by their fruites. . . . But I saye yᵗ euery elect, whyle he is in this present lyfe, being come to the yeres of discression, maye, and ought to know it of himself. . . .[73]

In stressing the this-worldly unknowability of the elect's identity, he concluded that all are to be treated "as if they were brethern," and thus, presumably, included in the church. Only "in the ende," by which in context he clearly meant the end of the world, will the wheat and tares be separated. His language is strongly inclusivist; though adult believers should know their own election, a continuing state of assurance is not necessary to salvation, since all who have had a genuine faith for as little as a minute of their lifetime will finally be saved: "al they which in this present lyfe do beleue liuely in Christ (yea were it for a moment of time) shalbe sauid," and he who sees "him selfe in Chryst saued, . . . seethe the truthe, and," he added with a distinctive type of logic, "that which is once trewe although it were but for the twincke of an eie must be said to be euer true."[74] This is a radical mode of expression, pregnant with both liberal and antinomian possibilities; for now, it is sufficient to note the inclusivist emphasis of Ochino's version of secret predestination.

Jean Veron, writing in London in 1561, was to argue for an inclusive church along lines that were more orthodox. He cautioned against any hasty judgment concerning who was, or was not, a reprobate when he wrote that

> all the godlye shall be ware, that they do not rashly iudge of the reprobate, but committe the judgemnt [sic] of them vnto him who alone doeth knowe the names of them, whom he hathe afore the foundacions of the worlde were laid . . . separated from the number of his elect & chosen. As for vs, it is our part as much as in vs doth lye to saue all men, to praye for all men, louyngely to embrase all men, and to doe good vnto all men, nor wythoute a iuste cause to dyspayre of anye, syth that it is hydden from vs what god did fynally appoint of euery man.[75]

This predestinarianism is inclusivist in its implications; none can know the identity of the saved or of the lost, so the working assumption of those who know themselves to be among the elect is that others are also. No person, claimed Veron, is to be despaired of "wythoute a iuste cause," which suggests that it is the reprobate who will stand out from the crowd by their extreme ungodliness, rather than envisaging the crowd as being itself godless, from which the elect are the ones who stand out. Indeed, this assumption, that the ungodly are the minority, was imputed to God himself, since "afore the foundacions of the worlde," he "separated" the godless "from the number of his elect & chosen," rather than the other way around. Veron's mode of expression in *A frutefull treatise of predestination* is even more strongly inclusivist in its implications; he argued that "wher we do se ye calling whiche is done by the preachinge of Gods word, and by the working of the holy ghost and iustification are moste infallible tokens and signes of our election."[76] The word *calling* here seems to be used, not in the frequent Reformed sense of "effectual calling" (i.e., God converting a person), but simply to refer to the "preachinge of God's word"; simply living where true faith is preached is a sign of one's own election. That this is what Veron here meant by "calling" is reinforced by his following sentences:

> On the contrary side, whome he dothe . . . appoynt and ordain unto
> death and condempnation, . . . them doth he most commonly depriue
> of the benefit of his worde, that it be not preached vnto them. . . . It
> is most plaine, that the holye ghoste dyd forbid the worde to be
> preached in Asia. . . .

He seems to have been implying that those are elect, or at least
likely to be elect, who live where the Gospel is preached. This
is an exceptionally strong example, of course, but it powerfully
illustrates the inclusive nature of the magisterial Protestants'
predestinarianism.

Beza did not go this far, but he agreed with Veron that the elect
could not be identified: "Election . . . is reuealed to vs by the
spirite of God within our selues, not in others, whose hearts we
can not know."[77] Expounding the Thirty-Nine Articles of the Elizabethan Church of England in 1579, Thomas Rogers, later chaplain
to Archbishop Bancroft and an advocate of the doctrine of limited
atonement, condemned "such as either curiously enquire who, and
how many, shall be saved or damned; or give the sentence of reprobation upon anyman whatsoever; as do the Papists upon Calvin,
Beza, and Verone, when they call them reprobates."[78]

For Catholics to have given such a definite pronouncement, even
in respect of their archenemies, was somewhat against their principles. If the inability to know the state of grace of one's neighbors
be thought limiting, it should be remembered that there was no
Catholic doctrine of assurance even in respect to oneself. Gardiner
was shocked to come across a Protestant sufficiently certain of his
standing before God as to feel able to say, "I knowe my selfe
predestinate." Gardiner would have ruled out inquiry as to how
God's "secret works of election and predestinacion" was to be
reconciled with "our worke in free choyse and free wyll" as "aboue
our capacite," but he was certain that, whatever predestination did,
it did not create any "necessitie in man," and never permitted one
to have certainty of one's salvation.[79]

The corollary of predestination's inscrutability is the abandonment of any hope, or even intention, that the church might consist
of saints only. As Calvin said,

> In this [visible] Church there is a very large mixture of hypocrites,
> who have nothing of Christ but the name and outward appearance. . . .
> it is necessary to believe [in] the invisible Church, which is manifest
> to the eye of God only.[80]

He insisted that it was "the special prerogative of God to know those who are his," and this fact acted as "a check on human rashness, the experience of every day reminding us how far his secret judgments surpass our apprehension."[81] For even the worst sinners may yet be converted, while among those "who openly bear his badge, his eyes alone see who of them are unfeignedly holy, and will persevere"; instead of certainty, God had ordered

> the judgment of charity, by which we acknowledge all as members of the Church who by confession of faith, regularity of conduct, and participation in the sacraments, unite with us in acknowledging the same God and Christ.[82]

It was taken for granted that, where such a theology prevailed within a state church, then the entire population would be required to confess such a faith, and to "acknowledge the same God and Christ"; only irregularity of conduct would, in general, exclude a person from the visible church.

Zwingli had been of the same mind. "The Church in yᵉ scriptures," taught an English translation of his works by Thomas Cottesford of 1550,

> is diuersly takē. Fyrst it is takē for those chosē, which by yᵉ wyl of God are appointed to eternal lyfe. . . . Thys Church is knowen only vnto God. For he only . . . hath knowen the hertes of the chyldren of men. But neuerthelesse, they that are members of thys churche knowe verely that they themselues are electe . . . because they haue fayth in Christ. But they know none other mēbres therof besyde themselues. . . . But who truly beleueth, no man knoweth but he that beleueth.[83]

The invisible church, then, consisted of individuals each of whom, for all practical purposes, was the only knowable member; the Christian's duty was to participate in the true visible church, identifiable by preaching of the word and right administration of the sacraments, aware that each of the members of the visible church may, or may not, be a fellow-member of the invisible church. "Of thys knowen and sensible church . . . are al that with mouth cōfesse Christ, althoughe there be many reprobates amonge them."[84] Zwingli explained that Peter, writing to "the elect" scattered throughout Pontus etc. (1 Pet. 1.1–2), meant all people "of the cōgregacions, to the whiche he wrote, and not them only whiche properly are chosen of the Lorde. For as they were vnknowē vnto Peter, so could he not wryte vnto them."[85]

The English reformers took the same view as the Continental leaders. Robert Barnes, taking continuity between the Old Testament Israel and the New Testament *ecclesia* for granted, insisted that it often referred to "the holle multitude of ye people bothe good and bad. . . . for in this church are Juys and Saracens | Murtherars ād theuys | baudys and harlotes though we knowe them not."[86] However, he added, there is "a nother holy churche" which "stondythe by Christis eleccion," and "cā not be perfytly knowen | by oure exterior senses."[87] The believer was forced to rely upon what he could see of the outward signs of a true visible church to deduce that at least some true believers (although one could not tell which) were present. Sir Thomas More scoffed at "this imaginary church" whose members "be each to other unknowen."[88] John Frith understood

the cōgregacion of God . . . euē somewhat largely y^t is for all thē y^t are thought or coūted to be mēbers of Christ as it is taken mathewe .xiii. where Christ cōpareth it vnto a nette whyche receyueth bothe good fishe and euil.[89]

He insisted that "oure iudgement recoūteth [i.e., accounteth] al faythful & chosē y^t seme to be," which may be interpreted as implicitly permissive of a stricter judgment than many of the other reformers would have countenanced.[90]

*   *   *

This chapter has sought to make evident three propositions. Firstly, that the English magisterial reformers and their Continental mentors whose works they published believed, virtually to a man, in "predestination" as simplistically defined at the outset of this chapter. Whether or not they understood this to comprehend sub- or supralapsarianism (the idea that God had elected and reprobated after or before the fall of Adam), or in a limited atonement (the idea that Christ had died only for the sins of the elect), they agreed on the central content of this dogma. Secondly, they were agreed that this predestination was secret to man, and that one could be assured of one's own salvation, but could do no more than surmise about the state of one's neighbor. Indeed, since the heart was unsearchable, and since the greatest apparent saint may be a hypocrite in that inner citadel, and the greatest malefactor may convert on his deathbed, some reformers taught that even such surmizing was as impermissible as ill-advised. Thirdly, this nescience concerning the elect's identity led in practical terms, to a church whose spiritual authority lay, not in the sainthood of its membership, but in the purity of its preaching and its administration, and perhaps also (Elizabethan Puritanism was to contend for the point) in its discipline against outward moral offenders. However one believed respecting the last point, inclusivism was implied, since "the discipline" was envisaged as a weeding out of the notoriously unworthy from a (presumably) worthy mass, not as an exercise in membership working upward from a zero base. The church was a mixed multitude. As William Turner put it, "in the cōmon wealth of christianes, is the cōmon & outwarde church."[91] Entry into that church, via baptism, was open to babies, and therefore to all inhabitants of the "Christian commonwealth," since one could no more be sure which adult was, or was not, elect than which baby, and there was no fear about including reprobates within the visible church since this was inevitable in any case. Secret predestination had done much more for the doctrine of salvation by faith than simply act as a sheet-anchor for it, by taking any element of human response out of the soterial transaction; the former doctrine had rescued the latter for official Christendom and the state church.

The situation was not quite so neat and tidy as this of course; no historical generalization ever is. Hooper and Latimer seem to have been anxious in some respects to play down the usual Protestant understanding of predestination altogether. Not only Catholics like Thomas More, but religious conservatives like Henry VIII and Stephen Gardiner, flatly denied it. Moreover, there were a very few of the earliest English Protestants who, while accepting the first of our two propositions, and most likely the third as well, were yet sufficiently inconsistent—or perhaps just lacking in political realism—to hope that Reformed doctrine would not lead to religious coercion in a state church. Tyndale's argument for toleration, seized upon with delight by the Familists, has already been referred to.[92] Even so, there is no evidence that he ever developed this idea along Anabaptist or modern lines, and in any case, as has been mentioned earlier, there is some ambiguity as to what relationship this idea had with Tyndale's belief in the secrecy of election. John Frith was the other exception to the norm though, like Tyndale, there is no evidence that his opposition to religious coercion materially affected his ecclesiology. His argument from secret predestination to refraining from persecution is sufficiently striking to be worthy of quoting in full.

with violence wyll god haue no man compelled vnto his lawe. . . . As no man can serche the herte but onlye god | so can no man iudge or ordre faythe but onlye god thorow his holy sprete. Furthermore | faythe is a gyfte of god | which he destributeth at his owne pleasure |. Corinthiãs, 12. If he geue it not this day | he maye geue it to morow. And yf thou perceyue by any exterior worke that they [sic] neighbour haue it not | enstruct hī with godsworde [sic] & pray god to geue hī grace to bileue: that is rather a poynte of a chrysten man thē to compell a man by deeth or exterior violēce. Fynallye | what doth thy cōpulsion and violēce? Verely nothinge but make a starke hypocrite. For no man can cōpell the harte to beleue a thynge. . . . [93]

The argument is enough to gladden the heart of a modern Reformed Baptist. But only for a moment. As Hooper and Latimer are insufficiently representative to bear the weight of Hargrave's case, so are Tyndale and Frith sufficiently exceptional as to be unable to do more than dent the argument outlined here. Both men were active before Henry VIII's break with Rome, let alone before any recognizably Protestant church was established in England. Unburdened by any prospect of actual power, they could afford these outbursts of idealism, while continuing to hold theologies appropriate to an ecclesiological inclusivism that would render toleration for dissent redundant. Frith's belief in secret predestination was in any case sufficiently thorough to make the Anabaptist idea of a visible congregation admitting only true believers seem ridiculous to him; baptism could not testify that one was elect, "seeing many which are baptised fal afterward into . . . death euerlastynge," and he cut short his discussion of the point because "I truste yᵉ englishe vnto whome I wryte this haue no such opiniōs."[94] Even the exceptions to the general rules delineated in this chapter were, it seems, very moderate indeed in their deviation from the general Protestant norm.

6

Radical Doctrines: The Common Concerns of the Sectarians

God's Injustice and the Unpopularity of Predestination

DESPITE the essential unanimity of the magisterial Protestant reformers in endorsing some version of predestinarian teaching, many were uncomfortably aware of the doctrine's unpopularity with the wider public, and not a few felt the need to stress the positive aspects. Nicholas Lesse, who translated a work of Augustine on the subject in 1550, confessed that his object was to demonstrate that "this doctryn of predestination . . . is no straunge & new doctryn, but siche as the old church hath alway firmly beleued & constantly defendid."[1] Tyndale was anxious that his readers come to the doctrine from a favorable angle, or they would never be able to endure it; they should first ground themselves in the realization of their own helplessness and the wonder of Christ's sacrifice on the cross. Come to the teaching any other way, he worried, and "it shall not be possyble for the to thnynke that God is ryghteous & iuste."[2] He realized that many thought that "god is vniuste to damne vs afore we do any actuall deade," and excused himself simply by positing that "our darkenes can not perceyue his lyght."[3] John Stockwood, Beza's translator, was well aware that "there bee others whiche are vtter enemies vnto this doctrine, and do thinke all writinges hereof more meete for the fire, then for the reading of God his children"; he was thereby conceding the point made by the anonymous *Copie of an answere* that the predestinarians themselves expected "disfauorers of theyr fantesye" to have "credite amonge the people."[4] Ochino, too, knew that many were "offended wyth predestinacion," and "thyncke God to be parciall."[5] He answered that God did not merely will what was right, but that right became right by virtue of the fact that God had willed it. Anthony Gilby agreed: God "offendeth against no lawe, bicause his godly wyll is the lawe it selfe."[6]

213

Even Ochino, however, conceded that his censures applied only to those who reacted against the doctrine "preached in the maner it ought to be."[7] There seems to be something in the discussion of predestination by many predestinarians that implicitly recognized the need to present it in a particular way, and to approach it from a particular point of view, and not to encourage too close an inquiry about hows and whys and wherefores. Anthony Gilby, in a work appended to Whittingham's—and then Stockwood's—translation of Beza's *Treasure of Trueth touching the grounde worke of man his salvation, and chiefest pointes of Christian Religion; with a briefe summe of the comfortable doctrine of God his providence,* well expressed this concern, when he cautioned that "this secrecie of Election must onely bee lefte to the Maiestie of God, where, when, howe, and whome he thereby saueth and sheweth his mercy."[8] Stockwood likewise counseled the reader to avoid "all curious and needlesse questions," in case he "wrappeth and entangleth himselfe" in agonies of conscience.[9] Above all, there was care taken not to give occasion to the kind of unpredictable behavior that might be provoked by the conviction that one was saved, do what one would, or, conversely, by the despair that one was ineluctably damned.[10]

The thought that all acts were finally acts of God was never far below the surface of any strongly predestinarian system, and this carried with it the peril of concluding that God was the author of sin. Whenever supralapsarians urged, as Peter Martyr did, that original sin "goeth not before predestination or reprobation; but of necessitie followeth it," the danger point was uncomfortably close.[11] Erasmus Sarcerius had already pointed out where the road led: "if p̄destinaiō taketh away the libertie of our wyll (as Valla & others haue thought) I se not howe god can be excused that he is notcauser [sic] of synnes."[12] Thomas More had argued similarly that "this execrable heresy maketh God the cause of all evil," and that the damned in such a universe as the predestinarians posited would suffer for God's "own deeds wrought in them by himself."[13]

Radicals felt themselves justified in seizing upon the same point. John Trew believed that the predestinarians made God "author of all the sin and abomination that is done and committed on the earth, clean discharging the devil and man thereof."[14] Thomas Cole, in his recantatory sermon of 1553, noted that this was a favored line of radical attack upon official Protestantism.[15] William Laurence and John Barre insisted that Bernhere's contention—"y^t in respect of godes comanndymēt it was not godes wyll y^t Adam shuld syñe but in respect of godes secret will, god would haue Adam to syñe"—was "A blasphemy against god, making him ye autor of syñe & affirme his worde to be untre."[16] The anonymous author of *The Copie of an answere* made the same accusation to John Knox.[17] Seen in this aspect, the predestinarian emphasis of the reformers must have seemed to some like a betrayal of the Reformation itself; preaching, turning services into the vernacular, putting the Bible into the hands of everyman, and destroying priestcraft and the magic of the mass had seemed to bring God nearer to ordinary people. The doctrinally pivotal position of predestination, on the other hand, required learned men to explain its parodoxical ramifications, and made God mysterious and remote once again. Furthermore, it appeared to make him arbitrary and unjust.

Quite apart from the effects which "Reformed" views on predestination might have upon the doctrine of God, many radicals worried about the effect on Christian believers themselves. But not all did so. Those radicals who leaned either in a rationalist or a Gnostic direction, such as the Arians or the Family of Love, found a modus vivendi with predestination, while men like Hart, Champneys, Cooche, Trew, "Cerberus," and (if it was not Cooche) the author of *The cõfutation of the errors of the careles by necessitie,* whose concerns were primarily moralistic or biblicist, could not. None of these epithets can be applied without qualification, of course, for the categories "rationalist," "biblicist," and so on, could overlap somewhat in the case of given individuals or groups, but with the cautionary terminology of "leaning," and adjectives like "primarily" the dangers of such a generalization need not outweigh its usefulness. Arianism tended to emphasize the "otherness" and transcendence of God, Gnostic groups such as the Family of Love his mysteriousness; in either case, a belief in ineluctable providence seemed to be a natural concomitant. Familism was almost bound, by its very nature, to imply that ultimate truth was revealed only to the favored few, who had been granted spiritual insight and the capacity to penetrate the mysterious verbiage of the sect (or at any rate, to appear to have done so while living happily with its opaqueness). For the biblicists, on the other hand, predestination seemed to undercut the Scripture's moral imperatives to the individual believer, and the ability of every person to meet those imperatives.[18] It also suppressed the possibility of discerning the sheep from the goats in this life, thus perpetuating the frustration of those who sought to erect a thoroughly cleansed and purified church well away from the rotten foundations of the ruined medieval structure.[19] In this, the biblicist radicals displayed similarities to Continental Anabaptists.[20] Certainly their magisterial Protestant opponents noticed and expected a connection between "anabaptism" and opposition to Reformed doctrines of predestination.[21]

However tempting, the urge to assign to the biblicist radicals a constant and conscious equation between free-will theology and separatist ecclesiology would be a mistake. By their writings they do not appear to have held some inevitable connection between the two at the forefront of their minds, though it may be possible to argue that the later Champneys and Cooche saw such a connection. Their disputes with magisterial Protestantism were, in their own minds, primarily theological and moral, rather than ecclesiological. It was, after all, the Puritan debates of the Elizabethan era, in which the Puritan radicals shared a common theology with their antagonists in the church hierarchy, that the focus of attention was upon ecclesiology itself, and which ultimately led some of them not only to separate from the Church of England but, even more significantly, to construct a theoretical rationale for having done so. The generality of the earlier radicals surveyed in the present work were, by contrast, less sophisticated, less well educated and, more importantly for our present purposes, less obsessed with ecclesiology than those Elizabethan Puritans who eventually turned to separatism. Indeed, their leaders' general lack of sophistication (only "Cerberus" seems to have had the benefit of any extensive formal education) undoubtedly inhibited them from inferring an explicit separatism from their own radical theological views; the failure of Hart to spell out the ecclesiology that was implicit in his ideas has already been commented upon in the present work.[22] The free-will men, Lollard survivalists, and quasi-Anabaptists, concentrated upon attacking the Reformed theology of the Protestant hierarchy; the later, Elizabethan separatists, by contrast, formally espoused that theology themselves. The former were more often separatist by implication than by injunction; theirs was a separatism in practice rather than by precept.

That there is a correlation between the theology of the midcentury radicals and an inclination toward, if not a clear conception of, a gathered church would seem undeniable. It may just be possible to envisage a national, coercive church run along lines that would have suited John Trew or Joan Bocher; the same can definitely not be said for Henry Hart, Robert Cooche, the author of *The cōfutation of the errors of the careles by necessitie,* John Champneys, or the Family of Love. Non-Catholic varieties of anti-predestinarianism were only the most frequent badge of religious radicalism that pointed in the direction of a sectarian ecclesiology.

Millenarianism, perfectionism, Gnosticism, antiintellectualism and the relentless pursuit of the principle that all believers were priests, even opposition to religious coercion (though that was occasionally espoused by some of the better men among the magisterial Protestants[23]): all were basically incompatible with the stability essential to a uniform, regulated, compulsory, and officially sponsored church. Of these, the search for perfection or the expression of dissatisfaction with the moral standards engendered by Protestantism was the most widely felt concern. This concern tended to crystallize into the conviction among many radicals that conservative Protestants' belief in predestination was leading, if not to libertinism, then at least to moral complacency.

Walking Worthy of the Call: The Radicals and Purity of Life

It should ever be borne in mind that the sixteenth-century Reformation made its appearance by combining the denunciation of long-standing moral abuses and laxity with a claim to be returning to the doctrines of the primitive, or at least of the immediately post-Constantinian, church. The reformers could capitalize on the natural human tendency to draw conclusions from the observable behavior of moral agents about the purity of the doctrines they propound. The behavior of the generality of people being what it is, it could not be otherwise than that the official Reformation would fail to deliver its apparent promises in the area of morality. As this became apparent, radicals, from the earliest Anabaptists onward, drew the appropriate inferences about the purity of the reformers' own doctrines. The reformers could hardly avoid this difficulty without actually enforcing higher moral standards on an unwilling public by moving toward some kind of disciplinarian or theocratic tyranny, a direction that was to appeal to those earnest Elizabethan Puritans who were not yet disillusioned with the enterprise of a godly commonwealth. The less sanguine realized more quickly that holiness was unlikely to be instituted by Caesar, and not likely to take effect if he tried (or concurred). Groups of such people were likely to conclude that holiness was best sought apart from the official structures, and to call into question the new doctrinal systems that those structures imposed.

The Familist "E.R.," who wrote to Rogers in December 1578, appealed to James 1.22 and Rom. 2.13, which emphasize the doing of the commands of God over against mere hearing, thereby illustrating the moralistic tendency in Familism, though it would have been equally typical of any of the radical groupings discussed here.[24] The frequent appeal to James by the pre-Reformation Lollard groups has been noted in an earlier chapter.[25] None of the other radicals considered here, not even Hart, appears to have made disproportionate use of its authority in their writings, but the anonymous former free-willer, tentatively identified in the present work as "Master Gibson," whose letter to his former colleagues was published by Strype, complained that one of the chief hindrances to his conversion had been to "understand S.Paul and S.James to make them agree together."[26]

All of the radicals shared a concern with expressing personal holiness of life well above the standards of behavior in the official church. Heretics condemned in 1535 in London were said to have insisted that "whosoeuer sinneth wittingly after baptisme, cannot be saued," while "anabaptists" encountered by John Hooper in 1549 argued the same concerning those who sin after receiving the Holy Ghost.[27] Champneys considered it to be a hallmark of the doubting Thomases of the official church to deny that there was any "spirit geuen vnto man wherby he should remaine righteous alway in Christ."[28] Veron noted that the "Anabaptistes and free will men" appealed constantly to 1 John 5.3: "This is the love of God, that we keep his commandments, and his commandments are not heavy."[29] There was an expectation among dissenters that the truly godly could and would keep the scriptural injunctions, and that the doctrines of the official church were simply an excuse for equivocation on this point that made magisterial Protestantism but little better than the corrupt Catholicism which it claimed to have replaced. The author of *The cōfutation of the errors of the careles by necessitie* asked rhetorically: "How many of thē [the predestinarians] cā we perceave by their conversatiō, that they have cast of the old mā ād put on the new mā, walking sincerely in their vocation ād the true feare of God"; clearly, he believed that they had not generally done so.[30] John Knox warned his brethren in Scotland against sectaries who were "bold to affirme, that amangis us thair is no trew Kirk, be reasone that oure lyvis do not agrie with the Word whilk we profess"; he added that "thai wold aspyre and contend for a greatter perfectioun than the commoun beleiveris culd have, and thairfoir did thai devyd thame selves apart . . . but to what haliness thai ar atteaynit let the warld witnes."[31]

Even Knox himself was not necessarily as skeptical of the sectaries' moral attainments as this remark suggests; he saw the dissenters as "mair dangerous and mair to be feirit" than the papists because of their "clok of mortification of the flesche, of godlie lyfe, and of Christian justice."[32] Other adversaries felt keenly the danger and persuasive power, in the battle for public support, of the radicals' own good example. Nicholas Lesse, writing in 1550, felt that the "anabaptysts and frewyl masters" were "so mych more dangerouse" precisely because "their myschefe is cloked with a dobl face of holiness ten tyme more religious . . . than were yᵉ superstitious & arrogant papystes"; they were "cloked ouer with goodly wordes . . . and sanctimony of lyfe."[33] John Philpot made the same point.[34] Certainly Peter Franke, the Dutch Anabaptist burned in Colchester in 1536, left an outstanding reputation to the extent that even John Bale was prepared to defend his reputation and take it as a sign that he had possessed true faith.[35] In this untypically generous response, however, it was perhaps Bale, rather than Franke, who was unusual.

The radicals did not speak with one voice on how far to take this insistence upon an upright life in the believer. Knox's Anabaptist adversary believed good works to be an indispensable sign of true discipleship, as did the author of *The Copie of an answere*.[36] Hart appears to have believed them indispensable for salvation itself.[37] Champneys clearly believed in a *posse non peccare,* that there was indeed a "spirite geuen vnto man wherby he should remaine righteous alway in Christ," while the Family of Love and some of the Edwardian radicals referred to by Hooper seem to have believed in a *non posse peccare*.[38]

Degrees of Nicodemism

Nicodemism is the blanket term that has been used here to refer to practices aimed at minimizing the effects of persecution while continuing to practice a dissident faith. The Lollards had established a record, though not perhaps quite a principle, of willingness to recant followed by relapse into "heresy;" Thomas More, writing in 1529 about the still new phenomenon of Protestantism, seems to have been thinking of them when he charged that

> this church that we be of, that take your church for heretics, have had many such martyrs therein; . . . whereas of your secret church I never yet found or heard of anyone in all my life, but he would forswear your faith to save his life.[39]

Joan Bocher and George van Parris did not, of course, abjure (though Joan had done so in the 1520s) but Michael Thombe, John

Assheton, and John Champneys, who were also all arrested in Edward VI's reign, did so, and Champneys at least returned to radical activism.[40] He had claimed in the first place that Christ's religion had been so persecuted from the time of the apostles, that "no man myght be suffred opēly to folow it."[41] Though none of Cooche's extant remarks mentions the subject of secret discipleship, his own example speaks volumes; he remained a singer in the royal chapel for years while continuing to propound Anabaptist ideas.[42] According to John Rogers, Christopher Vitel had held firmly Nicodemist ideas while still in his Arian phase.[43] It was the Family of Love's elevation of Nicodemist practice to the level of principled mendacity that most worried the Elizabethan government, whose chief implement of repressing dissent was thereby taken from its hands.[44]

Biblicism and Antiintellectualism

Biblicism was no new phenomenon to the sixteenth-century radicals, and may have been in part an inheritance from the "known men" who preceded them. Bishop Pecock, writing in the fifteenth century, had complained that the prime heresy of the Lollards with whom he came into contact was the belief "that no gouernaunce is to be holde of Cristen men the seruice or the lawe of God, saue it which is groundid in Holi Scripture."[45] The appeal to the Scripture was a constant with all of the groups discussed here, as it was with the state-church that was attempting to suppress them. Even the publications of the Family of Love contained copious scriptural references in the margins, though the methodology of interpretation was as unusual as the conclusions thereby reached.

The other radicals were more predictable in this respect. Hart's appeal to "common-sense interpretation" of the Scripture over against the complex theological constructs of the learned has been discussed here at some length.[46] John Champneys despised "clerckly lernynge" and repeatedly appealed to "the true literall sence of the holy scriptures" as the source of religious authority.[47] Proctor's Arian defined "right faith" as that "which the scriptures do testify . . . with one and the same perpetuall tenor and concent."[48] "S.B.," the English Anabaptist arguing with William White in 1575, saw the Scriptures as the sole authority in matters of religion.[49] Paul Baughton, apprehended in the 1530s for handling "books of Anabaptists' Confession," "will believe nothing but scripture without exposition," while his colleague John Raulinges believed that the "scripture is not to be expounded but believed."[50] All of these would have agreed with Bishop Pecock's Lollards that true exegesis was to be found, not by the educated, but by ordinary people whose hearts were right before God, and that "what euer Cristen man or woman be meke in spirit . . . schal without fail and defaut fynde the trewe vndirstonding of Holi Scripture in what euer place he or sche schal rede and studie."[51] For reasons that have already been mentioned, no credence can be given to Robert Parsons's report that Joan Bocher's final speech included the exhortation to "goe read Scriptures," or that she smuggled Bibles into the royal court, but Joan's concern with the centrality of the Scripture is evident from her earlier career with the Lollards of Essex.[52] Jean Veron, in the preface to his 1548 translation of one of Bullinger's works, sneered at the lack of theological sophistication of radicals who relied on a literal exegesis of the Scripture and, writing in the 1560s, he took it for granted that Champneys and his ilk were "enemies vnto learning."[53] John Philpot called the scripturalism of uneducated radicals a "beggar's cloak."[54] Robert Cooche and the author of *The Copie of an Answere* were not antiintellectual, of course, though they were biblicist. Both showed an appreciation of learning, and an awareness of major writers of the early church and of their own days.[55] That they were exceptional in this is shown by William Turner's mock surprise at Cooche's appeal to Cyprian: "Ye hadde wont to . . . crake nothing but scripture, scripture."[56]

Melchiorite Christology

Another frequent tenet of the radicals was the conviction of Melchior Hoffmann, that Christ took no flesh of his mother but brought it with him from heaven. This was the heresy for which Joan Bocher was put to death in 1550. Paul Baughton, like the Dutch Anabaptists with whom he met, held "strange opinions," almost certain Melchiorite, concerning the humanity of Christ, and Michael Thombe in 1549 did likewise, but recanted.[57] There are hints in the writings of the free-will men that Hart may have come to share the same views; certainly he moved in circles in which such ideas were reasonably common currency, and John Hooper experienced "much trouble" in debating with advocates of this Christology.[58] Two of the Dutch Anabaptists belonging to the group to which "S.B." was attaching himself in 1575, suffered martyrdom for beliefs "touching the truth of Christ's incarnation" and so, as

William White not unreasonably inferred, "very likely you your self allso do . . . deny" orthodoxy on this point.[59]

John Champneys did not espouse Monophysitism, however, and both John Trew and Nicholas Sheterden expressly repudiated it.[60] More significantly, the avowedly Anabaptist Robert Cooche said nothing on the matter either, but perhaps his rejection of original sin obviated the need for any radical Christology; the danger which Hoffmann had perceived in traditional orthodoxy was that it made Christ's human nature identical with that of the inherently sinful people whom he came to redeem since, as Joan Bocher said, Mary's "seed and flesh was sinful, as the seed and flesh of others," and this would render him disqualified to act as redeemer.[61] Cooche's denial of the transmission of sin by physical generation might, perhaps, be thought to have relieved the problem. Hendrik Niclaes did not teach Melchiorite views, but it seems that individual Familists, such as John Bourne of Wisbech, may have done so.[62] In sum, it must be concluded that Melchiorite Christology was a persistent, but by no means ubiquitous, thread of radical opinion.

Persecution: Theories and Realities

That dissenters oppose persecution of their own views is axiomatic, but many of the sixteenth-century radicals seem to have opposed all compulsion in religion. Trew and his fellows had sought to prove the unlawfulness of persecution, and Hart had criticized the clergy who "teache their flocke by poure and penaltie" rather than by example.[63] The Anabaptist against whom John Knox wrote, repeatedly equated Reformed theology with religious persecution, and denounced both, while Robert Cooche accused William Turner of seeking to achieve by fire what he could not by argument.[64] "S.B." thought that the "spirituall temple" which was the New Testament church "must be builded with spirituall weapons" only; "a true Christian must be a spirituall man" who "must have spirituall weapon to fight with spirituall enemies."[65] The Family of Love also recorded their horror at enforcing orthodoxy by the sword.[66]

The climate in favor of toleration, however, was not great. The Familists could quote Tyndale on the subject, but he had been writing at a time when it might have been possible for the idealism of English Protestants to be helped along by the lack of any taste of power.[67] John Foxe, to be sure, had a distaste for the execution of heretics by Protestant governments, and William Turner, in one of his better moments, asserted that only "the sworde of goddes word" was to be used.[68] Robert Crowley even urged that no one be "cōpelled by fyre, fagots, or swerde, to speake or wryte any thyng cōtrary to the conscience."[69]

Crowley's sentiments were exceptional, and most magisterial Protestants were more insistent on the traditional concern to enforce orthodoxy by any means available. Turner himself agreed that Cooche, as "an open felon against the kyngis lawes," "iustly deserued" to pay the full civil penalty for his transgressions, and Turner's anti-Catholic views were certainly no more tolerant.[70] John Trew and his friends were told that they "were like to die" for their opinions "if the Gospel should reign again," and John Philpot expressed the view that Joan Bocher's burning was a wholly justifiable action.[71] John Proctor was in no doubt that the Arian against whom he wrote deserved to be severely punished, and John Knewstub was anxious to see the Family of Love suffer "punishment and affliction."[72] John Knox threatened action against his Anabaptist antagonist in any "comonwelth where iustice against blesphemers may be ministered," and Jean Veron despised Champneys for failing to "playe the man" and to emerge from hiding to suffer for his antipredestinarian publication of the early 1560s.[73] Indeed, it was Veron who gave perhaps the best expression of the "spiritual" reason for persecuting radical heretics when, in his prologue to a translation of Bullinger, he urged magistrates to "spare theym not," for "better it is that fewe doo peryshe, then that all the whole countrey should through theyr wycked perswasion, be brought to naught."[74]

The remarkable thing is how little zeal most of these avid would-be persecutors had for the actual pursuit and punishment of the heretics known to them personally. In this they perhaps reflected the ambivalence of the population at large: disapproval of heresy, and a desire for its suppression, coupled with an unwillingness to destroy the lives or careers of given individuals for their religious aberrations. William Wilkinson was eager to warn the populace about the views of the Family of Love, but did not say "so much as I might truely, . . . hauyng refrayned for their sakes especially, which are my very frendes beyng somewhat ouertaken with the lime of that secte."[75] William Turner claimed that he could have obtained Cooche's prosecution had he so wished, and the drawn-out efforts of three Elizabethan bishops to turn him from his heterodoxy suggest that they, too, were not anxious to seize the first opportunity to clap this dissenter into irons.[76] Even Knox, for all his fire-breathing, was remarkably coy about betraying the identity of the "Anabaptist" who was clearly known to him personally. John Rogers did not publish the name of a single Familist whose identity was not already common knowledge, even though—or probably because—he was "familiarly acquainted" with a number of them, and he often referred to individuals only by their initials.[77] John Proctor did not name his Arian, for fear of displeasing him *in case* he had recanted, "as some saye that he hathe"; it rather sounds as though Proctor was ready to seize upon the slenderest reason that might excuse him from getting someone into trouble! All, it seemed, wanted the punishment of heretics in general, until confronted with some specific heretic. Proctor confessed that "I greatly detest & abhor the opinion and sect, | whiche can not to sharply be touched: for to your p^{er}son I owe no displeasure or malice at al." He clearly spoke for many.[78]

The activities of Henry Hart and company in Kent, and of Thomas Upchard and his fellows in Essex, were apparently conducted on a scale that would have been noticeable by their neighbors well before Christmas 1550, and yet it was not until those activities took a form too big to ignore—like sixty people crowding into a house for "talke of Scriptures"—that trouble ensued.[79] Joan Bocher, whose heresies were deemed so serious by the ecclesiastical authorities, was kept for a year, allowing strenuous efforts to convert her, before she was finally burned, and when she was, no one seems to have been anxious to authorize the deed. The customers of an inn at Colchester in Mary's reign were appalled at Vitel's apparently successful denial of the deity of Christ in debate with John Barre, but no one seems to have rushed to inform officialdom.[80] Hooper debated with the "anabaptists" who flocked to his sermons in 1549; he did not send for the constables.[81] It hardly seems credible that the highly organized radical conventicle meeting in Surrey, two of whose members were arrested in 1561, had been able to meet regularly since at least "the beginning of Queen Mary's reign" and to keep in contact with similar groups in six other counties as well as London without awakening in their neighbors anything more substantial than "suspicion."[82]

The surest way to come to offical attention, it seems, was to publish a book; this is what got John Champneys into trouble in 1549. The Family of Love lived a quiet and relatively undisturbed existence in England until the flood of Niclaes's books, translated by Vitel, began pouring into England from the mid-1570s; only then did the authorities react with the prosecution of Robert Sharpe and others in 1575, the publication of several attacks on the Family in late 1570s, the issuing of a proclamation against them in 1580, and the setting up in the same year of commissions under the bishops of Ely and Norwich to inquire into and suppress Familism in their districts.[83]

The anonymity of several of the tracts discussed in this thesis—Knox's Anabaptist and the author of *The Copie of an answere*—tells its own story, of course; radicals were aware of the dangers inherent in the publishing enterprise. Champneys attempted anonymity in his second foray into print, in 1561, but when his printer was arrested his identity was revealed.[84] Robert Cooche's work and that of Knox's Anabaptist do not seem to have been printed at all.

Sects in a Corner and Public Doctrine

To many critics, the proof that the dissenters were in the wrong was astonishingly simple: they were in a tiny minority. As Thomas Cole said in his recantatory sermon of 1553, it was a "stinkyng floure" to claim "y^t it is lawful to euery man to make peculiar orders to him self" concerning religion "in contempt of the cōmon order."[85] Though in many ways empathic and understanding of the Familists, Rogers showed a degree of baffled incomprehension of their refusal to comply with "publick doctrine," that which "everybody knew": "Alas, why are you so bewitched, or so bereft of sense, so to imagine, that a mortall man, an obscure Authour, whome you neuer sawe nor knewe, hath onely the truth: and all the world else seduced and deceiued."[86] Where theological reasoning was insufficiently persuasive, psychological pressure to social conformity might succeed. Credal deviants from socially accepted norms were, as they still are, confronted with Charles V's reasoning in respect to Luther: a single monk must err.

It was a powerful argument, and surprising people were prepared to use it. Even William White, sitting in his prison cell in 1575 for his illegal religious activities, saw no incongruity in telling "S.B." that "you thinke of yourself and your owne secte to be wiser and to vnderstand more then the whole world besides."[87] The Anabaptist's ignorance stemmed from the fact that he deprived himself of "publique doctrine."[88] Knox, though he would have nothing to do with Roman Catholic services or ceremonies, still thought it a point worth making against Anabaptists that they would frequent no congregation but their own.[89]

Jean Veron depicted the sectaries as typically lower class: "these men syttynge upon there ale benches," ready, like Champneys,

to distribute their pernicious books "in hugger mugger."[90] Robert
Crowley similarly felt it distasteful for writings presuming to propound God's truth to be "cast about in the streates of Londō,"
rather than sold at a recognized bookseller's shop.[91] William White
called the Anabaptists whom "S.B." so admired, "your owne sect
in a corn[er]," and Nicholas Lesse complained that the sectaries
"lork ī cornars" and "crep secretly into mens bosoms"; genuine
espousers of God's truth would do no such thing.[92] John Philpot
insisted that "the truth seeketh no corners," which is where he
said the sectarians went about "to pervert you from the
true faith."[93] The dissenters' separation from the all-embracing
church and their claims to a religious elitism were breaking social solidarity.

It was a betrayal of the rest of society to insist, as did the Familists whom William Wilkinson encountered, that "they onely are
the Church."[94] When Robert Sharpe abjured Familism in 1575, his
declaration of recantation criticized H.N. for "segregating vnto him
selfe a priuate Conuenticle," and the Privy Council in March 1579
worried about those who keep "conventicles a parte"; true religion
was, after all, as Professor Collinson has said, "a public duty, not
a private opinion or a voluntary profession."[95] Nicholas Lesse saw
this as clearly as anyone when he compared the Roman Catholic
church favorably with the horrible specter of "anabaptism" and
free-will.

> Papistes althoughe they were right nought for yᵉ soul yet were they
> good and profytable for the body for ciuil common welthes, for the
> mētinaunce of cyuil iustice, & al good politique orders. But asfor [sic]
> thes, thei ar nether good for yᵉ body nor for the soule yea they ar most
> mortal enemies and cruell murtherers to both.[96]

Lesse was right; unbridled expressions of religious faith under-
mined the very foundations of social order in the early modern
period, a social order for which both Catholicism and state-church
Protestantism acted as supports. The double murders that Lesse
anticipated have long since been accomplished. "Public doctrine"
now takes another form, but religious faith or unbelief is, de facto
if not quite de jure in Britain, on the basis which many of the
radicals studied here advocated. Social solidarity, hierarchy, and
uniformity have given way to an atomized society based on rough
egalitarianism. These changes—the deaths of the "politique order"
and of the corporate social "soule" for which Lesse contended—
have been brought about, of course, by a complex mass of later

developments. They were not caused by the sixteenth-century radicals. Even so, it is high time to examine closely the ideas of those who, if they did not succeed in murdering monolithic religion and the "politique order" which that monolith underpinned, nevertheless began to contemplate the deed.

Appendix: A Modern Historiography of Mid-Sixteenth-Century Dissent

MUCH of the historiography for this study has been done, as it were, on the hoof, with comments upon the work of other historians made in passing or in relation to some specific point under discussion. What follows here will, for that reason, be of the nature of a brief summary.

The scientific era, as far as Hart and company are concerned, commences with the work of Champlin Burrage in 1912. His reproduction of the depositions of 1550 and 1551 allowed these conventiclers to emerge from the obscurity of rare documents (and historians' comments thereon) into the light of day, and this fact has ensured that his *Early English Dissenters in the Light of Recent Research* would remain the foundational work on the subject, to which subsequent historians have consistently referred.[1] Nevertheless, Burrage was of the opinion that to call the free-willers separatists was "not quite sufficiently supported by the evidence,"[2] a view that has been called into question here, where it has been suggested that the conventiclers' theology pointed to an (admittedly incoherent) separatist ecclesiology.

Since Burrage, a number of historians have given (mostly brief) consideration to the Kent and Essex free-willers. M. M. Knappen, writing in 1939, devoted less than two pages to them in his introduction to a chapter on Congregationalism. In describing the conventiclers as "primitive Arminians," he was confounding terminology appropriate to antipredestinarianism of the right with that of the left, but in his designation of them as "halfway Anabaptists," he was correctly reflecting the radical nature of their distinctive tenets.[3] A. G. Dickens struck the same note in the first edition of his masterly book, *The English Reformation*.[4] In the second edition, he opines that the group as a whole gives "the impression of a discussion-group rather than that of an integrated sect under imperious or charismatic leadership," and he concludes that such a group "stood little chance of longevity amid the forces of Tudor religion and society."[5] The characterization of Hart and Trew's circles as a "discussion-group" is perhaps a little harsh, but it is certainly true that the free-willers were no closed world unto themselves, and that this, together with their failure to expand to any great size, probably sealed their fate once the formidable persecution of Mary's reign set in. Strangely, Dickens refers to John Champneys as being "a Melchiorite Anabaptist" in 1549; the likeliest explanation for such a statement is perhaps a confusion between Champneys and Michael Thombe, whose cases appear near one another in Cranmer's Register.[6] Dickens sees the Family of Love as "the most important direct offshoot of Anabaptism in England"; the "incursion of continental sectarianism" in general he believes to hold "no little significance for the later history of religion."[7]

In 1978, Michael Watts, in his work *The Dissenters from the Reformation to the French Revolution,* drew attention to an impressively wide range of information in the mere seven and a half pages which he devoted to what he calls "the earlier, radical, stream" from which the river of later English dissent partly derives. His judgment is, for the most part, wisely cautious, referring to the free-willers simply as "radicals" or "conventiclers."[8] Watts accepts the designation "Anabaptist" for Joan Bocher, as well as for Robert Cooche, who surely deserves it more than any other English radical, while his comments on Familism are fairly perfunctory.[9]

A fairly extensive study of the free-willers was published in 1967 by O. T. Hargrave in the journal *Church History* entitled "The Free-Willers in the English Reformation." Hargrave, however, considered his work to be a part of the search "for the sources and origins of the liberal theology which toward the end of the sixteenth and the beginning of the seventeenth century came to occupy an increasingly important position in English religious thought." In fact, the article seems to be an offshoot of his doctoral research on the doctrine of predestination in the English Reformation, and his interest is confined to Hart and the free-willers, rather than extending to the subject of dissent as a whole. The free-willers, he thought, were "Arminians *avant la lettre.*" Although Hargrave did not ignore the ecclesiological significance of the conventiclers' views (he described them as "separatist in activity and radical in opinion"), he clearly felt that this could be kept distinct from their theological antipredestinarianism. To this latter characteristic he gave more weight, praising their contribution "to the evolution of a liberal tradition in English religious thought."[10] In this enterprise, he came close to the position of Archbishop Laurence a century and a half before, who sought in the radicals a rescue from the uniform predestinarianism of magisterial Protestant origins. Hargrave was mistaken, however; D. D. Wallace was only stating the obvious when he wrote that "the view of O. T. Hargrave . . . seems wide of the mark in regarding these free-willers as forerunners of later English Arminianism—they were far closer to Lollards, certain representatives of the Continental Radical Reformation, and later English "free-willing" Separatists than to seventeenth-century Laudians."[11] It has been argued in the present study that, in the minds of Trew and his fellows, at least, their belief in free-will was part and parcel of their essential evangelicalism.[12] The anti-Calvinists who constitute the subject matter of N. Tyacke's recent study would have contemplated the activities of the free-will men, if they did so at all, with disdain.[13] For the Laudians, the denial of predestination was a part of their sacramentalism, and of a partial return to the religion of hierarchy, ritual, and tradition of the Middle Ages; it implied a downplaying of salvation by faith. For Hargrave, it is the "liberal tradition in English religious thought" which is the thing presupposed, not any link between radical, de facto separatists and Laudians, two groups who had nothing in common; the antipredestinarianism of the right must be firmly differentiated from that of the left, even if both chose their ground, in part at least, because the doctrine of predestination was so precious (and even vital) to the center.

One of the best brief surveys of the whole field of mid-Tudor radicalism is the 1979 article, "Anabaptism and English Sectarianism in the Mid-Sixteenth Century," by D. M. Loades. This emphasizes the diversity of dissent in the period. Loades accepts contemporary descriptions of this dissent as "Anabaptism," though as a term of convenience, not with any illusions as to its strict accuracy.[14] He concludes that "it cannot be positively proved that any 'gathered' congregation, rejecting the whole concept of a state church, existed in England at any time between 1530 and 1570."[15] He does not mention Robert Cooche, whose likely following in Edward's reign appears to have been thoroughly Anabaptist. Depending on the rigor of one's definition of "positive proof," it would be hard to quarrel with Loades's contention. Rather, one would have to argue, as this study has sought to do, that the ideas of the radicals often led in a sectarian direction, even if, Cooche excepted, that sectarianism was neither systematic nor explicit.

Strangely for one as understandably skeptical as Loades, he is inclined to accept as genuine the account given by Miles Hogarde, in his *Displaying of the Protestantes,* of a radical Protestant congregation in Marian London, which rejected alike Catholicism and the religion of the Edwardian bishops. Hogarde, the Catholic apologist, described the supposed activities of one "Father Brown" and his group in 1555, but his account is so jaundiced as to amount to caricature, and few historians have given much credence to the group's existence.[16] Loades himself admits that "it is difficult to know how seriously to take all this," but thinks that "the circumstantial detail of the episode is convincing, and makes it very unlikely that the author simply invented it."[17] Whether or not that is so, the account as a whole is such blatant propaganda that, given the complete absence of supporting information from other sources, Hogarde's story falls well short of most tests of "positive proof" of radical activity.

Some mention must be made of those historians of Anabaptism who have given consideration in their writings to developments in England. Unfortunately, in respect to Henry Hart and his fellows, there has been a tendency on the part of some of these writers to quote one another's work as authoritative in such a way as to perpetuate errors. W. R. Estep's book, *The Anabaptist Story,* states that "Hart spent much time in prison," citing Horst's article on Anabaptism in England in *The Mennonite Encyclopedia* as authority. Horst's article claims that "two Anabaptist ministers, Henry Hart and Humphrey Middleton, were imprisoned in Mary's reign"; both Hart's supposed imprisonment and the "Anabaptism" of himself and his followers are claims which lack any basis in documentary evidence.[18]

Concerning religious radicalism in England generally during this period, Estep has little to say, but he is rather too hopeful that the dislike of the institution of godparents by the members of Richard Fitz's privy church in London in the 1560s "might imply some question about the propriety of infant baptism."[19] This is clutching at straws, for Fitz's church consisted of Puritans impatient with the slowness of Elizabeth's "reformation," and their criticism comes from a background of hostility to all "superstitious ceremonies." Although he accepts that the matter cannot be proved, he clearly still hankers after the idea that English separatism was closely related to Anabaptism, and followed it in all but the issue of believers' baptism, though how this is compatible with his admission of the former's "Calvinistic tendency" is unclear.[20]

G. H. Williams, in his magnum opus *The Radical Reformation,* finds a "close interrelationship" between "Libertinism, anti-Trinitarianism, Anabaptism of the Melchiorite strain, and Spiritualism," and that "its anti-Trinitarianism seems to have been more prominent than in the Netherlands."[21] Certainly all of the elements Williams mentioned were present; occasionally more than one of these was exhibited by a given dissenter or group, but whether or not this amounts to an "interrelationship" as if there were some inevitability about the matter, is harder to judge. Clearly, those who had entered into the religious underworld by opening themselves to one strain of proscribed thought might be prepared to entertain others, but of the radicals discussed in the present work, it is doubtful whether more than one of the labels mentioned by Williams can really be attached to any but Vitel and his flock of English Familists.

Speaking of historians of Anabaptism, some mention must be made of I. B. Horst and his 1972 book, *The Radical Brethren: Anabaptism and the English Reformation to 1558,* of which the present study has voiced much criticism already. As will have become apparent, there are many errors, both of judgment and of fact, in Horst's book. Even so, Horst deserves recognition for having drawn attention to much important material. His keenness to perceive genuine Anabaptism in England is sometimes a little overenthusiastic, but he is arguably the first of several recent historians to delve into the amorphous radicalism of this period in real depth, and so can be credited, perhaps, with helping to awaken interest.

What Anabaptism is to Horst, Lollardy is to J. F. Davis, whose book, *Heresy and Reformation in the South East of England, 1520–1559,* is concerned with emphasizing the Lollard contribution to English Protestantism in general. His knowledge of the legal documentation of the period appears to be vast, but he shows little interest in the actual writings of the various "heretics." Davis is no more at fault here than other historians of this subject; narrative, not theology, has held the center of the field in almost all studies of midsixteenth-century sectarianism. Like Hargrave, Davis describes the view of the free-willers as "a prefiguring of Arminianism that became one of the principal opponents of Puritanism."[22] But the free-willers' antipredestinarianism was a move beyond that religious outlook that was to become Puritanism, and was hence a species of radicalism. When Robert and Thomas Cole, both former members of the group, became Puritan clergymen under Elizabeth, they were moving in a conservative direction from their previous views, not becoming more radical, which they certainly would have been had they been coming to their Puritanism from a "foreshadowing" of the Laudian era. Despite these criticisms, *Heresy and Reformation* remains a fine book, and presents a wealth of material.

Mention must also be made of the work of the American scholar, J. W. Martin. He has written a number of articles for academic journals over the past fifteen years, and these have recently (1989) been republished in one volume under the title *Religious Radicals in Tudor England*. This represents excellent research, and it can justly be claimed that Martin is, to date, the leading authority on many of the radicals discussed in the present thesis. Any disagreements with Martin in these pages are fairly trivial; the differences are those of approach, with Martin choosing a narrative base coupled with sociological commentary on the effects of printing, of the vernacular Bible, and the phenomenon of the conventicle. As A. G. Dickens comments in the preface, in dealing with Tudor religious activists Martin has been "placing them in their social context."[23]

As the acknowledgements section of *Religious Radicals in Tudor England* makes plain, some passages of the original articles have been condensed or deleted; for this reason, citations given here from the 1976 article entitled "English Protestant Separatism at Its Beginnings: Henry Hart and the Free-Will Men" refer to that piece in its article form, not to chapter 4 of the book, since much of the former has, in fact, been eliminated from the latter.[24] The 1976 article, though it concentrates primarily on the person of Henry Hart, stands head and shoulders above anything else published on the subject since Burrage. Martin sees Hart as an earnest but relatively undoctrinaire layman impelled to exhort his fellows by the force of his own discovery of the Bible.

Concerning many of the other subjects of this study, Martin's book is less enlightening. He says little of Joan Bocher, and does not even mention Robert Cooche. His coverage of John Champneys, though more extensive than any before him, remains sparse, and does little more than point out Champneys's biblicism and anticlericalism. He also thinks, mistakenly, that Champneys was the "Cerberus" attacked by Robert Crowley in 1566.[25]

E. Belfort Bax in his *Rise and Fall of the Anabaptists,* published in 1903, described Hendrik Niclaes's *Evangelivm Regni* as "nothing but a turgid mass of theological maunderings, which drones on page after page without apparently coming to any intelligible point."[26] It is easy to sympathize with this view of Niclaes's writings, though the section devoted to the Family of Love in the present work is based on the premise that there is at least some "intelligible point"! Precisely because the literature of the sect appears so impenetrable, however, few historians have considered the rewards of entering the mental world of the Familists worth the effort.

This lack of interest certainly obtained until recent times, but since the 1970s there has been a spate of articles and longer pieces concerning the English aspect of this most idiosyncratic of sixteenth-century sects. Lynnewood F. Martin produced an article, "The Family of Love in England: Conforming Millenarians," in 1972, which concluded that "the key doctrine in Familist theology is this millenialism which they saw as a continuity with Mediaeval Catholicism."[27] As L. F. Martin sees it, the Family of Love considered itself to have the same relationship with official Christianity as the New Testament church had had with Judaism; the old, which was passing away, was but a type of the new.[28] Furthermore, the disciples of the new way might freely participate in the rites of the old without fear of contamination, for these were harmless in themselves, and mere shadows of the new order that God was even now revealing in and through them. This seems to be a very keen insight into the self-image of the Familists, and one which fits well the actual tone of their writings.

J. D. Moss and A. A. H.Hamilton both produced full-length works in 1981. Both are excellent in their different ways, but it is Moss who concentrates more on the English experience of the Family. Hamilton's book, called simply *The Family of Love,* is mostly interested in the sophisticated, humanist Familism of the Netherlands and the Dutch in England, in their relationships with one another, with printers and artists. Even so, he does devote some space, later on in his work, to English Familism, and this is a very good account. His conclusion, however, seems at once too vague and too magniloquent concerning the significance of the group: that the Familists made a contribution to "the atmosphere of greater toleration which permitted the philosophers of the Enlightenment to express their ideas as boldly as they did."[29] Moss's book, *Godded with God: Hendrik Niclaes and his Family of Love,* is also very thorough, and has the merit of reproducing some of the key documents of English Familism at the back. Her account begins by looking at Niclaes and the growth of interest in him on the Continent, and then moves on to consider his following in England, the increasing opposition, and finally the movement's decline.

The Family of Love is the subject, apart from Hart's free-willers, about which J. W. Martin's work is particularly strong. He notes that historians of Tudor religious history "have tended to view the Familists as an imported group that does not quite fit into the English picture."[30] There are certain respects, of course, in which the Familists do not fit, or at least do not fit easily, but they cannot for that reason simply be ignored, and Martin has sought to show, as has the present study, the extent to which Familism adopted a specifically English form related to the origins of its English support. He stresses the extent to which the Family's English following was not dependent on Dutch Familists in England, and that the split caused in about 1573 by Barrefelt (also known as Hiël), who left to form his own sect, had virtually no repercussions in England.[31]

*   *   *

There has been a noticeable growth in recent years in the volume of literature devoted to sixteenth-century religious radicalism. This is encouraging, and gives cause for hope that understanding of all aspects, whether narrative, sociological, or theological, will at least grow in proportion with this increase in output. It is perhaps a sign, too, that the men and women who dared to move outside of the accepted orthodoxies of their day are beginning to receive the recognition which they deserve.

Notes

Introduction

1. J. A. F. Thomson, *The Later Lollards, 1414–1520,* passim; A. Hudson, *Lollards and their Books,* pp. 227–48; M. Aston, *Lollards and Reformers,* pp. 219–42.

2. J. F. Davis, *Heresy and Reformation,* p. 149.

3. R. Pecock, *The Repressor of Over Much Blaming of the Clergy,* p. 53.

4. B. R. White, *The English Separatist Tradition;* S. Brachlow, *The Communion of Saints;* pp. 114–56.

5. E. S. Morgan, *Visible Saints,* pp. 34–35.

6. J. Robinson, *Works,* ii 332.

7. J. W. Martin, *Religious Radicals in Tudor England;* A. G. Dickens, *The English Reformation,* 2d ed. pp. 258–68.

8. A. A. H. Hamilton, *The Family of Love;* J. D. Moss, *Godded with God.*

9. M. R. Watts, *The Dissenters,* pp. 7, 14.

10. B. R. White, *The English Separatist Tradition,* pp. 1–43 is both judicious and clear. A. Peel, *The First Congregational Churches,* provides an excellent account of the little-studied 1560s. Given the paucity of historians' references to it, however, this 1920 publication is apparently little known itself, though P. Collinson (*The Elizabethan Puritan Movement,* p. 475) has built on Peel's work to some extent, as has H. Gareth Owen ("A Nursery of Elizabethan Nonconformity, 1567–72," a study of the parish of the Minories in London). J. W. Martin, *Religious Radicals in Tudor England,* pp. 125–46, gives an account of the underground Protestant congregations in Mary's reign.

Chapter 1. The Free-Will Men

1. J. Veron, *A frutefull treatise of predestination,* preface (unnumbered page).

2. J. Veron, *Against the fre wil men,* Aii^v.

3. Augustine, *A worke of the predestination of saints,* Aii^r.

4. Ibid., Aiii^v.

5. J. Bale, *A mysterye of inyquyte contayned within the heretycall Genealogye of Ponce Pontolabus.* Hv^r.

6. See H. Denck, *Whether God is the Cause of Evil,* and Balthasar Hubmaier, *On Free Will,* in G. H. Williams and A. M. Mergal, eds., *Spiritual and Anabaptist Writers,* chaps. 4 and 5, pp. 86–135; Menno Simons, *Complete Works,* I. 221b.

7. J. M. Cramp, *Baptist History,* pp. 215–23.

8. E. C. Pike, *The Story of the Anabaptists,* pp. 95–111. Pike stated that "little is recorded concerning the Anabaptists during the later years of Queen Elizabeth's reign. Judging from such glimpses of them as we get, they were quiet people who met in secret and out-of-the-way places to worship according to their

conscience" (p. 110). This comes close to an explicit confession that hard documentary evidence of native Anabaptism is almost totally lacking.

9. W. R. Estep, *The Anabaptist Story,* pp. 206–15. Estep tries to be fair to the actual evidence, noting that Fitz's church is "Calvinistic in tone and not Anabaptist" (p. 212), and questioning the "close similarity which Scheffer saw between Browne and the Mennonites" (p. 208) (the reference is to J. De Hoop Scheffer, *History of the Free Churchmen,* p. 30). However, he is still certain that "Anabaptists and Anabaptist ideas were current in England for the greater part of the sixteenth century" (p. 210); I. B. Horst, *The Radical Brethren,* passim.

10. G. H. Williams, *The Radical Reformation,* pp. 778–90. Williams describes Henry Hart as an "antipedobabtist" and Humphrey Middleton as an "Anabaptist minister."

11. H. Robinson, ed., *Original Letters,* i. 65, 86–87.

12. J. Philpot, *Examinations and Writings,* p. 55.

13. J. Bale, *A Declaration of Edmonde Bonners articles,* Si[r]

14. Ibid., Si[v]

15. M. R. Watts, *The Dissenters,* p. 11.

Thomas Cole: born in Lincolnshire, graduated B.A. in 1546, and M.A. in 1550, at King's College, Cambridge. He was master of Maidstone School in 1552, and dean of Sarum at some point during the reign of Edward VI. Having been apprehended with the conventiclers in 1550/51, he preached his sermon of recantation before Cranmer in 1553, and emigrated to Frankfurt sometime before September of the following year, after the accession of Mary. There he took Whittingham's side in the ensuing troubles, but did not, apparently, leave for Geneva with the rest of his faction, although his name is absent from any Frankfurt register after the autumn of 1555. On his return, he was made rector of High Ongar, Essex, in 1559, and archdeacon of Essex the next year. In this capacity, he preached before Elizabeth I a sermon which was subsequently published, entitled *A Godlie and Learned Sermon, made this laste Lent at Windesor before the Queenes maiestie, on vvednesday the firste of Marche, 1564.* This is a tedious work, but is of interest in that it reveals its author as a conforming churchman of Puritan tendencies. In it, he preached election, speaking of "the mercye of God working all good about them whom he loveth, and to whom it is given to love him" (Aiiij). He was presumably targeting contemporary radicals when he praised King Jehu for rejecting "rash heads that would go farther than Goddes word willed" (B.i). But he warned that princes "must mainteine true Religiō without anye mingle mangle of their owne inventions" (B.ij), which sounds like the sort of expression he might have picked up from John Knox! He reinforces the point later by claiming that "all kings, Princes & Magistrates are bounde to maintaine the true Religiō of Christe prescribed oute of hys boke unto them w̄out any alteration." This style is resonant with the Puritan challenge to the Elizabethan settlement, and suggestive of the concern for purity of doctrine and ceremonies, rather than for exclusivity of membership. Cole died in 1571. (See *Dictionary of National Biography* and also C. Garrett, *The Marian Exiles,* pp. 122–3).

16. Foxe, vii.307. For a more detailed discussion of Melchiorite Christology, see pp. 67–68, 90–91.

Sheterden gave a spirited and astute defense of his views to his persecutors, despite his lack of a formal education (he knew no Latin—ibid., vii.311), and was one of the addressees of two letters by John Bradford (Bradford, ii. 113, 194); clearly, he was considered one of the more prominent members of the group.

17. M. M. Knappen, *Tudor Puritanism,* pp. 149–50.

18. J. Strype, *Ecclesiastical Memorials:* "The congregation in Essex was mentioned to be at Bocking: that in Kent was at Feversham, as I learn from an old

register. From whence I also collect, that they held the opinions of the Anabaptists and Pelagians; that there were contributions made among them for the better maintaining of their congregations. . . . Their teachers and divers of them were taken up, and found sureties for their appearance, and at length brought into the ecclesiastical court, where they were examined in forty-six articles, or more" (II, i, pp. 369–70); Foxe, viii. 164; Bradford, i. 306.

19. *EED*, ii. 1. The depositions of 1550/51 refer to him simply as "Cole of Fauersham," but Stephen Morris, a priest and informant of the bishop of London in the Marian persecution, told Bonner that "Robert Coles and his wife, John Ledley and his wife, William Punt, a bachelor: these three do lie at the sign of the Bell in Gracechurch-street, in a common inn. And two of those, namely, John Ledley, and Robert Coles, are great counsellors, and do resort much unto the King's Bench, unto the prisoners, about matters of religion" (Foxe, viii.384). Furthermore, John Bradford, from his prison cell in the King's Bench, addressed several letters to him, three of these being addressed to Cole jointly with others of the "free-willers" with whom Bradford was carrying on a debate (Bradford, i. 591, ii. 133, 194, 215, 233). It seems, therefore, that the "Cole of Fauersham" mentioned in the depositions is this Robert Cole(s), and not the Thomas Cole of Maidstone mentioned in the same depositions (*EED*, i. 3). To confuse matters further, Robert Cole, like Thomas, graduated M.A. from King's College, Cambridge, in 1550 and went into exile during Mary's reign. J. Strype mentions him as being a messenger for the exiles (J. Strype, *Ecclesiastical Memorials,* III. ii. 63–64). He was appointed rector of St. Mary-le-Bow, to which was added the benefice of All Hallows, Bread Street, in 1569. His earlier radicalism subsided to the extent that in 1564 Grindal was able to point to Cole as a good example for the more troublesome clergy, who refused to wear the prescribed vestments, to imitate (J. Strype, *Life of Archbishop Grindal,* p. 145). Born at Biggleswade, Bedfordshire, about 1524, he died in 1576. (See C. Garrett, *The Marian Exiles,* pp. 121–2.)

20. M. M. Knappen, *Tudor Puritanism,* p. 150; J. E. Oxley, *The Reformation in Essex,* p. 192.

21. H. Hart, *A godly newe short treatyse;* H. Hart, *A consultorie for all Christians.*

22. J. Lamberd, *Of predestinacion & election.*

23. "Myare" would seem here to equal "mere."

24. *EED*, ii. 1–4; H. Hart, *A godly newe short treatyse,* A iiij^v–v^r.

George Brodbridge was said by Foxe to be "of Bromfield" in the diocese of Canterbury. This almost certainly refers to one of the two villages in Kent named Broomfield, one of which is near Herne Bay and the other between Lenham and Maidstone. Of these, the latter must be considered the more probable, by dint of its location in the middle of the Kentish "conventiclers' triangle" of Faversham, Ashford, and Maidstone. Brodbridge was arrested under Mary and questioned by Thornton, bishop of Dover, on 3 August 1555. He told his inquisitors "that he would not be confessed of a priest because he could not forgive his own sins. And further said, that in the sacrament of the altar there is not the real body of our Saviour Christ, but bread given in the remembrance of him. 'Morever as for your holy bread, your holy water, and your mass, I do,' quoth he, 'utterly defy them.'" He was burned at Canterbury, together with four others, on or about 6 September. (See Foxe, vii. 383.)

Humphrey Middleton, who, from his presence at "Coles house at fauersham" on 1 August 1550 (*EED*, ii. 3), would seem to have been one of the Kentish, rather than of the Essex, conventiclers, was imprisoned again under Mary. He was condemned by the bishop of Dover on 25 June 1555, and was burned at Canterbury, together with Nicholas Sheterden and two others, on 12 July (See John Foxe, *The Acts and Monuments* vii. 312.)

25. Robert Crowley, *The confutation of .xiii. Articles,* Hviii^v, Iviii^v.

26. John Foxe, *The Acts and Monuments* v. 704–5.

27. *EED,* ii. 6; Maidstone PRC 3/12, fol. 89^r, PRC 3/18, fol. 89^r, PRC 17/41, fol. 164^{4-r}. Two Sybley widows, Joan Sybley and Bennett, both of Lenham, died within a year of one another. Joan Sybley died intestate in 1569, and so was perhaps younger, but Bennett Sybley clearly anticipated her death, which occurred the following year, and seems to have had a lively Protestant faith since she left a will containing more than perfunctory religious remarks; she described herself as "Trustynge assuredlye by his mercye & by the deathe and passyon of our savyor Jesus Chryst to obtayne remyssyon & forgyvenes of all my synnes." She appears to have had only one surviving child, her son John, which might also be consistent with a marriage which had been cut short by the early death of a husband.

28. R. Laurence, *Authentic Documents,* p. 56.

29. Foxe, viii. 164, 166. Careless, a married man with children, was first imprisoned in November 1553 at Coventry, where he was so trusted by his jailer, that he was temporarily released to take part in a city pageant. Moved to the Gatehouse shortly afterward, he was later transferred to the King's Bench, where he carried on an extensive correspondence with other Protestant prisoners, including John Bradford and John Philpot, and played a leading role in a protracted debate with John Trew, an imprisoned Protestant exponent of free-will, and his companions. Though not a scholar, Careless felt sufficiently sure of himself to insist, against his interrogators, that the writings of the early church fathers supported the Protestant cause, and to give advice to Harry Adlington, a genuinely unlearned man imprisoned for his faith. He won the grudging admiration of his inquisitor, Dr. Martin, and although he was willing, but not eager, to die for his faith, succumbed to illness in prison on 1 July 1556. See John Foxe, *The Acts and Monuments* vi. 411, viii. 163–201, and John Trew's account of the dispute among the Protestants in prison, *The Cause of Contention in the King's Bench,* Bodleian MS.53, fols. 116–24, edited by R. Laurence in *Authentic Documents,* pp. 37–69.

30. R. Laurence, *Authentic Documents,* pp. 56–57, but M. M. Knappen (*Tudor Puritanism,* p. 150, n.2) points out that Laurence has incorrectly transcribed "belief's" as "believers." Bodleian MS.53, fol. 121^v reads "Beleves" and, since "beleve" is a variant of the Middle English "bilēafe" (= belief), Knappen's correction, which in any case makes better sense, has been adopted here. John Clement, in opening his confession of faith, rendered Rom. 10.10 as "the believe of the harte justifieth" (J. Strype, *Ecclesiastical Memorials,* III.iii.446). For the relationship between John Trew and the Kent and Essex conventiclers, see pp. 77–88.

31. Bradford, ii. 165.

32. Ibid., ii. 134.

33. Ibid., ii. 133, 135, 194, 244. O. T. Hargrave expresses the view that these conciliatory gestures by Bradford are further evidence that the free-willers were not considered to be Anabaptists. "Statements such as these would be difficult to understand apart from a mutual acceptance which in this period would scarcely have existed between a former royal chaplain and a group of Anabaptists" (O. T. Hargrave, "The Freewillers in the English Reformation," p. 279). "Mutual accep-

tance" is probably too strong an expression in view of the degree of acrimony present in the overall relationship; however, the essential point is clearly valid.

34. John Bradford, *Writings* ii. 170–71.

35. Ibid.

36. Ibid., i. 318–30; R. Laurence, *Authentic Documents,* p. 37. A. Townsend, editor of Bradford's *Writings,* claimed variously that the date of Trew's writing was 1 January 1555 (i. 318) and 30 January 1555 (i. 306). The work dates itself as "the 30th of January, Anno Dom. 1555" (R. Laurence, *Authentic Documents,* p. 37). But Trew was using the old dating method; the *Cause of Contention* must thus be assigned to 1556 in modern dating.

37. John Bradford, *Writings* i. 309.

38. Nicholas Ridley, *Works,* p. 379.

39. John Bradford, *Writings* i. 327; J. W. Martin, "English Protestant Separatism at Its Beginnings," pp. 70–71.

40. John Bradford, *Writings* i. 328.

41. Henry Hart, *A godly newe short treatyse,* Av^v.

42. *EED,* ii. 4, 6; H. Hart, *A godly newe short treatyse,* Bv^r.

43. *EED,* ii. 3; J. E. Oxley, *The Reformation in Essex,* p. 4, n.2: "The term 'Known Men' is said to have been derived from the Wycliffite translation of 1 Corinthians xiv.38, 'If any man unknoweth, he shall be unknown', but it may have been due to secret signs and passwords by which they recognized one another. The ease with which persecuted Lollards found refuge in various parts of England suggests that they must have had some means of recognition"; J. A. F. Thomson, *The Later Lollards,* p. 115, cites a number of examples of the use of the term *known man.*

44. R. Laurence, *Authentic Documents,* pp. 56–57; H. Hart, *A godly newe short treatyse,* Biij^v–iiij^r, Bv^{r-v}.

45. Ibid., A. iij^{r-v}. See also *Bibliotheca Reformatoria Neerlandica,* v. 188, 194.

46. T. Cole, *A godly and frutefull sermon,* Diij.

47. Ibid., Aij.

48. I. B. Horst, *The Radical Brethren,* pp. 123–24.

49. T. Cole, *A godly and frutefull sermon,* Aij.

50. Ibid., Cviij.

51. I. B. Horst, *The Radical Brethren,* p. 124.

52. T. Cole, *A godly and frutefull sermon,* Diij.

53. Ibid., Cv; *EED,* ii. 3.

54. John Bradford, *Writings* i. 320.

55. H. Hart, *A godly newe short treatyse,* Aiij^v.

56. T. Cole, *A godly and frutefull sermon,* Bv, Ciiij.

57. Ibid., Bv.

58. Ibid., Cv.

59. R. Laurence, *Authentic Documents,* p. 55. The question of whether or not the church of Rome was a true church, and consequently whether or not its baptism was a true baptism, was one which was to plague Francis Johnson, who led the English separatist church in Amsterdam, in the early years of the next century. If the answer was in the negative, then Anabaptism, or at least Catabaptism, was the logical outcome. (See B. R. White, *The English Separatist Tradition,* pp. 145–8.)

60. *EED,* ii. 4–6; T. Cole, *A godly and frutefull sermon,* Cv.

61. *EED,* ii. 4.

62. *EED,* ii. 1–2.

63. Henry Hart, *A consultorie*, Aiiij^v; H. Hart, *A godly newe short treatyse*, Aviij^r.

64. Foxe, vii. 315; Bradford, ii. 171.

65. M. Coverdale, ed., *Certain most godly, fruitful, and comfortable letters*, p. 359.

66. J. Philpot, *Examinations and Writings*, p. 305.

67. Ibid., pp. 306, 308.

68. Bodleian MS. 53, fols. 138^v–139^r. For the identity of Laurence and Barre, see p. 53.

69. Ibid., fol. 139^r.

70. *The Second Parte of a Register*, i.575 (see pp. 171–76); *EED*, ii. 328.

71. B. Reay, *The Quakers and the English Revolution*, p. 34.

72. H. Hart, *A godly newe short treatyse*, A. iiij^r.

73. R. Laurence, *Authentic Documents*, pp. 45, 66.

74. Ibid., pp. 44–45, 53–54.

75. J. Philpot, *Examinations and Writings*, p. 247.

76. Bradford, ii. 170–71; Foxe, viii. 164.

77. Bradford, ii. 358.

78. J. Strype, *Ecclesiastical Memorials*, III. ii. 325–26.

79. Ibid., pp. 328–29.

80. Ibid., p. 327.

81. Ibid., p. 329.

82. Foxe, viii. 384.

83. Bradford, ii. 244.

84. J. Strype, *Ecclesiastical Memorials*, III. ii. 334.

85. Ibid., p. 327.

86. Foxe, vii. 315; J. W. Martin, *Religious Radicals in Tudor England*, p. 68.

87. Foxe, vii. 304, 312, 383.

88. Ibid., viii. 151; see p. 81.

89. Bradford, ii. 243; Foxe, vii. 242; Emmanuel College MS.260, fol. 239.

90. W. Wilkinson, *A Confutation of Certaine Articles*, ←iij^v; Foxe, viii. 384.

91. Bradford ii. 194; Foxe, viii. 384, 164; M. Coverdale, ed., *Certain most godly, fruitful, and comfortable letters*, p. 470.

92. J. Foxe, 1576 edn., pp. 1975–77.

93. Ibid., p. 1977; R. Laurence, *Authentic Documents*, pp. 67–68.

94. *EED*, ii. 4; R. Laurence, *Authentic Documents*, p. 57.

95. C. Garrett, *The Marian Exiles*, pp. 316–17.

96. Foxe, viii. 183–85, 189–91.

97. Ibid., viii. 765.

98. Emmanuel College MS.260, fol. 239; R. Laurence, *Authentic Documents*, p. 69; Bradford, ii. 243.

99. Emmanuel College MS.260, fol. 239^v.

100. Bradford, ii. 194.

101. Ibid., ii. 108, 117.

102. Foxe, viii. 576–77.

103. Ibid.; J. Strype, *Life of Archbishop Grindal*, pp. 54, 58.

104. Maidstone PRC 17/40, fol. 225^r; Thomas Cole, *A Godlie and Learned Sermon*, A. iiij.

105. John Bradford, *Writings* ii. 244.

106. John Foxe, *The Acts and Monuments* viii. 436.

107. John Bradford, *Writings* ii. 237.

108. John Foxe, *The Acts and Monuments* viii. 433, 436–43.

109. Ibid., viii. 164; W. Wilkinson, *A Confutation of Certaine Articles*, ←iiij^v

110. John Bradford, *Writings* ii. 194.

111. J. W. Martin, *Religious Radicals in Tudor England*, p. 66.

112. *EED*, ii. 1–6.

113. *EED*, ii. 6. Barrey may well be identical with the "Iohn Barrett" (*EED*, ii. 5), just listed, but if not—and perhaps even if he is—it seems that this Barrey is the John Barry (or Barre) mentioned in the 1557 letter of Stephen Morris, the informant priest, as servant to "master Laurence of Barnhall" (John Foxe, *The Acts and Monuments* vii. 384). Barnhall is located near the east coast of Essex between Tolleshunt Knights and Great Wigborough, and is some twelve miles from Bocking.

114. The place of residence of this person is not given, but may be inferred from that of the persons in connection with whom he is mentioned in the Depositions and/or Privy Council Minutes.

115. The expression "of the same sorte" used of him in the depositions of 1550/51 (*EED*, ii. 4) might be taken to imply that he was of the same place and trade as the person mentioned before him, who was the Bocking weaver Thomas Upchard. Nevertheless, he may be the husbandman John Simson of Great Wigborough who was martyred in Rochford in June 1555 (John Foxe, *The Acts and Monuments* vii. 86–90). The undated letter from the imprisoned John Simson of Wigborough to his coreligionists (Emmanuel College MS. 260, fol. 252b) is full of significance, for it was addressed to "the congregation dispersed in Suffolk, norfolk, essex, kente & elles where." Not only are these the counties in which George Eagles, known as Trudgeover, was hunted (see p. 54), but the singular noun "congregation" suggests that the addressees are not simply Protestants in general, of whom there were several congregations, but an organized sectarian grouping.

116. R. Laurence, *Authentic Documents*, p. 69.

117. John Foxe, *The Acts and Monuments* viii. 384.

118. John Bradford, *Writings* ii. 194.

119. C. Garrett, *The Marian Exiles*, p. 262.

120. Ibid., p. 258; Maidstone PRC 17/40, fols. 225^r–226^r.

121. John Bradford, *Writings* ii. 194; Emmanuel College MS. 262, fol. 32; M. Coverdale, ed., *Certain most godly, fruitful, and comfortable letters*, p. 470.

122. John Foxe, *The Acts and Monuments* viii. 384; John Bradford, *Writings* ii. 194, i. 591. See n. 113.

123. Bodleian MS. 53, fol. 138^v.

124. Ibid.

125. D. P. Walker, *The Decline of Hell*, p. 3.

126. J. W. Martin, *Religious Radicals in Tudor England*, p. 47 n. 24; pp. 63–70.

127. John Foxe, *The Acts and Monuments* viii. 384.

128. M. R. Watts, *The Dissenters*, p. 12; John Foxe, *The Acts and Monuments* viii. 386–97.

129. *EED*, ii. 5; John Foxe, *The Acts and Monuments* viii. 393–94.

130. John Foxe, *The Acts and Monuments* viii. 388, 392, 395.

131. R. Laurence, *Authentic Documents*, p. 69; *EED*, ii. 4; John Foxe, *The Acts and Monuments* viii. 384.

132. John Foxe, *The Acts and Monuments* viii. 384.

133. Ibid., vii. 289–90.

134. Ibid. vii. 287–91.

135. *EED*, ii. 1–2.

136. John Foxe, *Acts and Monuments* vii. 291.
137. *LPFD*. xviii (ii), 546 (p. 311).
138. Ibid., p. 312.
139. Ibid.
140. J. F. Davis, *Heresy and Reformation*, p. 37; *LPFD*, xviii (ii), 546 (pp. 314–15).
141. *LPFD*, xviii (ii), 546 (p. 315).
142. *EED*, ii. 4; W. Turner, *A preseruatiue.*
143. See pp. 230–31.
144. D. Witard, *Bibles in Barrels*, p. 21.
145. PROO, PCC-F, 8 Tashe, fol. 52.
146. *EED*, ii. 4; PRO, PCC-F. 8 Tashe, fol. 52; see n.115.
147. *EED*, ii. 7–8.
148. D. Witard, *Bibles in Barrels*, p. 22.
149. W. Turner, *A preseruatiue*, Kvij^v.
150. *EED*, i. 60.
151. *EED*, ii. 4.
152. PRO, PCC-F, 8 Tashe, fol. 52.
153. L. E. Whatmore, ed., *Harpesfield's Visitation, 1557*, i. 120; John Bradford, *Writings* ii. 194.
154. John Foxe, *Acts and Monuments* viii. 384.
155. *EED*, i. 51.
156. R. Laurence, *Authentic Documents*, pp. 67–68.

Chapter 2. Three Leaders: Henry Hart, John Trew, and Joan Bocher

1. *EED*, ii. 5; T. Cranmer, *Works*, ii. 367.
2. F. Haslewood, *Memorials of Smarden, Kent*, pp. 20–21, 78.
3. *LPFD*, xviii (ii), 546 (p. 306–7).
4. T. Cranmer, *Works*, ii. 367.
5. J. W. Martin, "English Protestant Separatism at its Beginnings," p. 58.
6. *EED*, ii. 3.
7. M. R. Watts, *The Dissenters*, pp. 10–11.
8. John Bradford, *Writings*, ii. 173.
9. Ibid., ii. 135.
10. *EED*, ii. 1–2.
11. *EED*, ii. 5.
12. J. W. Martin, "English Protestant Separatism at its Beginnings," p. 58.
13. *The Mennonite Encyclopedia*, ii. 217.
14. I. B. Horst, *The Radical Brethren*, p. 127.
15. John Bradford, *Writings* ii. 194.
16. John Foxe, *The Acts and Monuments* viii. 384.
17. L. E. Whatmore, ed., *Harpesfield's Visitation, 1557*, i. 120; H. R. Plomer, ed., *Index of Wills and Administrations at Canterbury 1396–1558 and 1640–1650*, p. 234.
18. Maidstone PRC 3/15, fol. 22^r.
19. Maidstone PRC 17/34, fols. 214^v–215^r.
20. R. Laurence, *Authentic Documents*, pp. 59–62.
21. John Foxe, *The Acts and Monuments* viii. 164. Careless was almost cer-

tainly referring to Hart's activities when he wrote to William Tyms early in 1556 that "you have also a full strong bulwark to beat back this pestiferous pellet [i.e., temptation] . . . even our best works are polluted and defiled in such sort as the prophet describeth them. With which manner of speaking our free-will Pharisees are much offended, for it felleth all man's righteousness to the ground. . . ." (John Foxe, *The Acts and Monuments,* viii. 182).

22. Ibid., viii. 105–21, 167.

23. Emmanuel College MS. 260, fol. 87.

24. M. Hoffmann, *Warhafftige erklerung* (Straßburg, 1531), A8a, cited in K. Deppermann, *Melchior Hoffmann,* p. 225. Martin Bucer cited Hoffmann as arguing that, if Christ had taken flesh of Mary, "so were es das verflůcht Adams fleisch | iñ dem er vns nit hette mögen erlösen." (M. Bucer, *Handlung inn dem offentlichen gesprech zů Straßburg,* Biᵛ.)

25. K. Deppermann, *Melchior Hoffman,* p. 226; J. F. Davis, *Heresy and Reformation,* p. 38.

26. H. Hart, *A godly newe short treatyse,* B. iiijᵛ.

27. See pp. 56–57, p. 83.

28. R. Laurence, *Authentic Documents,* p. 63.

29. H. Hart, *A godly newe short treatyse,* A. iijᵛ, B. iiijᵛ, Cʳ.

30. H. Hart, *A consultorie,* B. vᵛ–vjʳ, C. iijʳ.

31. John Foxe, *The Acts and Monuments* viii. 310; R. Laurence, *Authentic Documents,* p. 69.

32. John Foxe, *The Acts and Monuments* viii. 163, 105.

33. Ibid., viii. 106.

34. John Bradford, *Writings* ii. 171; John Foxe, *The Acts and Monuments* viii. 164.

35. H. Hart, *A consultorie,* A. viijᵛ.

36. Ibid., A. vijʳ⁻ᵛ, C. iijᵛ.

37. Ibid., B. vijᵛ.

38. Ibid., A. viijʳ.

39. Ibid., A. viijʳ⁻ᵛ.

40. Emmanuel College MS. 260, fol. 87.

41. J. W. Martin, "English Protestant Separatism at its Beginnings," p. 68.

42. J. Strype, *Ecclesiastical Memorials,* 3:ii. 328.

43. H. Hart, *A godly newe short treatyse,* A. iijʳ.

44. H. Hart, *A Consultorie,* E. iijᵛ.

45. Ibid., E. iijʳ.

46. G. H. Williams and A. M. Mergal, eds., *Spiritual and Anabaptist Writers,* pp. 141, 156. Franck's statement on the matter is fairly close to Hart's, if less crude. "Consider as thy brothers all Turks and heathen, wherever they be, who fear God and work righteousness, instructed by God and inwardly drawn by him, even though they have never heard of baptism, indeed, of Christ himself, neither of his story or scripture, but only of his power through the inner Word perceived within and made fruitful. . . . there are many Christians who have never heard Christ's name."

47. R. Laurence, *Authentic Documents,* p. 57; *EED,* ii. 4–5. For a discussion of the identity of "Simson," see p. 80.

48. R. Laurence, *Authentic Documents,* p. 69; *EED,* ii. 1–5.

49. W. Wilkinson, *A Confutation of Certaine Articles,* →iijᵛ.

50. R. Laurence, *Authentic Documents,* p. 42.

51. John Foxe, *The Acts and Monuments* viii. 164–67, 384.

52. R. Laurence, *Authentic Documents,* p. 38.

53. Ibid., p. 46. John Laurence and John Barre, probably coaddressees with Hart of Bradford's letter of 16 February 1554/55, (John Bradford, *Writings* ii. 194), also implied a belief in salvation by faith which, while less clearly expressed than Trew's, was nevertheless distinct from Hart's generally Pelagian tone. "We hold none to be in ye electiō but thos y^t be sanctified by ye spirite & beleve ye truth as ye holighost saythe. And sometyme ye saye y^t we sett up mañes fre will & merites of workes . . . wch ys farre from us!" (Bodleian MS. 53, fol. 138^r).

54. R. Laurence, *Authentic Documents,* p. 66.

55. Ibid., pp. 63, 65–66.

56. John Foxe, *The Acts and Monuments,* viii. 189.

57. Ibid., viii. 163, 168.

58. Harleian MS. 416, fol. 124^v.

59. John Foxe, *The Acts and Monuments,* viii. 151, 380, 430.

60. Ibid., viii. 306–10.

61. Ibid., viii. 242–43.

62. E. Farr, ed., *Select Poetry,* i. 168.

63. J. W. Martin, *Religious Radicals in Tudor England,* p. 177, n.20.

64. Emmanuel College MS. 260, fol. 239^r.

65. Ibid., fol. 239^v.

66. R. Laurence, *Authentic Documents,* p. 37.

67. John Foxe, *The Acts and Monuments* viii. 166–69.

68. R. Laurence, *Authentic Documents,* p. 38.

69. Ibid., p. 57. For Upchard, see pp. 46–47.

70. John Foxe, *The Acts and Monuments* viii. 334.

71. *EED,* i. 54.

72. *EED,* i. 53–54. Burrage's "over-zealous historians" were T. Crosby and J. Ivimey; T. Crosby, *The History of the English Baptists,* i.63; J. Ivimey, *A History of the English Baptists,* i.97–98.

73. Gonville & Caius College MS.218/233, fol.35.

74. Ibid., fol. 28.

75. Ibid., fol. 38.

76. John Foxe, *The Acts and Monuments* vii. 89–90.

77. Ibid. viii. 454, 456, 558.

78. Ibid., viii. 454–60.

79. R. Laurence, *Authentic Documents,* p. 57.

80. John Bradford, *Writings* ii. 128.

81. J. F. Davis, "Joan of Kent, Lollardy and the English Reformation," pp. 225–233.

82. *LPFD,* vol. iv, pt. 2, 4254. 3.

83. Ibid.; J. Strype, *Ecclesiastical Memorials,* I. ii. 59.

84. *LPFD,* vol. iv, pt. 2, 4175. 2.

85. Ibid.

86. Ibid.

87. E. G. Rupp, *Studies in the Making of the English Protestant Tradition,* p. 5.

88. However, this was an area which gave John Knox a friendly reception in Edward VI's time (John Foxe, *The Acts and Monuments* iv, 176, 222, 224, 228, 233, 235, 236; J. Strype, *Ecclesiastical Memorials,* II. ii. 73).

89. A. G. Dickens, *Lollards and Protestants,* p. 10, n.3.

90. E. G. Rupp, *Studies in the Making of the English Protestant Tradition*, p. 5.
91. A. G. Dickens, *Lollards and Protestants*, p. 10, n.3.
92. *LPFD*, vol. iv, pt. 2, 4175.2; J. Strype, *Ecclesiastical Memorials*, I. ii. 53.
93. *LPFD*, vol. iv, pt. 2, 4175.2.
94. *LPFD*, vol. xviii, pt. 2, 546 (p. 312).
95. Ibid., pp. 313–14.
96. Ibid., p. 314.
97. Ibid., p. 312.
98. Ibid., p. 314.
99. Ibid.
100. Ibid., p. 312, Cleopatra E. v., fol. 397[r].
101. *LPFD*, vol. xviii, pt. 2, 546 (p. 300).
102. Ibid., p. 307.
103. *LPFD*, vol. iv, pt. 2, 4254. 3.
104. R. Parsons, *A Treatise of Three Conversions of England*, i. 592.
105. *LPFD*, vol. xviii, pt. 2, 546 (pp. 314, 353–54, 366).
106. *Journal of King Edward VI*, p. 17; Edmund Becke, *A brefe coñfutacion*, title page.
107. *LPFD*, vol. xviii, pt. 2, 546 (p. 314).
108. Ibid., p. 354.
109. M. Hogarde, *The displaying of the Protestantes*, 75[r–v.]
110. Cranmer, *Works*, ii. 390, 392.
111. *LPFD*. vol. xviii, pt. 2, 546 (p. 314).
112. Ibid.
113. Ibid., p. 366.
114. Ibid., p. 331.
115. Ibid., p. 291.
116. I. B. Horst, *The Radical Brethren*, passim.
117. J. F. Davis, *Heresy and Reformation*, passim.
118. Lambeth Palace Library, Register Warham, i, fol. 175[r].
119. John Foxe, *The Acts and Monuments*, v. 44; *LPFD*, vol. viii. 317.
120. *LPFD*. Addenda, 1. i, 809 (pp. 281–82).
121. Ibid.
122. John Bale, *A mysterye of inyquyte*, Hvi[v].
123. Ibid., Hvi[v]–vii[r].
124. Ibid., Hviii[r].
125. John Hooper, *A Lesson of the Incarnation of Christe*, Aij[v]–Aiij[r].
126. H. Robinson, ed., *Original Letters*, ii. 560.
127. *Calendar of State Papers, Foreign*, i. 122.
128. J. Bale, *A declaration of Edmonde Bonners articles*, Si[r].
129. Register Cranmer, fol. 74[r].
130. *LPFD*, vol. xviii, pt. 2, 546 (p. 312).
131. Register Cranmer, fol. 74[r].
132. *LPFD*, vol. xviii, pt. 2, 546 (p. 312).
133. Register Cranmer, fol. 73[r].
134. *LPFD*, vol. xviii, pt. 2, 546 (p. 312); Register Cranmer, fols. 74[r]–75[r].
135. Register Cranmer, fol. 74[r]; J. Gairdner, *Lollardy and the Reformation*, iii. 317–88; A. G. Dickens, *The English Reformation*, p. 327.
136. I. B. Horst, *The Radical Brethren*, pp. 1–3, 111.
137. *Publications of the Huguenot Society*, x. i. 49, x. ii. 94, x. iii. 382.

138. Ibid., viii. 232, x. i. 471, x. ii. 104.
139. M. Hogarde, *The displaying of the Protestantes*, 47ᵛ.
140. Register Cranmer, fol. 75ʳ.
141. Ibid., fol. 75ᵛ; J. G. Nichols, ed., *Chronicle of the Grey Friars of London*, p. 58; J. Strype, *Ecclesiastical Memorials*, II. i. 336.
142. R. Hutchinson, *Works*, pp. 145–46.
143. Register Cranmer, fol. 72ʳ.
144. H. Latimer, *Sermons and Remains*, ii. 114.
145. J. Philpot, *Examinations and Writings*, p. 55.
146. Ibid.
147. *APC*, iii (1550–52), 15, 19.
148. Foxe, v. 699.
149. G. Burnet, *History of the Reformation*, II. i. 207.
150. R. Hutchinson, *Works*, pp. ii–iii; J. Strype, *Ecclesiastical Memorials*, II. i. 335.
151. Foxe, v. 699.
152. Ibid., v. 860.
153. *The Journal of King Edward's Reign*, p. 17 (original in British Museum, Cotton, Nero. c. 10).
154. M. Hogarde, *The displaying of the Protestantes*, 47ʳ⁻ᵛ.
155. E. Becke, *A brefe cõfutacion*.
156. J. F. Davis, "Joan of Kent, Lollardy and the English Reformation," p. 233.
157. R. Parsons, *A Temperate Vvard-vvord*, pp. 16–17.
158. Ibid., p. 17; R. Parsons, *Three Conuersions of England*, Hh89ᵛ.
159. R. Parsons, *Three Conuersions of England*, frontispiece.
160. R. Parsons, *A Temperate Vvard-vvord*, p. 17.
161. R. Parsons, *Three Conuersions of England*, Hh8ᵛ.
162. Ibid., i. 592–93.
163. Robert Parsons, *A Temperate Vvard-vvord*, p. 16.
164. Ibid.
165. J. Strype, *Ecclesiastical Memorials*, II. i. 335.
166. Robert Parsons, *A Temperate Vvard-vvord*, p. 17; Robert Parsons, *Three Conuersions of England*, Hh8ᵛ.
167. Robert Parsons, *Three Conuersions of England*, Hh8ᵛ.
168. M. Hogarde, *The displaying of the Protestantes*, 48ʳ.
169. J. F. Davis, "Joan of Kent, Lollardy and the English Reformation," p. 231.
170. R. Hutchinson, *works*, p. 147.
171. Ibid.

Chapter 3. Radical Writers

1. J. Champneys, *The Harvest is at Hand*, Aiiiᵛ.
2. Register Cranmer, fol. 72ʳ.
3. J. Champneys, *The Harvest is at Hand*, Dviiʳ⁻ᵛ.
4. Ibid., Dviiiʳ.
5. Ibid., Dviiiʳ⁻ᵛ.
6. Register Cranmer, fol. 72ʳ; J. Strype, *Memorials of Thomas Cranmer*, i. 254–55; J. Veron, *An Apologye or defence of the doctryne of Predestination*, Bviiiʳ.
7. Register Cranmer, fol. 72ʳ; J. Champneys, *The Harvest is at Hand*, Dviiʳ, Biiiiʳ.

8. J. Champneys, *The Harvest is at Hand,* Evii^v–Eviii^r.

9. Register Cranmer, fol. 72^r; J. Champneys, *The Harvest is at Hand,* Eiiii^v.

10. J. F. Davis, *Heresy and Reformation,* p. 103; J. Champneys, *The Harvest is at Hand,* Aii^v (mislabeled Bii).

11. Register Cranmer, fol. 72^r.

12. J. Champneys, *The Harvest is at Hand,* Dv^v.

13. Ibid., Bvii^r.

14. Register Crannmer, fol. 72^r.

15. J. Champneys, *The Harvest is at Hand,* Dvii^r.

16. Ibid., Ciii^{r–v}.

17. Ibid., Ciiii^v.

18. Register Cranmer, fol. 72^r; J. Champneys, *The Harvest is at Hand,* Bii^r.

19. Admittedly, in its context the statement had been "balanced" immediately afterward by an assertion that the church would soon become extremely visible: "Now God wyll glorifye all theim that loue it [the Gospel], for euer and euer. . . . And wyl clerely destroy the whole power of all the enemyes thereof. Esay. lx. b" (J. Champneys, *The Harvest is at Hand,* Bii^r). But this, in its turn, was an expression of Champneys's apocalypticism (see pp. 122–23) that would hardly have relieved official anxieties about the implications of his opinions.

20. Ibid., Dv^r.

21. Ibid., Fiiii^r, Giii^{r–v}.

22. Ibid., Av^{r–v}.

23. Ibid., Aviii^v.

24. Ibid., Aviii^r.

25. Ibid., Aviii^r.

26. Ibid., Aii^r (mislabeled Bii), Gii^v–Giii^r.

27. Ibid., Aii^r (mislabeled Bii), Diii^v, Dvii^v.

28. Ibid., Aii^r (mislabeled Bii).

29. Ibid., Aiiii^v–Av^r.

30. Ibid., Av^v–Avi^r.

31. The translator's preface to H. Bullinger, *A moste sure and strong defence of the baptisme of children* (J. Veron, trans.), Aiiij^r.

32. J. Champneys, *The Harvest is at Hand,* Evii^{r–v}.

33. Ibid., Giii^v.

34. Ibid., Diii^v.

35. Ibid., Avii^r.

36. Ibid., Giii^r; H. Bullinger, *An holsome Antidotus or counterpoysen, agaynst the pestylent heresye and secte of the Anabaptistes.*

37. J. Champneys, *The Harvest is at Hand,* Bi^v.

38. Ibid., Fvi^v.

39. Ibid., Bii^r.

40. Ibid., Fvii^v, Fviii^v.

41. Register Cranmer, fol. 72^r.

42. J. Champneys, *The Harvest is at Hand,* Dvi^v; J. F. Davis, *Heresy and Reformation,* p. 105.

43. J. Champneys, *The Harvest is at Hand,* Dvi^v.

44. Register Cranmer, fol. 72^r.

45. Ibid.

46. I. B. Horst, *The Radical Brethren,* pp. 114–15. Whether or not Horst is right on this point, the *DNB*'s reference (iv. 36) to "extreme Calvinistic opinions" is clearly an overstatement.

47. J. Champneys, *The Harvest is at Hand,* Cviii^v–Di^r, Diii^v.
48. Ibid., Bv^r, Cvi^r, Giii^r.
49. Ibid., Biv^r.
50. Ibid., Cv^v.
51. J. Veron, *An Apologye or defence of the doctryne of Predestination,* Ev^v.
52. Ibid., Bviii^v.
53. Ibid.
54. Ibid., Evi^r.
55. Ibid., Bvii^v, Eviii^v–Fi^r.
56. Ibid., Fi^v.
57. Ibid., Fii^r.
58. Ibid., Evi^r.
59. Ibid., Evi^{r-v}.
60. Lists of contents, *The Byble,* trans., Thomas Matthew; *The Byble in Englyshe* (Great Bible).
61. R. Crowley, *An apologie,* p. 28^v; *The Copie of an answere,* Bi^v.
62. A. W. Pollard and G. R. Redgrave, *A Short-Title Catalogue,* 1.258, item 5742.10.
63. R. Crowley, *An apologie,* pp. 1^{r-v}.
64. Ibid., p. 1^r.
65. Ibid., frontispiece, p. 46^v.
66. Ibid., pp. 6^r, 28^v, 34^{r-v}, 58^r, 62^v; *The Copie of an answere,* Bi^v, Biij^v–Biiij^r, Ci^r, Cij^r.
67. R. Crowley, *An apologie,* p. 1^v; *The Copie of an answere,* frontispiece.
68. R. Crowley, *An Apologie,* p. 2^r; *The Copie of an answere,* Aij^r. No copy of Samuel's work is extant.
69. R. Crowley, *An apologie,* p. 3^v; *The Copie of an answere,* Aij^v.
70. R. Crowley, *An Apologie,* p. 3^v; *The Copie of an answere,* Aiij^v.
71. R. Crowley, *An Apologie,* pp. 4^v–24^r, especially 24^r; *The Copie of an answere,* Aiij^v–Bi^r, especially Bi^r.
72. R. Crowley, *An Apologie,* pp. 28^v, 34^{4-v}; *The Copie of an answere,* Bi^v, Biij^v–Biiij^r.
73. R. Crowley, *An Apologie,* p. 45^r; *The Copie of an answere,* Bv^r.
74. R. Crowley, *An Apologie,* p. 73^r; *The Copie of an answere,* Cvi^{r-v}.
75. R. Crowley, *An Apologie,* pp. 58^r–62^v; *The Copie of an answere,* Ci^r, Cij^v.
76. R. Crowley, *An Apologie,* pp. 73^v, 90^v–91^r; *The Copie of an answere,* Cij^v–Ciij^r, Dv^v–Dvi^{r}L; T. Beza, *A Briefe declaration of the chiefe poyntes of Christian Religion,* Aiiij^r, Avj^{r-v}; A. W. Pollard and G. R. Redgrave, *A Short-Title Catalogue,* i. 83, item 2001.
77. R. Crowley, *An Apologie,* pp. 97^v–98^r; *The Copie of an answere,* Ei^r.
78. J. Ailward, *An Historicall Narration,* pp. 1–66.
79. Ibid., p. 1.
80. W. Prynne, *a Quench-Coale,* p. 23.
81. Ibid., p. 24.
82. Ibid., frontispiece.
83. J. W. Martin, *Religious Radicals in Tudor England,* pp. 47–78, and n.28.
84. W. Prynne, *A Quench-Coale,* p. 25; J. Veron, *An Apologye or defence of the doctryne of Predestination,* Ev^v, Eviii^r.
85. Ibid., Bviii^r, Ev^v, Evi^r; Robert Crowley, *An apologie,* pp. 1, 4^v–5^r, 29^r, 93^r; *The Copie of an answere,* Aiiij^{r-v}, Av^r, Avi^r, Bij^v, Dij^v, Dvij^v.
86. J. Veron, *An Apologye,* Bviii^r.

87. Ibid., Fii^r.
88. P. Heylyn, *Ecclesia Restaurata*, p. 73.
89. J. Ailward, *An Historicall Narration*, p. 1; W. Prynne, *A Quench-Coale*, p. 23.
90. R. Crowley, *An apologie*, pp. 24^r, 28^v, 34^{r-v}, 58^r, 61^r, 62^v, 84^r; *The Copie of an answere*, Bi^{r-v}, Biij^r–Biiij^r, Ci^r, Cii^v–Ciij^r, Diij^r, Dv^v–Dvi^r.
91. J. Champneys, *The Harvest is at Hand*, Aiii^v, Dviii^r.
92. R. Crowley, *An apologie*, pp. 48^v, 49^r; *The Copie of an answere*, Bvij^r, Bviij^r.
93. See pp. 132–33.
94. See p. 58.
95. *EED*, ii. 7–8.
96. P. Martyr, *The common places*, pp. 113–15.
97. Ibid., p. 113.
98. Ibid., pp. 113, 115.
99. Ibid., p. 115.
100. Ibid., pp. 113–14.
101. Ibid., p. 114.
102. Ibid.
103. P. Martyr, *The common places*, p. 114.
104. W. R. D. Jones, *William Turner*, pp. 19, 34; *Calendar of State Papers, Domestic, 1547–80*, pp. 18, 32–33.
105. W. Turner, *A preseruatiue*, Fviij^r.
106. Ibid., Bi^{v}ff.
107. W. R. D. Jones, *William Turner*, p. 183.
108. W. Turner, *A preseruatiue*, Eiij^r, Kiij^r.
109. J. Bale, *A declaration of Edmonde Bonners articles*, Si^r.
110. W. Turner, *A preseruatiue*, Kiij^r.
111. Ibid., Kiij^r, Kiiij^v.
112. Ibid, Avij^v.
113. Ibid., Evij^r.
114. *EED*, ii. 7.
115. W. Turner, *A preseruatiue*, Aiii^r.
116. P. Martyr, *The common places*, p. 114.
117. W. Turner, *A preseruatiue*, Aiii^{r-v}.
118. Ibid., Nvj^r.
119. Ibid., Kvij^{r-v}.
120. Ibid., Fj^r.
121. Ibid., Mvij^v.
122. Ibid., Iiiij^v, Gvij^r, Gvi^v.
123. Ibid., Miij^v.
124. See pp. 127–28, 132–33.
125. W. Turner, *A preseruatiue*, Bviij^r ff.
126. Ibid., Cviij^r, Ej^r.
127. Ibid., Cviij^r.
128. Ibid., Ej^v.
129. Ibid., Bvij^v–viij^r.
130. Ibid., Cj^r.
131. Ibid., Dvij^v.
132. Ibid., Giij^r.
133. Ibid., Ivj^{r-v}.

134. Ibid., Lij^r.
135. Ibid., Ivij^r.
136. Ibid.
137. Ibid., Iviij^r.
138. Ibid., Fij^v.
139. Ibid., Fiij^{r-v}.
140. Ibid., Fiij^v.
141. Ibid., Fv^r.
142. Ibid., Fviij^r.
143. Ibid., Gj^r.
144. Ibid., Hvj^r.
145. Ibid., Fj^v.
146. Ibid., Fvij^v.
147. Ibid., Hv^v.
148. Ibid., Giiij^v.
149. I. B. Horst, *The Radical Brethren*, p. 125; J. W. Martin, "English Protestant Separatism at its Beginnings," p. 59.
150. W. Turner, *A preseruatiue*, Avij^r.
151. Ibid., Kv^v, Mv^{r-v}.
152. Ibid., Lij^r.
153. Ibid., Mviij^r.
154. H. Hart, *A godly newe short treatyse*, Aiij^v; John Bradford, *Writings*, i. 320.
155. W. Turner, *A preseruatiue*, Hviij^v.
156. Ibid., Kiij^r, Miij^v, Kiij^v.
157. *TBHS*, 4 (1914–15), p. 89; *EED*, i. 62.
158. A. G. Dickens, *The English Reformation*, pp. 327, 481; G. H. Williams, *The Radical Reformation*, p. 781; *TBHS*, 4 (1914–15), p. 90.
159. D. Witard, *Bibles in Barrels*, p. 21.
160. J. H. Shakespeare, *Baptist and Congregational Pioneers*, pp. 15–16, 147.
161. *TBHS*, 4 (1914–15), pp. 89–90.
162. Foxe, vii. 267–68; Bradford, ii. 133.
163. *EED*, i. 63.
164. H. Robinson, ed., *The Zürich Letters*, ii. 236–37.
165. Ibid., ii. 237.
166. *EED*, ii. 7–8.
167. H. Robinson, ed., *The Zürich Letters*, ii. 236.
168. W. Turner, *A preseruatiue*, Gvij^{r-v}.
169. W. R. D. Jones, *William Turner*, p. 180.
170. H. Robinson, ed., *The Zürich Letters*, ii. 237.
171. See pp. 22–25.
172. J. Knox, *An Answer to . . . an Anabaptist*, p. 106.
173. Ibid., p. 8.
174. J. Knox, *Works*, iv. 261–75.
175. Ibid., iv. 270.
176. Ibid., iv. 271.
177. Ibid., v. 15*.
178. J. Ridley, *John Knox*, p. 290.
179. *Registres de Conseil*, Archives, Hotel de Ville, fol. 141, cited by D. Laing, ed. in J. Knox, *Works*, v. 15*–16*.
180. Ibid. fol. 144.

181. J. Knox, *Works,* v. 16; *EED,* i. 63.
182. J. Knox, *Works,* v. 16; J. Strype, *Ecclesiastical Memorials,* ii(i), 111–12.
183. *EED,* ii. 8.
184. J. Knox, *An Answer to . . . an Anabaptist,* p. 207.
185. Ibid., p. 112.
186. J. Knox, *Works,* v. 13*–14*.
187. J. Knox, *An Answer to . . . an Anabaptist,* p. 41.
188. Ibid., p. 40.
189. Ibid., p. 213.
190. *EED,* ii. 7.
191. *EED,* ii. 7.
192. W. Turner, *A preseruatiue,* Bi^v.
193. J. Knox, *An Answer to . . . an Anabaptist,* p. 226.
194. Ibid., pp. 167, 207.
195. P. Martyr, *The common places,* pp. 113–15.
196. J. Knox, *An Answer to . . . an Anabaptist,* p. 96.
197. *TBHS,* 4 (1914–15), pp. 89–90.
198. Emmanuel College MS. 260, fol. 87.
199. J. Knox, *Works,* iv. 241–44.
200. J. Knox, *An Answer to . . . an Anabaptist,* p. 67.
201. J. S. McEwen, *The Faith of John Knox,* p. 78.
202. J. Knox, *An Answer to . . . an Anabaptist,* p. 191.
203. Ibid.
204. Ibid.
205. Ibid.
206. Bradford, i. 327–28.
207. J. Knox, *An Answer to . . . an Anabaptist,* p. 203.
208. Ibid.
209. Ibid.
210. Ibid., pp. 203–4.
211. Ibid., p. 204.
212. Ibid., pp. 46, 296.
213. Ibid., p. 46.
214. R. T. Kendall, *Calvin and English Calvinism to 1649,* passim.
215. J. Knox, *An Answer to . . . an Anabaptist,* p. 381.
216. Ibid., pp. 97–98.
217. Ibid., pp. 97, 295.
218. Ibid., p. 394.
219. Ibid., p. 378.
220. Ibid., p. 394; J. Ridley, *John Knox,* p. 293.
221. J. Knox, *An Answer to . . . an Anabaptist,* pp. 191–92.
222. Ibid., p. 192.
223. Ibid., p. 206.
224. Ibid., p. 207.
225. Ibid., p. 192.
226. Ibid.
227. Ibid., p. 216.
228. Ibid., pp. 215–16.
229. Ibid., p. 215.
230. Ibid.
231. Ibid., p. 192.

232. Ibid., pp. 408–47.

233. Ibid., p. 381.

234. *The Second Parte of a Register*, i. 546–80. The manuscript is in Dr. Williams's Library, London. The occupation of "S.B." as a carpenter is mentioned on i.576. The debate has been transcribed by A. Peel, in his "Conscientious Objector of 1575," *TBHS*, vii (1920–21), pp. 71–128, the article presumably being named for the immediate relevance to Peel's generation of the Anabaptist's pacifism to the recent experience of the First World War. The debate is summarized as item 64 in Peel's catalogue of the whole document, also entitled *The Seconde Parte of a Register*, i. 103–7.

235. *The Seconde Parte of a Register* (original), i. 546.

236. Ibid.

237. Ibid.

238. Ibid.

239. Ibid., i. 566–67.

240. Ibid., i. 555–56.

241. Ibid., i. 559.

242. Ibid., i. 551–52.

243. Ibid., i. 547, 553.

244. Ibid., i. 553–54.

245. Ibid., i. 561.

246. Ibid., i. 561–65.

247. Ibid., i. 565.

248. R. Pecock, *The Repressor of Over Much Blaming of the Clergy*, i. 5.

249. *The Second Parte of a Register* (original), i. 573.

250. Ibid., i. 555.

251. Ibid., i. 547, 574.

252. Ibid., i. 549.

253. Ibid.

254. Ibid., i. 546, 550, 567–68.

255. Ibid., i. 572.

256. Ibid., i. 546, 559.

257. Ibid., i. 559.

258. J. Knox, *An Answer to . . . an Anabaptist*, pp. 16–18.

259. *The Copie of an answere*, Bi^r.

Chapter 4. Shaking the Foundations: Arianism and English Familism

1. H. Robinson, ed., i. 65–66.

2. Harleian MS. 537, fol. 112^r.

3. Harleian MS. 421, fols. 94^r–95^r.

4. J. Philpot, *Examinations and Writings*, pp. 304–9.

5. Register Cranmer, fol. 73^r; D. Wilkins, *Concilia*, iv. 40–41. "Shiltelington" would seem to be Shillington, Bedfordshire, in the diocese of Lincoln.

6. *LPFD*, vol. xviii, pt. 2, 546 (p. 312).

7. J. Proctor, *The Fal of the Late Arrian*, Avii^r.

8. Ibid., Dv^r.

9. Ibid., Dv^{r-v}, Ei^v.

10. Register Cranmer, fol. 73^r; D. Wilkins, *Concilia*, iv. 41.

11. J. Proctor, *The Fal of the Late Arrian*, Ei[r].
12. Ibid., Dv[r], Eii[r–v].
13. Ibid., Eii[v].
14. Ibid., Lviii[r].
15. Ibid., Ivi[r].
16. Ibid., Gi[r].
17. Ibid., Kvii[r–v].
18. Ibid., Evii[v].
19. Ibid., Gii[r].
20. Register Cranmer fol. 79[r]; D. Wilkins, *Concilia*, iv. 45.
21. Register Cranmer fol. 78[r]; D. Wilkins, *Concilia*, iv. 44.
22. M. Hogarde, *The displaying of the Protestantes*, 47[r].
23. Ibid., 46[v]–47[r]; W. K. Jordan, ed., *The Chronicle and Political Papers of King Edward VI*, p. 58.
24. J. Strype, *Memorials of . . . Thomas Cranmer*, i. 505.
25. J. Philpot, *Examinations and Writings*, pp. 293–318.
26. Ibid., p. 297.
27. Ibid., p. 302.
28. Ibid., pp. 311–13.
29. Ibid., p. 314.
30. J. D. Moss, *Godded with God*, pp. 70–74.
31. H. Robinson, ed., *Original Letters*, i. 65–66.
32. J. Philpot, *Examinations and Writings*, p. 314.
33. W. Wilkinson, *A Confutation of Certaine Articles*, →iiij[r].
34. Ibid.
35. Ibid.
36. Ibid.
37. Ibid.
38. Ibid., Ai[r].
39. Ibid., →iij[v]–→iiij[r].
40. Bodleian MS. 53, fols. 138–39. See p. 53.
41. J. W. Martin, *Religious Radicals in Tudor England*, pp. 130, 139.
42. W. Wilkinson, *A Confutation of Certaine Articles*, Ai[r].
43. J. Rogers, *An Answere vnto a . . . Libel*, Lij[v].
44. Ibid., Liii[r].
45. J. Rogers, *The Displaying*, Diij[r].
46. A Hamilton, *The Family of Love*, p. 116.
47. W. Wilkinson, *A Confutation of Certaine Articles*. →iiij[v].
48. Ibid.
49. J. D. Moss, *Godded with God*; A Hamilton, *The Family of Love*.
50. J. D. Moss, *Godded with God*, p. 22.
51. W. Wilkinson, *A Confutation of Certaine Articles*, →iiij[r].
52. Ibid.; J. Rogers, *The Displaying*, Ivij[v].
53. J. Rogers, *The Displaying*, Ovij[v].
54. I. B. Horst, *The Radical Brethren*, p. 154.
55. Ibid.; J. Rogers, *The Displaying*, Hiv[v]–Hv[r]; J. D. Moss, *Godded with God*, p. 71.
56. J. Rogers, *An Answere vnto a . . . Libel*, Ki[r].
57. I. B. Horst, *Radical Brethren*, p. 154.
58. See pp. 64–65, 79–80, and chap. 1, n.115; L. E.Whatmore, ed., *Harpesfield's Visitation, 1557*, i. 120.

59. I. B. Horst, *Radical Brethren*, pp. 79, 154; G. Arnold, *Kirchen-und Ketzer-Historie*, ii. 711.

60. T. Wilson Hayes, "The Peaceful Apocalypse," p. 133.

61. Ibid.

62. J. Rogers, *The Displaying*, Ovij^v.

63. J. Rogers, *An Answere vnto a . . . Libel*, ¶ii^v.

64. J. Rogers, *The Displaying*, Diij^r.

65. J. Rogers, *An Answere vnto a . : . Libel*, Kvi^r.

66. Ibid., Ci^r.

67. Ibid., ¶ij^v.

68. J. Rogers, *The Displaying*, Bii^r.

69. W. Wilkinson, *A Confutation of Certaine Articles*, Kij^v.

70. Ibid.

71. J. Rogers, *An Answere vnto a . . . Libel*, Ciiij^v–Cv^r.

72. Ibid., Cij^r.

73. Ibid., Kiiij^{r-v}.

74. J. Rogers, *The Displaying*, Lij^v.

75. Ibid., Liij^v.

76. A. Hamilton, *The Family of Love*, p. 122.

77. Ibid., p. 123.

78. PRO, S. P. 12, 133, fols. 98^r–99^r, printed in J. D. Moss, *Godded with God*, pp. 80–81.

79. Bodleian MS. 53, fol. 138^v.

80. J. D. Moss's transcription in her *Godded with God*, pp. 70–74.

81. Ibid., p. 71.

82. Ibid.

83. Ibid.

84. Ibid., *EED*, ii. 3.

85. J. Rogers, *The Displaying*, Hiij^r.

86. A. Hamilton, *The Family of Love*, p. 119.

87. Ibid.

88. J. Rogers, *The Displaying*, Gij^v; J. Rogers, *An Answere vnto a . . Libel*, Ki^v.

89. J. D. Moss, *Godded with God*, p. 74.

90. J. Rogers, *An Answere vnto a . . . Libel*, Ki^v.

91. Ibid., Kii^r; J. Rogers, *The Displaying*, Ovij^r; J. D. Moss, *Godded with God*, p. 74.

92. J. Philpot, *Examinations and Writings*, pp. 297, 302, 312–14.

93. Ibid., p. 314.

94. Ibid., pp. 313–14.

95. Ibid., p. 312.

96. Most of the medieval mystics were predestinarian in their outlook. (J. van Ruysbroeck, *The Chastising of God's Children and The Treatise of Perfection of the Sons of God*, pp. 156, 158, 243; J. van Ruysbroeck, *The Adornment of the Spiritual Marriage*, p. 109; H. Suso, *Little Book of Eternal Wisdom and Little Book of Truth*, p. 48). Julian of Norwich and the author of *The Cloud of Unknowing* also had a sense of "chosenness," teaching that it was grace that drew people to the life of contemplation. (Julian of Norwich, *Revelations of Divine Love* [also called *Showings*], chap. 39; *The Cloud of Unknowing*, chap. 34.) Eckhart had been an exception to the rule. (*Meister Eckhart*, p. 279.)

The most relevant precedent for Hendrik Niclaes and the Family of Love, of course, is the *Theologia Germanica,* and perhaps also that of Johannes Tauler, of whose teaching it has been considered largely a reflection. Neither the *Theologia Germanica* nor Tauler expressed any clear view on the subject of predestination, though both exude an atmosphere consistent with predestinarianism; in the former, the emphasis is placed firmly on the initiative of the Father in drawing men to Christ (chap. 54); self-will, or autonomy, is denounced as the commodity of which hell itself consists (chap. 47). There is an aversion, similar to that found among the Protestant reformers, to prying into "the hidden counsel and Will of God, desiring to learn why God has done this or that or left this or that undone" (chap. 48). Luther's favorable view of the *Theologia Germanica* is well-known; Matthias Flacius Illyricus also considered it sound on questions of grace and free-will.

97. G. H. Williams, *The Radical Reformation* pp. 839, 842–43.
98. Ibid., pp. 617–18.
99. H. Niclaes, *Evangelivm Regni,* 81ʳ, 11ʳ, 55ʳ, 57ʳ, 86ʳ.
100. H.Niclaes, *Dicta HN. Documentall Sentences,* 32ᵛ.
101. H. Niclaes, *The Glasse of Righteousnesse,* pp. 12–13.
102. Tobias, *Mirabilia opera Dei,* K4ʳ.
103. W. Wilkinson, *A Confutation of Certaine Articles,* →iiijʳ.
104. J. Rogers, *The Displaying,* Ivijᵛ.
105. Ibid., Kiᵛ.
106. Ibid., Nijᵛ.
107. Ibid., Nvᵛ.
108. Ibid., Mvijʳ⁻ᵛ.
109. Ibid., Kijʳ, Niijʳ.
110. A. Hamilton, *The Family of Love,* pp. 112–14.
111. J. D. Moss, *Godded with God,* p. 74.
112. J. Rogers, *An Answere vnto a . . . Libel,* Eviijᵛ.
113. J. Rogers, *The Displaying,* Hijʳ.
114. J. Rogers, *An Answere vnto a . . . Libel,* Diijᵛ.
115. J. Rogers, *The Displaying,* Bijᵛ–Biijʳ.
116. Ibid., Aviʳ; J. Rogers, *An Answere vnto a . . . Libel,* Dvijᵛ, Hviijᵛ–Hviijʳ.
117. J. Rogers, *The Displaying,* Diiijʳ⁻ᵛ.
118. J. Rogers, *An Answere vnto a . . . Libel,* Kviᵛ.
119. J. Rogers, *The Displaying,* Aviijᵛ.
120. Ibid., Liijᵛ.
121. J. Rogers, *An Answere vnto a . . . Libel,* Ciiijᵛ.
122. Ibid., Ciijᵛ–Cvʳ.
123. J. Rogers, *The Displaying,* Bijᵛ.
124. Ibid., Ovijᵛ.
125. H. Niclaes, *Evangelivm Regni,* 10ᵛ.
126. Ibid., 80ʳ.
127. J. Knewstub, *A Confutation of monstrous and horrible heresies,* 37ʳ⁻ᵛ.
128. J. Rogers, *An Answere vnto a . . . Libel,* Hviijᵛ.
129. H. Niclaes, *Terra Pacis,* 4ᵛ.
130. J. Knewstub, *A Confutation of monstrous and horrible heresies,* 19ᵛ, 31ᵛ–32ʳ, 34ᵛ, 35ʳ, 36ᵛ.
131. Ibid., 81ʳ.
132. Ibid., 17ʳ⁻ᵛ; H. Niclaes, *Evangelivm Regni,* 44ʳ.
133. J. Knewstub, *A Confutation of monstrous and horrible heresies,* 38ʳ–39ᵛ.
134. Ibid., 18ᵛ–19ᵛ; H. Niclaes, *Evangelivm Regni,* 44ʳ.

135. J. Knewstub, *A Confutation of monstrous and horrible heresies*, 19[v].
136. H. Niclaes, *Dicta HN, Documentall Sentences*, 4[v]; H. Niclaes, *Evangelivm Regni*, 88[r].
137. J. Rogers, *An Answere vnto a . . . Libel*, Cvij[r].
138. J. Rogers, *The Displaying*, Cviij[v].
139. J. Rogers, *An Answere vnto a . . . Libel*, Hviij[v].
140. J. Knewstub, *A Confutation of monstrous and horrible heresies*, *4[r-v].
141. J. D. Moss, *Godded with God*, pp. 76, 77.
142. Ibid., pp. 77–78.
143. J. Knewstub, *A Confutation of monstrous and horrible heresies*, 85[r].
144. W. Wilkinson, *A Confutation of Certaine Articles*, Piiij[v].
145. Ibid., Bi[r].
146. Ibid.
147. H. Niclaes, *Evangelivm Regni*, 2[r-v], 5[v].
148. Ibid., 80[r-v], 81[v].
149. Ibid., 80[v].
150. J. D. Moss, *Godded with God*, p. 76.
151. Tobias, *Mirabilia opera Dei*, A2[r].
152. W. Wilkinson, *A Confutation of Certaine Articles*, Piij[v].
153. J. Rogers, *An Answere vnto a . . . Libel*, Kvi[v].
154. Ibid., Kvi[r].
155. W. Wilkinson, *A Confutation of Certaine Articles*, Bi[r], Piiij[v].
156. H. Niclaes, *Evangelivm Regni*, 81[r].
157. Ibid., 81[r-v].
158. Ibid., 97[v].
159. W. Wilkinson, *A Confutation of Certaine Articles*, Ai[v].
160. J. Rogers, *The Displaying*, Eviij[r].
161. J. Rogers, *An Answere vnto a . . . Libel*, Ei[v]–Eij[r].
162. J. D. Moss, *Godded with God*, p. 76.
163. J. Rogers, *An Answere vnto a . . . Libel*, Cviij[v].
164. J. Rogers, *The Displaying*, Kiij[v]; J. Rogers, *An Answere vnto a . . . Libel*, Fv[v].
165. J. Rogers, *The Displaying*, Mvj[r].
166. J. Rogers, *An Answere vnto a . . . Libel*, Fv[v].
167. J. Rogers, *The Displaying*, Niij[r-v].
168. H. Ainsworth, *An Epistle Sent Vnto Tvvo daughters of VVarwick*, p. 15.
169. J. Rogers, *An Answere vnto a . . . Libel*, Aiiij[v].
170. J. D. Moss, *Godded with God*, p. 76.
171. H. Niclaes, *Dicta HN, Documentall Sentences*, 43[r-v].
172. J. Rogers, *An Answere vnto a . . . Libel*, ¶22j[r].
173. H. Niclaes, *Evangelivm Regni*, 3[v]–4[r].
174. Ibid., 91[v], 96[v]–97[r]. See similar claims in his *Glasse of Righteousnesse*, pp. 5–6; *Revelatio Dei*, p. 126.
175. J. Rogers, *The Displaying*, Bvi[v]–Bvij[r].
176. J. D. Moss, *Godded with God*, p. 74.
177. W. Wilkinson, *A Confutation of Certaine Articles*, *iij[v]–*iiij[r].
178. J. Rogers, *An Answere vnto a . . . Libel*, Iv[v]; W. Wilkinson, *A Confutation of Certaine Articles*, 30[v]; J. Knewstub, *A Confutation of monstrous and horrible heresies*, **4[v].
179. J. Strype, *The Life and Acts of Matthew Parker*, ii.382–85; R. Sharpe, *The Confession and Declaration of Robert Sharpe*.

180. J. D. Moss, *Godded with God*, pp. 70, 74.
181. Ibid., pp. 75–77.
182. J. Rogers, *An Answere vnto a . . . Libel*, Aij^v.
183. J. Knewstub, *A Confutation of monstrous and horrible heresies*, *6^v.
184. J. Rogers, *The Displaying*, Aiij^r, Mvj^v–Mvij^r, Nv^v.
185. J. Rogers, *An Answere vnto a . . . Libel*, Aiiij^v, Avj^r.
186. J. Knewstub, *A Confutation of monstrous and horrible heresies*, *6^v.
187. J. Rogers, *An Answere vnto a . . . Libel*, Hv^v–Hvj^r.
188. J. Rogers, *The Displaying*, Iviij^r.
189. S. Batman, *The Golden Booke of the Leaden Goddess*, 33^r; H. Niclaes, *A Figure of the True & Spiritual Tabernacle*, A8^v–B1^r; H. Niclaes, *Terra Pacis*, 7^r.
190. J. Rogers, *The Displaying*, Ivj^v.
191. Ibid.
192. Ibid., Iviij^v.
193. John Champneys, *The Harvest is at Hand*, Diii^v.
194. H. Niclaes, *Evangelivm Regni*, 79^v.
195. Ibid., 10^r.
196. J. Rogers, *The Displaying*, Gij^v.
197. H. Ainsworth, *An Epistle Sent Vnto Tvvo daughters of Vvarwick*, p. 25.
198. H. Niclaes, *Dicta HN. Documentall Sentences*, frontispiece; H. Niclaes, *The Prophecy of the Spirit of Love*, p. 5.
199. W. Wilkinson, *A Confutation of Certaine Articles*, Uij^v.
200. J. Rogers, *The Displaying*, Ivij^v.
201. Ibid., Kvj^v.
202. W. Wilkinson, *A Confutation of Certaine Articles*, *iij^v.
203. Ibid., Ui^v.
204. J. Rogers, *An Answere vnto a . . . Libel*, Aiiij^v.
205. W. Wilkinson, *A Confutation of Certaine Articles*, Tiiij^r.
206. H. Niclaes, *Cõmoedia*, 31^r.
207. W. Wilkinson, *A Confutation of Certaine Articles*, Qij^v.
208. J. Rogers, *An Answere vnto a . . . Libel*, Gj^v–Gii^v.
209. J. Knewstub, *A Confutation of monstrous and horrible heresies*, *4^r.
210. H. Niclaes, *Evangelivm Regni*, 73^r.
211. W. Wilkinson, *A Confutation of Certaine Articles*, Aiij^r.
212. Ibid., Aiij^{r-v}.
213. J. D. Moss, *Godded with God*, p. 79.
214. J. Rogers, *An Answere vnto a . . . Libel*, Hii^v.
215. H. Ainsworth, *An Epistle Sent Vnto Tvvo daughters of Vvarwick*, p. 55.
216. W. Wilkinson, *A Confutation of Certaine Articles*, Aiij^v.
217. J. Rogers, *The Displaying*, Nviij^r.
218. H. Ainsworth, *An Epistle Sent Vnto Tvvo daughters of Vvarwick*, p. 36.
219. J. Rogers, *The Displaying*, Ciij^v.
220. J. Rogers, *An Answere vnto a . . . Libel*, Iviij^r.
221. Ibid., Cviij^v.
222. Ibid., Lvj^r.
223. Ibid., Gj^v; G. Fox, *The Journal of George Fox*, p. 70.
224. J. Rogers, *The Displaying*, Niij^r.
225. J. D. Moss, *Godded with God*, p. 75.
226. E. Sandys, *Sermons*, p. 130.
227. J. Knewstub, *A Confutation of monstrous and horrible heresies*, *7^v.
228. H. Ainsworth, *An Epistle Sent Vnto Tvvo daughters of Vvarwick*, p. 7.

229. Foxe, viii. 164.
230. J. Rogers, *The Displaying*, Ivij^v.
231. H. Niclaes, *Dicta HN. Documentall Sentences*, 26^r.
232. Ibid., 26^r-v.
233. W. Wilkinson, *A Confutation of Certaine Articles*, Siiij^r.
234. J. Rogers, *An Answere vnto a . . . Libel*, Liij^r.
235. Ibid., Gij^v; W. Wilkinson, *A Confutation of Certaine Articles*, Sii^r; Bradford, ii. 300–51.
236. J. Rogers, *An Answere vnto a . . . Libel*, Eiij^r.
237. H. Ainsworth, *An Epistle Sent Vnto Tvvo daughters of Vvarwick*, pp. 31, 47.
238. Ibid., pp. 61–62.
239. J. Rogers, *An Answere vnto a . . . Libel*, Ki^v.
240. W. Wilkinson, *A Confutation of Certaine Articles*, Si^v.
241. R. Sharpe, *The Confession and Declaration of Robert Sharpe*, J. Strype, *The Life and Acts of Matthew Parker*, ii. 382–85.
242. J. Rogers, *The Displaying*, Dvij^r, Ovij^v.
243. Ibid., Mvj^v.
244. Ibid., Mvj^r.
245. Ibid., Aiij^v.
246. Ibid., Av^r.
247. J. Rogers, *An Anwere vnto a . . . Libel*, Gij^v.
248. J. Rogers, *The Displaying*, Kviij^r.
249. Ibid., Iii^v.
250. Ibid., Aij^r.
251. J. Rogers, *An Answere vnto a . . . Libel*, Ki^v; W. Wilkinson, *A Confutation of Certaine Articles*, Kij^v.
252. H. Niclaes, *Evangelivm Regni*, 78^v.
253. Ibid.
254. H. Niclaes, *Comoedia*, 31^v.
255. W. Tyndale, *Works*, i. 203; J. Rogers, *The Displaying*, Liiij^v–Lv^r.
256. J. Rogers, *The Displaying*, Ni^r.
257. J. Rogers, *An Answere vnto a . . . Libel*, Bvij^v.
258. J. Rogers, *The Displaying*, Mi^v.
259. W. Wilkinson, *A Confutation of Certaine Articles*, Uiii^v–Uiiij^r.
260. Ibid., Uiii^v.
261. Ibid., Piiij^v.
262. J. Knewstub, *A Confutation of monstrous and horrible heresies*, *7^v.
263. W. Wilkinson, *A Confutation of Certaine Articles*, Uiii^r-v.
264. J. Jones, *The Arte and Science of preseruing Bodie and Soule*, pp. 91–92.
265. H. Niclaes, *Evangelivm Regni*, 4^v.
266. Ibid., 91^v, 96^v.
267. J. Knewstub, *A Confutation of monstrous and horrible heresies*, 11^v.
268. H. Niclaes, *Terra Pacis*, 7^v.
269. J. D. Moss, *Godded with God*, p. 79.
270. W. Wilkinson, *A Confutation of Certaine Articles*, *ij^r.
271. G. E. Ladd, *The Presence of the Future*, passim.
272. W. Wilkinson, *A Confutation of Certaine Articles*, Aij^r.
273. H. Niclaes, *Evangelivm Regni*, 2^r, 89^r.
274. Ibid., 89^v–90^r; N. T. Burns, *Christian Mortalism from Tyndale to Milton*, p. 39.

275. H. Niclaes, *Evangelivm Regni*, 4ᵛ; J. Knewstub, *A Confutation of monstrous and horrible heresies*, 11ᵛ.
276. H. Niclaes, *Dicta HN. Documentall Sentences*, 16ᵛ.
277. H. Niclaes, *Evangelivm Regni*, 2ʳ, 5ʳ, 58ʳ, 81ᵛ, 82ʳ, 84ʳ, 95ᵛ 98ᵛ.
278. J. D. Moss, *Godded with God*, p. 78.
279. Ibid., p. 80.
280. J. Rogers, *An Answere vnto a . . . Libel*, Diᵛ.
281. W. M. Lamont, *Godly Rule*, pp. 23–24, 33–34, 42, 49.
282. See p. 175; J. Rogers, *The Displaying*, Niijʳ⁻ᵛ.

Chapter 5. Established Protestantism, Predestination and Ecclesiology

1. C. D. Cremeans, *The Reception of Calvinistic Thought in England;* O. T. Hargrave, "The Doctrine of Predestination in the English Reformation"; D. B. Knox, *The Doctrine of Faith in the Reign of Henry VIII;* D. D. Wallace, "The Doctrine of Predestination in the Early English Reformation"; D. D. Wallace, *Puritans and Predestination.*
2. *The Byble . . .* translated into Englysh by Thomas Matthew, **iiijᵛ.
3. Ibid., ***ijʳ.
4. Ibid., Hviʳ.
5. J. Frith, *A Mirroure to know thyselfe*, Aiiijᵛ.
6. J. Frith, *A myroure or lokynge glasse wherin you may beholde the Sacramente of baptisme described*, Aviiᵛ.
7. R. Barnes, *A supplicatyon . . . vnto . . . kinge henrye the eyght*, M6ʳ, M8ᵛ.
8. S. Fish, *The summe of the holye scripture*, Dviijʳ.
9. G. Joye, *George Joye confuteth | Vvinchesters false Articles*, ciiiᵛ.
10. G. Joye, *The letters whyche Johan Ashwell . . . sente*, Biiiᵛ.
11. G. Joye, *The refutation of the bishop of Winchesters derke declaratiō*, Gviiiᵛ, Hiᵛ.
12. L. Ridley, *A commentary . . . vpon . . . Ephesyans*, Aviiiʳ⁻ᵛ.
13. M. Coverdale, *A confutacion of . . . John Standish*, Ii.
14. Henry VIII, *A Necessary Doctrine and Ervdition for any Christen man*, Ziʳ.
15. Ibid., Yiiʳ.
16. O. T. Hargrave, "The Doctrine of Predestination in the English Reformation," p. 23.
17. D. D. Wallace, *Puritans and Predestination*, p. 4.
18. O. T. Hargrave, "The Doctrine of Predestination in the English Reformation," p. 23.
19. D. D. Wallace, *Puritans and Predestination*, p. 4.
20. O. T. Hargrave, "The Freewillers in the English Reformation," pp. 279–80.
21. J. Hooper, *A Declaration of the ten holy cōmaundementes*, Avijᵛ.
22. D. D. Wallace, "The Doctrine of Predestination in the Early English Reformation," p. 212, n.62.
23. J. Hooper, *Writings*, ii. 25.
24. J. Hooper, *A Declaration of the ten holy cōmaundementes*, Avijᵛ, Aviijᵛ.
25. H. Robinson, ed., *Original Letters*, i. 65.
26. Bodleian MS. 53, fols. 140ʳ–146ʳ; H. Latimer, *Works*, ii. 204.
27. Ibid., ii. 175.

28. J. Bale, *The Image of both churches*, Oovi[r].
29. Ibid.
30. J. Poynet, *A Short Catechisme*, Fvi[r], Fvii[r].
31. J. Philpot, *Examinations and Writings*, pp. 402–3.
32. Ibid., p. 46.
33. E. G. Rupp, "John Bradford, Martyr," p. 52.
34. Bradford, ii. 214, 220.
35. H. Robinson, ed., *Original Letters*, ii. 405–6.
36. Ibid, i. 326–27.
37. Ibid.
38. Ibid., ii. 704–7, 711, 737.
39. M. Bucer, *Metaphrasis et Enarratio in Epist. d. Pavli Apostoli ad Romanos*, pp. 410–11; M. Bucer, *In Sacra Qvatvor Evangelia*, p. 169.
41. M. Bucer, *Espitola d.Pavli ad Ephesios, . . . In eandem Commentarius*, D2[v].
41. P. Martyr, *Common Places*, pt. 3, p. 4(a); see also ibid., pp. 3–31.
42. Ibid., p. 11 (b).
43. B. Ochino, *Certayne Sermons*, Lvi[v].
44. Ibid., Lviii[v].
45. O. T. Hargrave, "The Doctrine of Predestination in the English Reformation," p. 49.
46. J. Ailward, *An Historicall Narration*, A3[r]–A4[r].
47. Ibid., pp. 106–8; T. Cranmer, *Works*, i. 6; J. Jewel, *works*, iii. 579.
48. R. T. Kendall, *Calvin and English Calvinism to 1649*, pp. 29–41.
49. T. Cranmer, *Works*, i. 6; Bradford, ii. 170–71, 173.
50. J. Ketley, ed., *Liturgies of King Edward VI*, p. 475.
51. C. Hardwick, *A History of the Articles of Religion*, p. 296.
52. Ibid., p. 298.
53. O. T. Hargrave, "The Doctrine of Predestination in the English Reformation," p. 239.
54. C. Hardwick, *A History of the Articles of Religion*, pp. 297, 299.
55. O. T. Hargrave, "The Doctrine of Predestination in the English Reformation," p. 240; C. D. Cremeans, *The Reception of Calvinistic Thought in England*, p. 34.
56. O. T. Hargrave, "The Doctrine of Predestination in the English Reformation," p. 241.
57. Ibid., p. 212.
58. O. Chadwick, "The Sixteenth Century," p. 61; O. T. Hargrave, "The Doctrine of Predestination in the English Reformation," p. 242.
59. O. T. Hargrave, "The Doctrine of Predestination in the English Reformation," p. 247.
60. D. D. Wallace, "The Doctrine of Predestination in the Early English Reformation," p. 203.
61. D. B. Knox, *The Doctrine of Faith in the reign of Henry VIII*, p. 66.
62. J. Veron, *A frutefull treatise*, preface (unnumbered page); P. Martyr, *The Common Places*, pt. 3, p. 3(b).
64. See chap. 4, n.96.
64. J. van Ruysbroeck, *The Treatise of the Perfection of the Sons of God*, p. 158.
65. J. van Ruysbroeck, *The Adornment of the Spiritual Marriage*, pp. 196–201.

66. J. Frith, *A myroure or lokynge glasse wherin you may beholde the Sacramente of baptisme described*, Avii^v.

67. Ibid., Bi^r.

68. Ibid., Bi^v.

69. Ibid., Bviii^r.

70. L. Ridley, *A commentary . . . vpon . . . Ephesyans*, Aviii^{r–v}.

71. W. Turner, *A preseruatiue*, Iviij^r.

72. Bradford, i. 328.

73. B. Ochino, *Fourtene Sermons*, B. vi^v.

74. Ibid., B. vii^{r–v}.

75. J. Veron, *An Apologye or defence of the doctryne of Predestination*, Fiii^{r–v}.

76. J. Veron, *A frutefull treatise*, Aviii^{r–v}.

77. Theodore Beza, *A briefe declaration of the chiefe poyntes of Christian Religion*, Dij^v.

78. T. Rogers, *The Catholic Doctrine of the Church of England*, pp. 148–49.

79. S. Gardiner, *A Declaration of such true articles as George Ioye hath gone about to confute as false*, Kii^r-Kiii^v.

80. J. Calvin, *Institutes*, IV.i.7.

81. Ibid., IV.i.8.

82. Ibid.

83. H. Zwingli, *The accompt rekenynge and confession of the faith of Huldrik Zwinglius*, C3^r.

84. Ibid., C4^v.

85. Ibid., C4^v, C5^r.

86. R. Barnes, *A supplicatyon . . vnto . . . kinge henrye the eyght*, H2^v.

87. Ibid., H3^r.

88. T. More, *Works*, ii. 140 (from the *Dialogue concerning heresies of 1529*).

89. J. Frith, *A myroure or lokynge glasse wherein you may beholde the Sacramente of baptisme described*, Bi^{r–v}.

90. Ibid., Bii^v.

91. W. Turner, *A nevv booke of spirituall Physik*, M7^v.

92. W. Tyndale, *Works*, i. 203; see p. 189.

93. J. Frith, *A disputacion of Purgatorye*, Liiii^{r–v}.

94. J. Frith, *A myroure or lokynge glasse wherin you may beholde the Sacramente of baptisme described*, Biii^r, Biiii^r.

Chapter 6. Radical Doctrines: The Common Concerns of the Sectarians

1. Augustine, *A worke of the predestination of saints*, Aii^v.

2. The Byble, trans. Thomas Matthew, Hvi^v.

3. W. Tyndale, *The Exposition of the fyrste, seconde and thyrde canonical epistles of s. Jhon wyth a Prologue before it*, Fi^v.

4. T. Beza, *The Treasure of Trueth*, Aiii^v–iiii^r; *The Copie of an answere*, Aiij^r.

5. B. Ochino, *Certayne Sermons*, Fviii^v.

6. A. Gilby, *A brief Treatise, with certayne Answers*, Pviij^v.

7. B. Ochino, *Certayne Sermons*, Fviii^v.

8. T. Beza, *The Treasure of Trueth*, Piii^v.

9. Ibid., Aiiii^v.

10. J. Veron, *A frutefull treatise*, Ci^v.

11. P. Martyr, *Common Places*, pt. 3, p. 24 (b).
12. E. Sarcerius, *Comon places of scripture*, Biiij^v.
13. T. More, *Works*, ii. 299.
14. R. Laurence, *Authentic Documents*, p. 42.
15. T. Cole, *A godly and frutefull sermon*, sig. B.v.
16. Bodleian MS. 53, fol. 138^v.
17. *The Copie of an answere*, Biij^v–Biiij^r.
18. J. Strype, *Ecclesiastical Memorials*, III.ii.328; R. Laurence, *Authentic Documents*, pp. 53–54; H. Hart, *A godly newe short treatyse*, Aiv^v–v^r.
19. Bradford, i. 327.
20. G. H. Williams and A. M. Mergal, eds., *Spiritual and Anabaptist Writers*, pp. 105, 115.
21. J. Veron, *An Apologye or defence of the doctryne of Predestination*, Eviii^v; J. Veron, *Against the fre wil men*, Aii^v; J. Knox, *Works*, iv. 270; J. Bale, *A mysterye of inyquyte*, Hv^r.
22. See pp. 33–34, 60–61.
23. J. Foxe, *Rervm in Ecclesia Gestarum*, pp. 202–3; R. Crowley, *The confutation of .xiii. Articles*, Bviii^r; W. Turner, *A preseruatiue*, Aiij^v.
24. J. Rogers, *The Displaying*, Lv^v.
25. See pp. 81–82.
26. See pp. 48–50; J. Strype, *Ecclesiastical Memorials*, III.ii. 328.
27. R. Parsons, *The Third Part Of A Treatise Intituled: of three Conversions of England*, G1^v–2^r; H. Robinson, ed., *Original Letters*, i. 65.
28. J. Champneys, *The Harvest is at Hand*, Eiiii^v.
29. J. Veron, *Against the fre wil men*, Ii^v.
30. J. Knox, *An Answer to . . . an Anabaptist*, p. 191.
31. J. Knox, *Works*, iv. 263, 267.
32. Ibid., pp. 269–70.
33. Augustine, *A worke of the predestination of saints*, Aiii^v, Aii^v.
34. J. Philpot, *Examinations and Writings*, pp. 306, 309.
35. J. Bale, *A mysterye of inyquyte*, Hvi^v.
36. J. Knox, *An Answer to . . . an Anabaptist*, p. 191; *The Copie of an answere*, Avii^v.
37. Emmanuel College MS. 260, fol. 87.
38. J. Champneys, *The Harvest is at Hand*, Eiiii^v; see pp. 184–85; H. Robinson, ed., *Original Letters*, i. 65.
39. T. More, *Works*, ii. 140.
40. See pp. 91ff., 100, 110, 147, 149–50.
41. J. Champneys, *The Harvest is at Hand*, Bii^r.
42. *EED*, ii. 7–8.
43. J. Rogers, *An Answere vnto a . . . Libel*, Liii^r.
44. J. D. Moss, *Godded with God*, p. 75; P. L. Hughes and J. F. Larkin, eds., *Tudor Royal Proclamations*, ii. 474–75.
45. R. Pecock, *The Repressor of Over Much Blaming of the Clergy*, p. 5.
46. See pp. 39–41, 66–73.
47. J. Champneys, *The Harvest is at Hand*, Av^v, Diii^v, Dvii^v, Dviii^r.
48. J. Proctor, *The Fal of the Late Arrian*, Evii^v.
49. *The Second parte of a Register*, i. 550.
50. *LPFD*, Addenda 1, 809 (p. 281).
51. R. Pecock, *The Repressor of Over Much Blaming of the Clergy*, p. 6.

52. See pp. 93–96; R. Parsons, *A Temperate Vvard-vvord*, pp. 16–17; *LPFD*, vol. iv, pt. 2, 4175.2.

53. H. Bullinger, *A moste sure and strong defence of the baptisme of children*, Aiiij^r; J. Veron, *An apologye or defence of the doctryne of Predestination*, Fii^r.

54. J. Philpot, *Examinations and Writings*, p. 306.

55. P. Martyr, *Common Places*, pp. 113–15; *The Copie of an answere*, Aij^r–Bi^v, Biij^v–Biiij^r, Diij^r.

56. W. Turner, *A preseruatiue*, Cviij^r, Dvij^v.

57. *LPFD*, Addenda 1, 809 (p. 281); Register Cranmer, fol. 74^r.

58. See pp. 56–57, 66–69; H. Robinson, ed., *Original Letters*, i. 65.

59. *The Second Parte of a Register*, i. 579.

60. R. Laurence, *Authentic Documents*, p. 63; Foxe, vii. 307.

61. M. Bucer, *Handlung inn dem offentlichen gesprech zů Straßburg*, Bi^v; R. Hutchinson, *Works*, p. 146.

62. J. D. Moss, *Godded with God*, p. 81.

63. R. Laurence, *Authentic Documents*, p. 57; H. Hart, *A consultorie*, Cv^v.

64. J. Knox, *An Answer to . . . an Anabaptist*, pp. 191–92; W. Turner, *A preseruatiue*, Ni^v.

65. *The Second Parte of a Register*, i. 555, 568–69.

66. H. Niclaes, *Evangelivm Regni*, 78^v; J. Rogers, *The Displaying*, Liiij^v–Lv^r.

67. J. Rogers, *The Displaying*, Liiij^v–Lv^r; W. Tyndale, *Works*, i. 203.

68. Foxe, v. 860; W. Turner, *A preseruatiue*, Aiij^v.

69. R. Crowley, *The confutation of .xiii. Articles*, Bviii^r.

70. W. Turner, *A preseruatiue*, Ni^v; W. Turner, *A new Dialogue*, Gii^v, Giii^r.

71. R. Laurence, *Authentic Documents*, p. 57; J. Philpot, *Examinations and Writings*, p. 55.

72. J. Proctor, *The Fal of the Late Arrian*, Ci^r; J. Knewstub, *A Confutation of monstrous and horrible heresies*, *7^v.

73. J. Knox, *An Answer to . . . an Anabapist*, p. 207; J. Veron, *An Apologye or defence of the doctryne of Predestination*, Ci^r.

74. H. Bullinger, *A most necessary & frutefull Dialogue*, Ci^r.

75. W. Wilkinson, *A Confutation of Certaine Articles*, →i^r.

76. W. Turner, *A preruatiue*, Ni^v; *EED*, ii. 7–8.

77. J. Rogers, *The Displaying*, Ivj^v, Kiij^v, Lij^v.

78. J. Proctor, *The Fal of the Late Arrian*, Dv^r, Svi^r.

79. *EED*, ii. 4–5.

80. W. Wilkinson, *The Confutation of Certaine Articles*, →iiij^v.

81. H. Robinson, ed., *Original Letters*, i. 65–66.

82. J. D. Moss, *Godded with God*, pp. 71, 74.

83. *APC*, xii. 232, 317.

84. J. Veron, *An Apologye or defence of the doctryne of predestination*, Ev^v.

85. T. Cole, *A godly and frutefull sermon*, sig. Cv.

86. T. Rogers, *The Displaying*, Eviij^r.

87. *The Second Parte of a Register*, i. 547.

88. Ibid., i. 569.

89. J. Knox, *An Answer to . . . an Anabaptist*, p. 208.

90. H. Bullinger, *A most necessary & frutefull Dialogue*, Biii^v; J. Veron, *An Apologye or defence of the doctryne of Predestination*, Bviii^v.

91. R. Crowley, *An Apologie*, p. 6.

92. *The Second Parte of a Register*, i. 574; Augustine, *A worke of the predestination of saints*, Aiiii^v.

93. J. Philpot, *Examinations and Writings,* pp. 313–14.
94. W. Wilkinson, *A Confutation of Certaine Articles,* *4^r.
95. R. Sharpe, *The Confession and declaration of Robert Sharpe; APC,* xi. 74; P. Collinson, *The Elizabethan Puritan Movement,* p. 25.
96. Augustine, *A worke of the predestination of saints,* Aiiii^v–Av^r.

Chapter 7. A Modern Historiography of Midsixteenth Century Dissent

1. For example, M. M. Knappen, *Tudor Puritanism,* p. 150; A. G. Dickens, *The English Reformation,* p. 481; O. T. Hargrave, "The Freewillers in the English Reformation," pp. 272, 279; J. W. Martin, "English Protestant Separatism at its Beginnings," pp. 59, 66–67.
2. *EED,* i. 51.
3. M. M. Knappen, *Tudor Puritanism,* pp. 149–51.
4. A. G. Dickens, *The English Reformation,* p. 328.
5. Ibid., 2d ed., p. 265.
6. Ibid., p. 263; Register Cranmer, fols. 72^r, 74^r.
7. A. G. Dickens, *The English Reformation,* 2d ed., pp. 266, 268.
8. M. R. Watts, *The Dissenters,* pp. 10–13.
9. Ibid., pp. 9, 189–90.
10. O. T. Hargrave, "The Freewillers in the English Reformation," pp. 271, 279–80.
11. D. D. Wallace, *Puritans and Predestination,* pp. 20–21.
12. See, for example, John Trew's confession of faith in his *Cause of Contention in the King's Bench,* Bodleian MS 53, fols. 116–24, edited by R. Laurence in *Authentic Documents Relative to the Predestinarian Controversy,* pp. 64–69.
13. N. Tyacke, *Anti-Calvinists.*
14. D. M. Loades, "Anabaptism and English Sectarianism in the Mid-Sixteenth Century," p. 60.
15. Ibid., p. 70.
16. M. Hogarde, *The displaying of the Protestantes,* pp. 122–31.
17. D. M. Loades, "Anabaptism and English Sectarianism in the Mid-Sixteenth Century," p. 67.
18. W. R. Estep, *The Anabaptist Story,* pp. 211, 233; *The Mennonite Encyclopedia,* ii. 217.
19. W. R. Estep, *The Anabaptist Story,* p. 212.
20. Ibid., pp. 211–15.
21. G. H. Williams, *Radical Reformation,* pp. 778, 790.
22. J. F. Davis, *Heresy and Reformation,* p. 148.
23. J. W. Martin, *Religious Radicals in Tudor England,* p. xii.
24. J. W. Martin, "English Protestant Separatism at its Beginnings."
25. J. W. Martin, *Religious Radicals in Tudor England,* pp. 45, 47, 73–74, 163.
26. E. Belfort Bax, *The Rise and Fall of the Anabaptists,* p. 359.
27. L. F. Martin, "The Family of Love in England," p. 108.
28. Ibid.
29. A. Hamilton, *The Family of Love,* p. 143.
30. J. W. Martin, *Religious Radicals,* p. 180.
31. Ibid., p. 181.

Bibliography

Acts of the Privy Council. 46 vols. London: 1890–1964.

Ailward, John. *An Historicall Narration of the Iudgement of some most Learned and Godly English Bishops, Holy Martyrs, and Others; . . . Concerning Gods Election, and the Merits of Christ his Death, &c.:* 1631.

Ainsworth, Henry. *An Epistle Sent Vnto Tvvo daughters of VVarwick . . . With a refutation of the errors that are therin.* Amsterdam: 1608.

Arnold, Gottfried. *Kirchen- und Ketzer-Historie.* 2 vols. Frankfurt-am-Main: 1729.

Aston, M. *Lollards and Reformers.* London: Hambledon Press, 1984.

Augustine, Saint. *A worke of the predestination of saints.* Translated by Nicholas Lesse. London: 1550.

Bale, John. *A declaration of Edmonde Bonners articles, concerning the cleargye of Lōdon dyocese whereby that excerable [sic] Antychriste, is in his righte colours reueled in the yeare of our Lord a. 1554.* London: 1561.

———. *The Image of both churches after the moste wonderful and heauenly Reuelacion of Sainct John the Euāgelist . . . Compiled by John Bale an exile also in this life for the faythfull testimonie of Jesu.* London: 1550.

———. *A mystery of inyquyte contayned within the heretycall Genealogye of Ponce Pontolabus.* Geneva, Switzerland: 1545.

Barnes, Robert. *A supplicatyon made by Robert Barnes doctoure in diuinite | vnto the most excellent and redoubted prince kinge henrye the eyght.* 1534?

Batman, Stephen. *The Golden Booke of the Leaden Goddess, Wherein is Described the Vayne imaginations of Heathē Pagans, and counterfaict Christians.* London: 1577.

Bax, E. Belfort. *The Rise and Fall of the Anabaptists.* London: Swan Sonnenschein & Co., 1903.

Becke. Edmund. *A brefe coñfutacion of this most detestable, & Anabaptistical opinion, that Christ dyd not take hys flesh of the blessed Vyrgyn Mary nor any corporal substaunce of her body For the maintenaunce whereof Jhone Bucher otherwise called Jhone of Kēt most obstinately suffered and was burned in Smythfyelde,* London: 1550.

Beza, Theodore. *A briefe declaration of the chiefe poyntes of Christian Religion, set foorth in a Table of Predestination.* Translated by William Whittingham. 1575?

———. *The Treasure of Trueth, touching the grounde worke of man his saluation, and chiefest pointes of Christian Religion: with a briefe summe of the comfortable doctrine of God his prouidence.* Translated by John Stockwood (another translation of *A Briefe declaration*): 1576?

Bible. *The Byble*. Translated by Thomas Matthew (M. Coverdale and W. Tyndale) 1537.

———. *The Byble in Englyshe* [Great Bible]: 1539.

Bibliotheca Reformatoria Neerlandica. 10 vols. 's-Gravenhage, Netherlands: 1903–14.

Brachlow, S. *The Communion of Saints: Radical Puritan and Separatist Ecclesiology 1570–1625*. Oxford: Oxford University Press, 1988.

Bradford, John. *The Writings of John Bradford*. Edited by A. Townsend. 2 vols. Cambridge, England: Parker Society, 1848 and 1853.

Brewer, J. S., J. Gairdner, and R. H. Brodie, eds. *Letters and Papers, Foreign and Domestic, of the Reign of Henry VIII*. 21 vols. in 36. Public Record Office London: 1862–1932.

Bucer, Martin. *Epistola d. Pavli ad Ephesios, Quarationem Christianismi breuiter iuxta & locuplete, vt nulla breuius simul & locupletius explicat, versa Paulo liberius, ne peregrini idiotismi rudiores scriptuarum offenderent, bona tamen fide, sententijs Apostoli appensis. In eandem Commentarius:* 1527.

———. *Handlung inn dem offentlichen gesprech zů Straßburg iüngst iṁ Synodo gehalten | gegen Melchior Hoffman | durch die Prediger daselbet | von vier fürnemen stuckē Christlicher leere vñ haltůg | sampt getrewem dargeben | auch der gründen | darauff Hoffman seine jrthumben setzet*. Straßburg: 1533.

———. *In Sacra Qvatvor Evangelia, Enarrationes Perpetvae, Secvndvm Recognitae*. Basel, Switzerland: 1536.

———. *Metaphrasis et Enarratio in Epist. d. Pavli Apostoli ad Romanos*. Basel, Switzerland: 1562.

Bullinger, Heinrich. *An holsome Antidotus or counterpoysen, agaynst the pestylent heresye and secte of the Anabaptistes*. Translated by Jean Veron. London: 1548.

———. *A most necessary & frutefull Dialogue, betwene yᵉ seditious Libertin or rebel Anabaptist, & the true obedient Christiā*. Translated by Jean Veron. Worcester, England: 1551.

———. *A moste sure and strong defence of the baptisme of children*. Translated by Jean Veron. Worcester, England: 1551.

Burnet, Gilbert. *History of the Reformation*. 3 vols. in 6, Oxford: 1816.

Burns, N. T. *Christian Mortalism from Tyndale to Milton*. Cambridge, Mass.: 1972.

Burrage, C. *The Early English Dissenters in the Light of Recent Research*. 2 vols. Cambridge, England: Cambridge University Press, 1912.

Calendar of State Papers, Domestic Series, of the Reigns of Edward VI, Mary, Elizabeth 1547–1580. Edited by R. Lemon. London: 1856.

Calendar of State Papers, Foreign Series. 23 vols. London: 1861–1950.

Calvin, J. *Institutes of the Christian Religion*.

Chadwick, O. "The Sixteenth Century." In *The English Church and the Continent*, edited by C. R. Dodwell. London: 1959.

Champneys, John. *The Harvest is at Hand, VVherin the Tares shall be Bovnd. and cast into the fyre and brent* Math.xiii. D.G. London: 1548.

The Cloud of Unknowing. Edited by J. Walsh, S. J. New York: Paulist Press, 1981.

Cole, Thomas. *A godly and frutefull sermon, made at Maydstone the fyrste Son-*

day in Lent by M. Thomas Cole Scholemayster there againste dyvers erronious opinions of the Anabaptistes and others. London: 1553.

———. *A Godlie and Learned Sermon, made this laste Lent at Windesor before the Queenes Maiestie, on vvednesday the firste of Marche, 1564.* London: 1564.

Collinson, P. *The Elizabethan Puritan Movement.* London: Cape, 1967.

The Copie of an answere. Netherlands? 1563? [STC 5742.10]

Coverdale, Miles. *A confutacion of that treatise which one John Standish made agaynst the protestacion of D. Barnes in the yeare .M.D.Xl.* Zürich, Switzerland: 1541?

———, ed. *Certain most godly, fruitful, and comfortable letters.* London: 1564.

Cramp, J. M. *Baptist History* London: 1871.

Cranmer, Thomas. *Works.* Edited J. E. Cox. 2 vols. Cambridge, England: Parker Society, 1844 and 1846.

Cremeans, C. D. *The Reception of Calvinistic Thought in England.* Urbana, Ill.: University of Illinois Press, 1949.

Crosby, T. *The History of the English Baptists.* London: 1738.

Crowley, Robert. *The confutations of .xiii. Articles, wherunto Nicolas Shaxton, late byshop of Salisburye subscribed . . . M.D.xlvi. whē he recanted in Smithfielde.* London: 1548.

———. *An apologie, or defence of those Englishe writers and preachers which Cerberus the three headed Dog of Hell chargeth wyth false doctrine vnder the name of Predestination.* London: 1566.

Davis, J. F. *Heresy and Reformation in the South East of England, 1520–1559.* Swift, London: Royal Historical Society, 1983.

———. "Joan of Kent, Lollardy and the English Reformation." *Journal of Ecclesiastical History* 33, no. 2 (1982): 225–33.

Deppermann, K. *Melchior Hoffman.* Edinburgh, Scotland: T. & T. Clark, 1987.

Dickens, A. G. *The English Reformation.* Glasgow, Scotland: 1967 and 2d ed., Batsford, London: 1989.

———. *Lollards and Protestants in the Diocese of York.* Oxford: Oxford University Press, 1959.

Eckhart. Meister. *Meister Eckhart: The Essential Sermons, Commentaries, Treatises and Defense.* Edited by E. Colledge and B. McGinn. London: 1981.

Edward VI. *The Journal of King Edward's Reign.* Clarendon Historical Society: 1884.

Estep, W. R. *The Anabaptist Story,* rev. ed. Grand Rapids, Mich.: Eerdmans, 1975.

Farr E. ed. *Select Poetry, Chiefly Devotional of the Reign of Queen Elizabeth.* 2 vols. Cambridge: Parker Society, 1845.

Fish, Simon. *The summe of the holye scripture | and ordinarye of the Christen teachyng | the true Christen faithe | by the which we be all iustified.* Antwerp, Belgium: 1529.

Fox, George. *The Journal of George Fox.* Edited by J. L. Nickalls. Cambridge, England: Religious Society of Friends, 1952.

Foxe, John. *The Acts and Monuments of the English Martyrs.* London: 1563, 1576 and ed. J. Pratt, London: 1870.

———. *Rervm i Ecclesia Gestarum* Basel, Switzerland: 1559.

Frith, John. *A disputacion of Purgatorye*. 1533?

———. *A Mirroure to know thyselfe*. Antwerp, Belgium: c. 1536?

———. *A myroure or lokyng glasse wherin you may beholde the Sacramente of baptisme described*. 1548?

Gairdner, J. *Lollardy and the Reformation in England*. 4 vols. London: Macmillan, 1908–13.

Gardiner, Stephen. *A Declaration of such true articles as George Ioye hath gone about to confute as false*. London: 1546.

Garrett, Christina. *The Marian Exiles*. Cambridge, England: Cambridge University Press, 1938.

Gilby, A. *A brief treatise, with certayne Answers* (included in John Stockwood's translation of *The Treasure of Trueth*— see Beza, 1576?).

Hamilton, A. A. H. *The Family of Love*. Cambridge, England: James Clark, 1981.

Hardwick, C. *A History of the Articles of Religion*. London: 1859.

Hargrave, O. T. "The Doctrine of Predestination in the English Reformation." Ph.D. diss., Vanderbilt University, 1966.

———. "The Freewillers in the English Reformation." *Church History* 37 (1968): 271–80.

Hart, Henry. *A consultorie for all Christians. To beware least they beare the name of christians in vayne*. Worcester, England: 1549.

———. *A godly newe short treatyse instructyng euery parson, howe they shulde trade theyr lyues in ye imytacyon of vertu and ye shewyng of vyce*. London: 1548.

Haslewood, F. *Memorials of Smarden, Kent*. Ipswich, England: 1886.

Hayes, T. Wilson. "The Peaceful Apocalypse: Familism and Literacy in Sixteenth-Century England." *Sixteenth Century Journal* 17, no. 2 (1986): 131–143.

Henry VIII, *A Necessary Doctrine and Ervdition for any Christen man*. London: 1543.

Heylyn, Peter. *Ecclesia Restaurata*. London: 1661.

Hogarde, Miles. *The displaying of the Protestantes, & sondry their practices, with a description of diuers their abuses of late frequented*. London: 1556.

Hooper, John. *A Declaration of the ten holy cōmaundementes of allmygthye God*. Zürich, Switzerland: 1549?

———. *A Lesson of the Incarnation of Christe, that he toke his humanite in and of the Blessed Virgine*. London: 1549.

———. *Writings*. Edited by S. Carr and C. Nevinson. 2 vols. Parker Society, Cambridge, England: Parker Society, 1843 and 1852.

Scheffer, J. De Hoop. *History of the Free Churchmen*. Edited by William Elliot Griffis. Ithaca, N.Y.: Andrus & Church, n.d.

Horst, I. B. *The Radical Brethren: Anabaptism and the English Reformation to 1558*. Nieuwkoop Netherlands: 1972.

Hudson, A. *Lollards and Their Books*. London: Hambledon Press, 1985.

Hughes P. L. and J. F. Larkin, eds. *Tudor Royal Proclamations*. 3 vols. New Haven and London: Yale University Press, 1969.

Huguenot Society. *Publications of the Huguenot Society*. 57 vols. London: 1887–1985.

Hutchinson, Roger. *The Works of Roger Hutchinson.* Edited by J. Brude. Cambridge, England: Parker Society, 1842.

Ivimey, J. *A History of the English Baptists.* 4 vols. London: 1811–30.

Jewel, John. *Works.* Edited by J. Ayre. 4 vols. Cambridge, England: Parker Society, 1845–50.

Jones, John. *The Arte and Science of preseruing Bodie and Soule in Healthe, Wisedome, and Catholike Religion: Phisically, Philosophically, and Diuinely.* London: 1579.

Jones, W. R. D. *William Turner: Tudor naturalist, physician and divine.* London: Routledge, 1988.

Jordan, W. K. ed. *The Chronicle and Political Papers of King Edward VI.* London: Allen and Unwin, 1966.

Joye, George. *The letters whyche Johan Ashwell Priour of Newnham Abbey . . . sente secretly to the Bishope of Lyncolne, in the yeare of our Lord M. D. xxvii. Where in the sayde pryour accuseth George Joye . . . of fower opinyons: wyth the answere of the sayde George Vnto the same opynyons.* Straßburg: 1531.

———. *George Joye confuteth | Vvinchesters false Articles.* Antwerp, Belgium: 1543.

———. *The refutation of the·byshop of Winchesters derke declaratiō of his false articles, once before confuted by George Joye.* London: 1546.

Julian of Norwich. *Showings (Revelations of Divine Love).* Edited by E. Colledge, O.S.A., and J. Walsh, S.J. New York: Paulist Press, 1978.

Kendall, R. T. *Calvin and English Calvinism to 1649.* Oxford: Oxford University Press, 1979.

Ketley J., ed. *Liturgies of King Edward VI.* Cambridge, England: Parker Society: 1844.

Knappen, M. M. *Tudor Puritanism.* Chicago: University of Chicago Press, 1939.

Knewstub, John. *A Confutation of monstrous and horrible heresies, taught by H.N. and embraced of a number, who call themselues the Familie of Loue.* London: 1579.

Knox, D. B. *The Doctrine of Faith in the Reign of Henry VIII.* London: J. Clarke, 1961.

Knox, John. *An Answer to a Great Nomber of blasphemous cauillations written by an Anabaptist, and aduersarie to Gods eternal Predestination.* Geneva, Switzerland: 1560.

———. *The Works of John Knox.* Edited by D. Laing. 6 vols. Edinburgh, Scotland: 1846–64.

Ladd, G. E. *The Presence of the Future.* London: 1980.

Lamberd, John. *Of Predestinacion & election.* Canterbury, England: 1550.

Lamont, W. M. *Godly Rule: Politics and Religion 1603–60.* London: Macmillan, 1969.

Latimer, Hugh. *Sermons and Remains of Hugh Latimer.* Edited by G. E. Corrie. 2 vols. Cambridge, England: Parker Society, 1844–45.

Laurence, R.———see John Trew.

Lesse, Nicholas———see Augustine.

Loades, D. M. "Anabaptism and English Sectarianism in the Mid-Sixteenth Century." In *Reform and Reformation: England and the Continent c. 1500–c. 1750,* edited by D. Baker *Studies in Church History: Subsidia 2.* Oxford: Blackwell, 1979, pp. 59–70.

McEwen, J. S. *The Faith of John Knox.* London: Lutterworth Press, 1961.

Martin, J. W. "English Protestant Separatism at its Beginnings: Henry Hart and the Free-Will Men." *Sixteenth Century Journal* 7 (1976): 55–74.

——. *Religious Radicals in Tudor England.* London: Hambledon Press, 1989.

Martin, L. F. "The Family of Love in England: Conforming Millenarians." *Sixteenth Century Journal* 3 (1972): 99–108.

Martyr, Peter——see Pietro Martire Vermigli.

The Mennonite Encyclopedia. 4 vols. Penn. Scottdale: Herald Press, 1956.

More, Thomas *The English Works of Sir Thomas More.* Edited by W. E. Campbell and A. W. Reed. 2 vols, London: Eyre and Spottiswoode, 1931.

Morgan, E. S. *Visible Saints: The History of a Puritan Idea.* Ithaca, N.Y.: Cornell University Press, 1963.

Moss, J. D. *Godded with God: Hendrik Niclaes and his Family of Love.* Transactions of the American Historical Society, vol. 71, pt. 8, 1981.

Nicholls J. G., ed. *Chronicle of the Grey Friars of London.* London: Camden Society, 1852.

Niclaes, Hendrik. *Comoedia. A worke in Ryme, contayning an Enterlude of Myndes, witnessing the Mans Fall from God and Christ.* 1574.

——. *Dicta HN. Documentall Sentences.* 1574.

——. *Evangelivm Regni. A Joyfull Message of the kingdom.* 1575?

——. *A Figure of the True & Spiritual Tabernacle.* London: 1655.

——. *An Introduction to the Holy Understanding of the Glasse of Righteousness.* London: 1649.

——. *The Prophecy of the Spirit of Love.* London: 1649.

——. *Revelatio Dei. The Revelation of God, and his Great Prophesie, Which God now (in the last day) Hath shewed unto His ELECT.* London: 1649.

——. *Terra Pacis. A True Testification of the spirituall Lande of Peace . . . or the heauenly Ierusalem.* 1575?

——. See also H. Ainsworth.

Ochino, Bernadino. *Certayne Sermons of the ryghte famous and excellente Clerk Master Barnadine Ochine, . . . an exyle in thys lyfe, for the faithful testimony of Jesus Christe.* London: 1551?

——. *Fouretene Sermons of Barnadine Ochyne, concernyng the predestinacion and eleccion of god.* Translated by A. Cooke, Lady Bacon. 1551?

Owen, H. Gareth. "A Nursery of Elizabethan Nonconformity, 1567–72." *Journal of Ecclesiastical History* 17 (1966): 65–76.

Oxley. J. E. *The Reformation in Essex.* Manchester, England: Manchester University Press, 1965.

Parsons, Robert. *A Temperate Vvard-vvord, to the Tvrbvlent and Seditiovs VVachword of Sir Francis Hastings knight, vvho indeuoreth to slaunder the vvhole Catholique cause, & all professors thereof, both at home and abrode.* Antwerp, Belgium, 1599.

——. *A Treatise of Three Conversions of England from Paganisme to Christian Religion.* St. Omer, France: 1603.

————. *The Third Part Of A Treatise Intituled: of Three Conuersions of England.* St. Omer, France: 1604.

Pecock, Reginald. *The Repressor of Over Much Blaming of the Clergy.* Edited by C. Babington. 2 vols. London: Rolls Series, 1860.

Peel, A. *The First Congregational Churches.* Cambridge, England: Cambridge University Press, 1920.

————. "A Conscientious Objector of 1575." *TBHS* 7 (1920–1): 71–128.

————. ed. *The Seconde Parte of a Register.* 2 vols. Cambridge, England: Cambridge University Press, 1915.

Philpot, John. *Examinations and Writings.* Edited by R. Eden. Cambridge, England: Parker Society, 1842.

Pike, E. C. *The Story of the Anabaptists.* London: National Council of Evangelical Free Churches, 1904.

Plomer, H. R., ed. *Index of Wills and Administrations at Canterbury 1396–1558 and 1640–1650.* London: British Record Society, 1920.

Poynet, John. *A Short Catechisme, or playne instruction, conteyninge the sūme of Christian learninge, sett fourth by the kings maiesties authoritie, for all Scholemaisters to teache.* London: 1553.

Proctor, John. *The Fal of the Late Arrian.* London: 1549.

Prynne, William. *A Quench-Coale.* Amsterdam: 1637.

Reay, B. *The Quakers and the English Revolution.* London: Temple Smith, 1985.

Ridley, Lancelot. *A commentary in Englyshe vpon Sayncte Paules Epystle to the Ephesyans.* London: 1540.

Ridley, Nicholas. *Works.* Edited by H. Christmas. Cambridge, England: Parker Society, 1841.

Ridley, J. *John Knox.* Oxford: Clarendon Press, 1968.

Robinson H., ed. *Original Letters relative to the English Reformation.* 2 vols. Cambridge, England: Parker Society, 1846–47.

————, ed. *The Zürich Letters.* 2 vols. Cambridge, England: Parker Society, 1842–45.

Robinson, John. *The Works of John Robinson.* Edited by R. Ashton. 3 vols., London: 1851.

Rogers, John. *The Displaying of an horrible secte of grosse and wicked Heretiques, naming themselues the Familie of Loue, with the liues of their Authours, and what doctrine they teach in corners.* London: 1578.

————. *An Answere vnto a wicked & infamous Libel made by Christopher Vitel, one of the chiefe English Elders of the pretended Family of Loue.* London: 1579.

Rogers, Thomas. *The Catholic Doctrine of the Church of England, an Exposition of the Thirty-Nine Articles.* Edited by J. J. S. Perowne. Cambridge, England: Parker Society, 1854.

Rupp, E. G. *Studies in the Making of the English Protestant Tradition,* mainly in the reign of Henry VIII. Cambridge, England: Cambridge University Press, 1947.

————. "John Bradford Martyr." *The London Quarterly and Holborn Review* 6th ser. 32 (1963): 50–55.

Ruysbroeck, Jan van. *The Chastising of God's Children and The Treatise of the*

Perfection of the Sons of God. Edited by J. Bazire and E. College. Oxford: Blackwell, 1957.

———. *The Adornment of the Spiritual Marriage.* Translated by C. A. Wynschenck. London: J. M. Watkins, 1951.

Sandys, Edwin. *The Sermons of Edwin Sandys.* Edited by J. Ayre. Cambridge, England: Parker Society, 1841.

Sarcerius, Erasmus. *Cōmon places of scripture.* Translated by R. Taverner. London: 1538.

Shakespeare, J. H. *Baptist and Congregational Pioneers.* London: National Council of Evangelical Free Churches, 1906.

Sharpe, Robert. *The Confession and Declaration of Robert Sharpe Clerke, and other of that secte, tearmed the Familie of Loue.* London: 1575. Society of Antiquaries Broadsides, Lemon 66.

Simons, Menno. *Complete Works.* Elkhart, Ind.: Herald Press, 1871.

Stockwood, John.—see Theodore Beza.

Strype, J. *Ecclesiastical Memorials.* 3 vols. in 6, Oxford: 1822.

———. *Life of Archbishop Grindal.* Oxford: 1821.

———. *Memorials of the Most reverend father in God, . . . Thomas Cranmer.* 2 vols. Oxford: 1840.

———. *The Life and Acts of Matthew Parker.* 3 vols. Oxford: 1821.

Suso, Henry. *Little Book of Eternal Wisdom and Little Book of Truth.* Translated by J. M. Clark. London: 1953.

The Theologia Germanica of Martin Luther. Translated by B. Hoffman. New York: Paulist Press, 1980.

Thomson, J. A. F. *The Later Lollards 1414–1520.* Oxford: Oxford University Press, 1965.

Tobias. *Mirabilia opera Dei: Certaine wonderfull Works of God which hapned to H.N. even from his youth: and how the God of Heaven hath . . . chosen and sent him to be a Minister of his gracious Word.* London: c. 1650.

Trew, John. *The Cause of Contention in the King's Bench,* Bodleian MS. 53, fols. 116–24. Edited by R. Laurence in *Authentic Documents Relative to the Predestinarian Controversy.* Oxford: 1819.

Turner, W. *A new Dialogue Wherein is conteyned the examination of the Messe, and of that kynde of Preisthode, whych is ordeined to say messe: and to offer vp for remyssyon of synne, the bodye and bloude of Christe agayne.* 1548.

———. *A preseruatiue, or triacle, agaynst the poyson of Pelagius, lately reneued, & styrred vp agayn, by the furious secte of the Annabaptistes.* London: 1552.

———. *A nevv booke of spirituall Physik for dyuerse diseases of the nobilite and gentlemen of Englande.* Emden, Germany: 1555.

Tyacke, N. *Anti-Calvinists: the Rise of English Arminianism c. 1590–1640.* Oxford: Oxford University Press, 1987.

Tyndale, William. *The Works of William Tyndale.* Edited by H. Walter. 3 vols. Cambridge, England: Parker Society, 1848–50.

Vermigli, Pietro Martire. (Peter Martyr). *The common places of the most famous . . . Diuine Doctor . . . P. Martyr.* Translated by A. Marten. 1583.

Veron, Jean. *An Apologye or defence of the doctryne of Predestination.* London: 1561.

————. *A frutefull treatise of predestination.* London: 1561.

————. *Against the fre wil men.* London: 1561.

————. see also Heinrich Bullinger.

Walker, D. P. *The Decline of Hell.* London: Routledge & Kegan Paul, 1964.

Wallace, D. D., Jr. *Puritans and Predestination: Grace in English Protestant Theology, 1525–1695.* Chapel Hill, N.C.: University of North Carolina Press, 1982.

————. "The Doctrine of Predestination in the Early English Reformation." *Church History* 43 (1974): 201–15.

Watts, M. R. *The Dissenters from the Reformation to the French Revolution.* Oxford: Oxford University Press, 1978.

Whatmore L. E., ed. *Harpesfield's Visitation, 1557* London: Catholic Record Society, 1950–51.

White, B. R. *The English Separatist Tradition.* Oxford: Oxford University Press, 1971.

Wilkins, D. *Concilia Magnae Brittanniae.* 4 vols., London: 1733–37.

Wilkinson, William. *A Confutation of Certaine Articles deliuered vnto the Familye of Loue, with the exposition of Theophilus, a supposed elder in the sayd Familye vpon the same Articles.* London: 1579.

Williams, G. H. *The Radical Reformation.* London: Weidenfeld and Nicolson, 1962.

————. and A. M. Mergal, eds. *Spiritual and Anabaptist Writers.* Philadelphia: LCC, The Westminster Press, 1957.

Witard, D. *Bibles in Barrels.* Essex Baptist Association, 1962.

Zwingli, Huldrych. *The Accompt rekenynge and confession of the faith of Huldrik Zwinglius byshop of Zuryk the chief town of Heluetia, sent vnto Charles the fyfte nowe Emperoure of Rome, holdynge a counsel wyth the moost noble Princes, Estates and learned men of Germany assembled together at Ausburgh, 1530, in the moneth of July.* Translated by Thomas Cotsforde. Geneva: 1555.

Manuscript Sources

Bodleian MS. 53.

Emmanuel College MSS. 260 and 262.

Gonville & Caius College MS. 218/233.

British Library Harleian MSS. 416, 421, and 537.

British Library Cotton MS. Cleopatra E. v.

Lambeth Palace Library, Register Cranmer and Register Warham.

Maidstone PRC 3 and 17.

Public Record Office (PRO), PCC-F. 8 Tashe.

The Second Parte of a Register, Dr. Williams's Library, London.

Index